In our time 'Englishness' has become a theme for speculation rather than dogma; twentieth-century writers have found it an elusive and ambivalent concept, a cue for nostalgia or for a sense of exile and loss. *Literary Englands* meditates on the contemporary meanings of 'Englishness' and explores some of the ways in which a sense of nationality has informed and shaped the work of a range of writers including Edward Thomas, Forster and Lawrence, Leavis and George Sturt, Orwell and Evelyn Waugh, Betjeman, Larkin and Geoffrey Hill. Through close engagement with the language and thought of these writers David Gervais shows the extent to which they have been influenced by the consciousness of working within a long-established, complex and sophisticated literary tradition. In the process he elucidates a nostalgia which lies at the heart of our culture.

LITERARY ENGLANDS
VERSIONS OF 'ENGLISHNESS' IN MODERN WRITING

LITERARY ENGLANDS

Versions of 'Englishness' in Modern Writing

DAVID GERVAIS

Honorary Fellow in English, University of Reading

CAMBRIDGE
UNIVERSITY PRESS

Published by the Press Syndicate of the University of Cambridge
The Pitt Building, Trumpington Street, Cambridge, CB2 1RP
40 West 20th Street, New York, NY 10011-4211, USA
10 Stamford Road, Oakleigh, Melbourne 3166, Australia

First published 1993

Printed in Great Britain at the University Press, Cambridge

A catalogue record for this book is available from the British Library

Library of Congress cataloguing in publication data

Gervais, David, 1943–
Literary Englands: versions of 'Englishness' in modern writing / David Gervais.
p.   cm.
Includes bibliographical references and index.
ISBN 0 521 44338 5 (hardback)
1. English literature–20th century–History and criticism.   2. English
literature–England–History and criticism.   3. National characteristics, English,
in literature.   4. England in literature.
I. Title.
PR478.n37g47   1993
820.9'355–dc20   92-47285   CIP

ISBN 0 521 44338 5 hardback

TAG

For Damien and Tristan

So everything, in its ruin, seems in England to live a new life; and it is only this second life, this cottage built in the fallen stronghold, that is English.

George Santayana, *Soliloquies in England*

Contents

Contents

Preface

It is a long time since we thought of England as a 'precious stone set in the silver sea' or even since we extolled its good fortunes in the manner of Mr Podsnap. We are more likely nowadays to find ourselves performing an autopsy on it. Since the Great War at least it has become a theme for nostalgia, a good belonging to the past like half-heard music that just carries from some distant room. England is too problematic now to inspire simple patriotism.

A full treatment of 'Englishness' would involve many different Englands. Instead, I have chosen to leave some gaps in the story, some of which may cause surprise and require explanation. John Cowper Powys might seem made for my theme and my only excuse for leaving him out is lack of space and my own unfitness to do him justice. I did intend to write more on T. F. Powys, still a too little-known writer, but I found that his way of imagining England, *sub specie aeternitatis*, fitted in with no one else's. Some readers will miss a fuller account of 'thirties' poetry but I preferred to keep my space for less studied writers. Besides, I have to confess that even when I enjoy Auden I have little wish to write about him and critics should keep silent when they can. Other lacunae loom even larger but I had no wish to seem to be writing a literary history of the period. With more space I would have included Angus Wilson and David Storey (both of whom have been acute monitors of how England has changed). The same goes for drama, particularly the recent 'political' playwrights whose own obsession with England has played a considerable part in prompting academic interest in the subject. There is also much to be said about the place of England in Ted Hughes's Poetry.

Bigger than any of these omissions, I have not discussed any English women writers. When I thought of doing so I began to wonder if their concern with 'Englishness' were not of a different

xiii

order, perhaps less public and less geared to nationalistic attitudes. The subject remains to be attempted. There is also scope for a book, along the lines of John Lucas's study from Dryden to Browning, of nineteenth-century versions of England. Another rich field would be the way English painters, particularly in the 'thirties', have responded to the theme.

But now it is too late to be listing either intentional or involuntary omissions. All I can do is to hope that they will at least provide a cue from which my reader will be able to refute or modify some of the arguments I derive from those writers I do discuss.

Acknowledgements

This book is indebted to many friends and colleagues, in particular Andy and Libby Gurr, H. A. Mason, Patrick Parrinder and Christopher Salvesen. Geoffrey Strickland read several chapters in an early draft and offered many useful criticisms of them. I also owe thanks to the editors of *Barcelona English Literature and Language Studies* (*BELLS*), *The Cambridge Quarterly*, *The Dutch Quarterly Review* and *English* for permission to quote passages of this book which first appeared in their pages. I am also very grateful for the suggestions made by my two (necessarily anonymous) publisher's readers.

Criticism is a communal activity and I would like to record a particular debt to two groups of people: my students on the Modern M. A. Course at Reading and my fellow editors of *The Cambridge Quarterly*.

James Nuttall's help with word-processing has been invaluable.

Abbreviations

BP   John Betjeman, *Collected Poems: Enlarged Edition*, compiled with
      intro. by the Earl of Birkenhead (John Murray, 1984).
HP   Geoffrey Hill, *Collected Poems* (Penguin, Harmondsworth, 1985).
LL   Geoffrey Hill, *The Lords of Limit: Essays on Literature and Ideas*
      (André Deutsch, 1984).
LP   Philip Larkin, *Collected Poems*, ed. with introd. by Anthony
      Thwaite (Faber, 1988).
SJ   *The Journals of George Sturt* 1890–1927, selected and edited by E.
      D. Mackerness in 2 vols. (Cambridge University Press, 1967).
TP   *The Collected Poems of Edward Thomas*, ed. R. George Thomas
      (Clarendon Press, Oxford 1978).

CHAPTER I

The nineteenth century: pastoral versions of England

To use the word 'pastoral' in a modern context is not necessarily to imply all the affectation and evasiveness it carries with it from earlier periods. Dr Johnson considered it the most insipid form of poetry but, conceived as a contrast to the new England of mills and railways, it could be as serious as more hard-bitten kinds of literature. There is nothing sentimental about Blake's 'rural pen'. In the sense in which it is used in the present chapter, 'pastoral' is as likely to be radical in import as conservative. In relation to the 'real' England of the time, far from being distanced and poetical, it was often a writer's means of confronting what was most problematic in the present. This does not mean, of course, that the pastoral of the period was free from nostalgia, though the word 'free' surely begs the question. For the nostalgia of writers like, say, George Eliot or William Morris, dissimilar as they seem, was itself a way of raising questions.

With an idea as large as 'England' there is always some earlier source to go back to: Drayton, Spenser, even Chaucer. Yet continuity cannot be taken for granted. Are Shakespeare's John of Gaunt and Sir Henry Newbolt really speaking about the same thing when they invoke 'England'? Every idea of England predicates a slightly different England. Only interested parties who have a large material stake in it need to pretend that it is one indivisible entity. Politicians may like to think it is but, when they do so, they usually take care to appeal to its past – to 'Victorian values' or 'the age of Drake' or the 'spirit of the Blitz' – rather than to the present where it is still in contention. Tradition can be an effective weapon against present doubts and divisions; most periods of English history have looked back to some earlier period to exemplify what England really is. Being finished, the past can be made to seem complete. Yet the idea of England has been more revealing when it has remained problematic, when, for instance, one version of it has been used to exclude another. Thus, an Edwardian writer like Hilaire Belloc contrived to make the England of the South Downs stand for the whole country. More profoundly, Dickens's later novels came increasingly to define one England *against* another. *Bleak House* depicts a society made up of several quite different Englands, which seem to have grown up in total ignorance of each other, and then makes them collide. Part of its interest (and its 'romantic side'), for its first readers, must have been that these Englands very rarely collided in their own lives. (They would not have wanted them to.) What Dickens tells us, more fully than any other writer of the period, is that England is not something that is simply *there* but something that we have to construct for ourselves. This process of construction was, however, well under way long before him. A better starting point is the poetry of Wordsworth, which already records – and tries to resist – the process of fragmentation that had become so acute by the time of *Bleak House*. For the disorientating shift from the country to the town that is central to the problems of characters like Trooper George and 'The Man from Shropshire' is already clear from a poem like 'Michael'.

In the sonnets he wrote during the Napoleonic wars, Wordsworth made a determined bid to revive the Miltonic notion of England as a 'noble and puissant nation rousing herself like a strong man after sleep'. But the continuity he hoped to cement was already broken:

> Milton! thou shouldst be living at this hour:
> England hath need of thee: she is a fen
> Of stagnant waters: altar, sword, and pen,
> Fireside, the heroic wealth of hall and bower,
> Have forfeited their ancient English dower
> Of inward happiness.

Even if such poems are more than the 'declamatory claptrap'[1] which Leavis dismissed them as being, they hardly succeed in creating a real sense of Milton himself:

> Thy soul was like a Star, and dwelt apart;
> Thou hadst a voice whose sound was like the sea

This lofty apartness is what really stirs the poet of solitude, not the prospect of national consensus. Milton may also be lowly, like Wordsworth's own shepherds, but what at first seems his 'majestic' public voice comes to seem very like a private one, though on the grand scale. Wordsworth's deepest versions of England, on the other hand, focus on some single haunting figure – a discharged soldier or a leech-gatherer – seen in some empty English landscape and evoked in language much less conscious of its audience, without the afflatus of a spiritual call to arms. This England is local and mundane, not clad in the formal robes of nationalism. A poem like 'Michael' describes a much closer attachment to place than any of the sonnets dedicated to 'National Independence and Liberty'.

This is not to say that the England of 'Michael' does not have its distance too. Though seemingly immemorial, it is in reality dying out. The sheepfold remains unfinished at the end and only nature, not human society, has any permanence:

> the estate
> Was sold, and went into a stranger's hand.
> The Cottage which was named the Evening Star
> Is gone – the ploughshare has been through the ground
> On which it stood; great changes have been wrought
> In all the neighbourhood

Only the 'boisterous brook of Green-head Ghyll', the non-human part of England, is unchanging. In the poem's closing lines it brings home to us the veil of distance through which we see the events of Michael's life. Nostalgia becomes a possibility, for all the poem's unique concreteness. More than that, the pathos of the ending encourages us to make a selection in our minds from what has actually happened: all the regret is for what had befallen Michael himself. There is none to spare for his son Luke who has come to a bad end in the city. It is as if that distant city, which has accelerated the passing of Michael's way of life, were not itself an authentic part of England. That is why Wordsworth is so unspecific about it despite the meticulous realism which he brings to the sheepfold. One England has cancelled out another and his allegiance is to the one that is disappearing.

Poetry after Wordsworth was to be full of contrasts between opposing Englands in which the absent one would also be the most poetically real. In 'Michael', though, both Englands are still real. The difference between them is simply that Michael's England is more English than Luke's is. That is a good enough reason for calling the poem a 'pastoral'. It is also what makes it such a pregnant anticipation of later literary Englands, such as *Lady Chatterley's Lover* (where one England 'blots out' another) or that of Orwell in *The Lion and the Unicorn* ('a family with the wrong members in control').[2] But by that time it was even clearer that the word 'England' was more likely to divide than unite the English people who tried to meet each other in it. 'Michael' is usually seen as a poem about actual rural life, purging pastoral of its previous artificiality, but in the century after it – from Tennyson's 'Dora' down to the bucolic escapism of the Georgians – simplicity became increasingly hard to tell from artifice. Whereas country life is essentially real for Wordsworth, his successors came to see it as a refuge from reality. Already Arnold's Scholar Gypsy loves 'retired ground':

> For early didst thou leave the world, with powers
> Fresh, undiverted to the world without,
> Firm to their mark, not spent on other things.

The attraction of his life is that it is 'unlike to ours', marginal and elusive. England is on the way to being Housman's 'land of lost content', not real but imaginary. But Rupert Brooke's Grantchester, which would have seemed like a fantasy to any farm worker who actually lived there, was luminously present to Brooke himself. Nostalgia could masquerade as observation, even if England had become as faraway as the 'foreign field that is forever England'. Not that Brooke's poem is *only* artificial, false as it seems now. Its version of England clearly answered to an emotional need and the emotion itself was real even if its embodiment was precious. Nostalgia may be insidious but it would be puritanical to repress it altogether. Without it, would there be any versions of England at all?

One of the revolutionary features of 'Michael' (but forgotten in Brooke) is the prominence it gives to hard manual work, not simply labour but work as a community's chief means of finding a cultural identity for itself. Such work becomes an intrinsic part of 'Englishness' after Wordsworth. Adam Bede, Gabriel Oak, even Sturt's real-life Bettesworth, are all offspring of Michael, grounded in reality on one side and shading into myth on the other. At a time when English workmen were leaving the land in droves to become railwaymen and industrial 'hands', such figures were offered as exemplary in their 'Englishness'. As late as *Howards End* and Edward Thomas's 'Lob', writers were prone to seeing the old yeoman class as more English than any other. By introducing its purposeful work – so unlike the songs a hundred leisured Strephons had sung to a hundred Chloës – pastoral could be renewed and a changing countryside immobilised whilst seeming real and unliterary. Not for nothing does *Silas Marner* take its epigraph from 'Michael'. Though steeped in actual rural experience (as the young George Eliot had been herself) its version of England is also a highly literary one. The two things were not necessarily incompatible. Part of the novel's complexity is that it circumvents the facile juxtaposition of the real and the ideal, as if they belonged to different realms. In *Silas Marner*, social history and legend are emotionally indissoluble, perhaps more strikingly than in *Adam Bede* or *The Mill on the Floss* but in a similar way. George Eliot clearly found this no more foreign to the spirit of realism which she had learnt from Ruskin's *Modern Painters* than Ruskin himself saw any contradiction between typology and naturalism in his interpretation of Turner.[3] Yet it is impossible to dissociate George Eliot's picture of 'Englishness' in *Silas Marner* from the fact that she chose to set her novel in the past. More subtly, she has made the progress of her story a reversal of actual English history between the time when it was set and the time when it was written. Unlike the majority of workers in that period, Silas moves from the town to the country. Moreover, having begun life a dissenter, he ends it in the bosom of a reassuringly broad Anglican Church. At the end of the book, he discovers with relief that Lantern Yard – the origin of all his troubles – has been 'swep' away'. Unlike less fortunate Englishmen, he runs no risk of having to work in the factory that has taken its place. His past (for them, the future) recedes and traditional Raveloe life comes to seem the norm. In other words, George Eliot has used social history to turn an exception into a rule. Her novel still glows with a conscious nostalgia. One readily understands why James spoke of its 'delightful tinge of Goldsmith'.[4] In the past, rural life seemed both mellow and more substantial.

Silas himself may be a very special case beside Michael but George Eliot nonetheless assimilates him to the same England. What is more, she invests his story with some of that 'healing power' which Victorians like Arnold and herself went to Wordsworth for.[5] If the novel says that this is what rural England was really like (as Mrs Leavis argued) it also speaks of how we would like it to be. In much the same way, Arnold could praise Wordsworth's poetry for its plainness and go on to single out its ability to turn sorrow into a form of consolation:

> The cloud of mortal destiny,
> Others could front it fearlessly,
> But who, like him, could put it by?

One answer to Arnold's question could be, 'George Eliot, when she treats history as she does in *Silas Marner*.' Her strategy, in a time of agricultural change and depression, of identifying rural England with the past has done yeoman service since then. Kipling's *Puck of Pook's Hill* and Edward Thomas's 'Lob' are just two versions of England which depend on a similar starting point. Not all conservatism sticks narrowly to the *status quo*. There is also a kind which exists to side-step it.

This is not to say that all Victorian Wordsworthians took a merely complacent view of country life. Ruskin, who used Wordsworth for the epigraph to all five volumes of *Modern Painters*, clearly had doubts about the sort of consolation that could be derived from figures like the Leech-Gatherer. In the final volume of that book he gives a brilliant and disturbing account of meeting an old watercress-picker in Derbyshire hill country. The passage is a pointed rewriting of 'Resolution and Independence'; the old man, who is from Skye and was 'bred in the Church of Scotland, sir', tells a harrowing tale of his life as a sailor and the death of his wife in childbirth: 'I never cared much what come of me since'. Ruskin never thinks of comparing him to a stone or sea beast or laughing his own 'despondency' to 'scorn' at the thought of him. He just attends to what the hills are really telling him:

Truly, this Highland and English hill-scenery is fair enough; but has its shadows; and deeper colouring, here and there, than that of heath and rose.
    Now, as far as I have watched the main powers of human mind, they have risen first from the resolution to see fearlessly, pitifully, and to its very worst, what these deep colours mean, wheresoever they fall; not by any means to pass on the other side, looking pleasantly up to the sky, but to stoop to the horror, and let the sky, for the present, take care of its own clouds. However this may be in moral matters, with which I have nothing here to do, in my own field of enquiry the fact is so; and all great and beautiful work has come of first gazing without shrinking into the darkness.[6]

Some readers will wonder if Wordsworth doesn't begin his poem by 'gazing ... into the darkness' and then, in the inimitable way envied by Arnold, 'shrinking' from it or, rather, putting it by. Ruskin, the only great Victorian who could have written this fine passage, begins where Wordsworth began only to go in a quite different direction: a page later we are in the thick of a comparison between the idea of 'fate' in Greek and Shakespearian tragedy. But the immediate point is that one can never see life's 'deeper colouring' without facing its 'darkness' and this is a condition for understanding not just tragedy but 'the spirit of the highest Greek and Venetian art' too. For Ruskin, Wordsworth, great as he is, is in danger of missing both, meeting 'darkness' but 'seeking pleasure only' from it. This is why, indirectly, the word 'pastoral' can still be applied to him. In the end, he is a modern – as the famous chapter on the 'Pathetic Fallacy' argues – and Ruskin chooses the 'impassive' Dante instead for his ideal of the great poet.

What is impressive in the account of the watercress-gatherer is Ruskin's alertness to suffering. Unlike Arnold, who was seduced by Wordsworth's 'healing power', he is more drawn to the sickness than the cure. Does anyone have the right to be uplifted by the fortitude of a man whose life has been so harsh? By the time he wrote volume v of *Modern Painters* in 1860, the year of *Unto This Last*, Ruskin not only knew that rural England was no longer the reassuring pastoral of the poets but that it could no longer be taken to epitomise modern England at all. In his final years, he became increasingly obsessed with the 'storm cloud of the nineteenth century', with the industrial pollution which he claimed to be able to see even over Lake Coniston. Whereas George Eliot still tried to cement the idea of England's traditional unity of culture – presenting it as distant but still accessible – the Ruskin of *Fors Clavigera* was haunted by his sense of its fragmentation.[7] Where she speaks for continuity (in broadly Wordsworthian terms), he tells of rupture. It has been a frequent debate since their time, as a comparison of, say, *Howards End* and *Lady Chatterley's Lover* also reminds us. After all, Wyndham Lewis's *Blast* came out only a few years after the National Trust was founded.

Though Ruskin gazed hard into England's 'darkness' (until he went mad with what he saw) he did not gaze in the spirit of a realistic novelist. As the founder and Master of the Guild of St George, he too mythologised England, every bit as much as George Eliot did. Both Raveloe and the land Ruskin bought for the Guild shared one thing in common with the creations of many other Victorian writers and artists: a need to re-constitute England in terms of another historical period. Tennyson did it in his *Idylls of the King* and Browning disguised all manner of current issues in renaissance drapery in *Men and Women*. When a pre-Raphaelite painter like Hunt did it in *The Light of the World* he made sure that his allegory was topical. For Tennyson, setting England in a remote past was a means of preserving the idea of its unity. It became notoriously easy to divide his poems into public and private versions of England – 'Ode on the Death of the Duke of Wellington' or *Maud*, for instance – though that kind of split was already present in Wordsworth. It is far from clear what Charles James Fox was expected to get from 'The Old Cumberland Beggar' since the social issues Wordsworth outlined in his letter to him hardly come up in the poem itself.[8] But England is still a thinkable idea for Tennyson and Wordsworth, even if it rarely occasions their best poetry. By the twentieth century, few poets beside Kipling and forgotten figures like Newbolt, Austin and Sir William Watson attempted as much. Edward Thomas's England, arguably *the* main theme of his poems, associates the rural with the private. At a time when more and more people had come to live and work in the towns, the country which Thomas himself had left London for became more and more identified with the solitary, Wordsworthian individual. Though it still seemed 'English', the England it stood for actually included less and less of England as it was, the England Thomas had escaped. Thomas, of course, probably owed more to Wordsworth than to any poet and he was also old enough to have heard William Morris speak at a street corner and to say that Morris was the only man he would have liked to be himself.[9] Not that Morris's England was inevitably Utopian, simply because its language was a far cry from the Victorian novel's, but one can see how his romances followed on from the Ruskin who criticised Wordsworth. For, by 1860, Ruskin had already foreseen what England would become and the only way poets would be able to make it tolerable.

To point out that the Victorians liked to see their England in terms of its past is not to say that they all used it in the same way. Browning clearly turned it to much more radical effect than Tennyson did. But even the old pastoral version of England could be deployed in quite different ways by the poets from Clare to Arnold. Ruskin himself invokes it, at the end of *Unto This Last* of all places, not out of nostalgia but to dream a dream of hope in troubled times. It is the kind of passage that mattered a great deal to Morris:

The desire of the heart is also the light of the eyes. No scene is continually and untiringly loved, but one rich by joyful human labour; smooth in field; fair in garden; full in orchard; trim, sweet and frequent in homestead; ringing with voices of vivid existence. No air is sweet that is silent; it is only sweet when full of low currents of under sound – triplets of birds, and murmur and chirp of insects, and deep-toned words of men, and wayward trebles of childhood. As the art of life is learned, it will be found at last that all lovely things are also necessary: – the wild flower by the wayside, as well as the tended corn; and the wild birds and creatures of the forest, as well as the tended cattle; because man doth not live by bread only, but also by the desert manna; by every wondrous word and unknowable work of God.[10]

The whole passage is one which probably speaks more clearly today than it did fifty years ago. The extraordinary charge of hedonism that Ruskin was able to inject into his idea of England, without betraying his sense of its communal and spiritual effort, is something few of his contemporaries knew how to cope with. Pastoral is usually an aristocratic form, or at at least a way of upholding the class structure, but Ruskin's robust way of introducing the idea of class into it is deliberately unsettling:

What is chiefly needed in England at the present day is to show the quantity of pleasure that may be obtained by a consistent, well-administered competence, modest, confessed and laborious. We need examples of people who, leaving heaven to decide whether they are to rise in the world, decide for themselves that they will be happy in, and have resolved to seek – not greater wealth, but simpler pleasure. (p. 227)

Perhaps the implications of this exhortation are conservative (though there is an important distinction between being at the bottom of society and *deciding* not to rise in it) but what is most striking is Ruskin's energy of tone. There is none of the usual wistfulness of pastoral. Arnold employs a very similar imagery in 'The Scholar Gypsy' but his ideal is located firmly in the past, somewhere between an old book in the Bodleian and the myth of 'Merrie England'. Ruskin's voice is positively abrasive in comparison with Arnold's urbane and impotent pensiveness. Yet it has, of course, been much more common for poets since Arnold to situate England in the past than in the future, as Ruskin does. I am not thinking simply of a poet like Betjeman. The attitude persists as recently as Donald Davie's collection about England, *The Shires*, which came out in 1973, the year of the three-day week:

> Slow and vocal
> Amber of a burring baritone
> My grandad's voice, not Hardy's, is what stays
> Inside me as a slumbrous apogee
> Meridional altitude upon
> Pastoral England's longest summer day.
> O golden age! Bee-mouth, and honeyed singer.[11]

It is a lovely poem but it has more to do with our memories than our
lives. Would even a peasant of Hardy's day have recognised this
glowing Dorset? 'Honeyed' is a word one more readily associates
with Elizabethan poetry. One also senses the presence of Virgil being
used to much the same effect that Arnold used him, for that classical
resonance which enables a modern poet to pass his feelings off as
universal. Enticing as Davie's Dorset is, there is no room in it for
'pleasure' in Ruskin's sense.

   Though they are very different, it would be a mistake merely to
contrast Ruskin and Arnold as if one could only subscribe to one of
them and not both. Arnold the poet is not really Arnold entire. As a
prose-writer, he was as capable as Ruskin of putting his finger on
what made the usual sort of middle-class 'Englishness' rebarbative.
He pointed out everything narrowly provincial in the Englishman's
pride in his country (and even, in *Essays in Criticism*, what was
provincial in Ruskin himself).[12] Both writers were well qualified to
relish Dickens's Mr Podsnap; indeed, they spent much of their own
time hunting down his absurdities too:

'In England, Angleterre, England, We aspire the "H", and we say
"Horse". Only our Lower Classes say,"'Orse!"''
   'Pardon,' said the foreign gentleman; 'I am alwiz wrong!'
   'Our language,' said Mr Podsnap, with a gracious consciousness of being
always right, 'is Difficult. Ours is a Copious Language, and Trying to
Strangers. I will not Pursue my Question ... It merely referred,' Mr Podsnap
explained, with a sense of meritorious proprietorship, 'to our Constitution,
Sir. We Englishmen are Very Proud of our Constitution, Sir. It was
Bestowed Upon Us By Providence. No Other Country is so Favoured as
This Country.'[13]

Mr Podsnap is still with us, wherever there is a four course dinner and
a politician with a speech to be made, but no one, save Dickens
himself, has been better at guying provincial self-congratulation than
Arnold was. What was less obvious was the provinciality of those
who, aghast at this public face of England, sought refuge from it in its
more congenial rural aspect. It seldom struck them that they might
be vulnerable to the charge of being provincial offshoots of something
that was already provincial. For if the public England was provincial,
wouldn't the private one be even more so? If the Arnold of the
criticism, the champion of French and German literature as well as
the classics, did not take this path it is arguable that the Arnold of
'The Scholar Gypsy', the friend of Clough who had such trouble

understanding Clough's poetry, probably did. The problem was that there were two Arnolds, just as it was becoming increasingly plain that there were two Englands. The task of the later Ruskin was none other than to put them together again, like Humpty Dumpty, and everything he wrote from *Unto This Last* up to his final silence shows just how difficult this was to do. Other versions of pastoral proved easier to sustain than the one he tried to pit against them, versions that also proved more popular with the reading public.

The usual strategy of pastoral is to make the part stand for the whole. In George Eliot and even the early Hardy realism is cushioned with pastoral which comes from the novel's being set either in a past England or in one remote enough to seem special. By treating locations like Loamshire and Wessex with what chapter 17 of *Adam Bede* calls a 'faithful' and 'Dutch' 'truthfulness' they can then be made to seem English in a general as well as a local way. The attraction of this approach is that it enables a writer to project an imaginary England whilst *at the same time* devoting a minute attention to England as it actually is. The novel is a flexible form and realism and pastoral can be made to serve each other in it, though they seem to be opposites. The whole conception of Wessex, for instance, depends on us recognising that Shaston, Casterbridge and the rest are fictions on the one hand and based on real places on the other. Similarly, Thomas's Lob is both a spirit or myth of the countryside and also 'as English as this gate, this mire'. There is much to be said for having it both ways in these cases. But by the time Hardy stopped writing novels, it might be said that the English countryside, however circumstantially perceived, really belonged for most readers to the realm of the imagination. This is where many modern readers, at least of the novels up to *Tess*, want to re-locate his Dorset. It was, in effect, no more than a step from the way rural England was represented in an ostensibly realistic novel like *Far From the Madding Crowd* (whose very title implies where Hardy expects his reader to be standing) to a fiction like *News From Nowhere* which turns it from an actuality into the substance of a dream.

It was not by chance that Morris pointedly chose to raise his Utopia on the grave of the nineteenth-century novel. One of the first people the Guest meets in Nowhere is called Mr Boffin, an overdressed figure who feels ill at ease with the new dispensation and spends his time 'writing reactionary novels, and is very proud of getting the local colour right.'[14] Mr Boffin pines for news of the same past that

the guest is so glad to have escaped from. Morris himself clearly
thinks Boffin's antiquarian delight in 'local colour' – or 'realism' –
is eccentric. Far from being a way of facing life as it is, reading
novelists like Dickens has become a form of escapism. Now that
English people dwell in 'the continuous life of the world of men' (p.
123), books have become mere substitutes for real living. As the
beautiful Ellen tells her bookish grandfather:

'Books, books! always books, grandfather! When will you understand that
after all it is the world we live in which interests us most; the world of which
we are a part, and which we can never love too much? Look!' she said,
throwing open the casement wider and showing us the white light sparkling
between the black shadows of the moonlit garden, through which ran a little
shiver of the summer night-wind, 'look! these are our books in these days!'
(p. 141)

Morris in fact bases his Communist Utopia on the England of the
Middle Ages, before the invention of the printing press, rather than
on the nineteenth century. (Though one must remember that the
Middle Ages were more alive to him than they are to most of us.) All
this seems a far cry from George Eliot. It explains why *Nowhere* is not
usually thought of as a novel at all. But Morris is not so much opposite
to her practice as taking it to its logical extreme. When he converts
medieval England into a vision of the future the result is not
fundamentally different from a book like *Silas Marner* which
transforms the 'organic community' of the past into the embodiment
of a rural reality which is still just within reach. There is far less
difference than meets the eye between Eppie and Aaron's happiness
at the end of her novel and the life Ellen and the rest lead in Nowhere.
If anything, George Eliot's picture is the rosier one, more purged of
sadness. But both writers make a selection from the actual in the
service of an ideal.

But though *News From Nowhere* presents an ideal, that does not
mean that it is idealised. It is less of an idyll than it seems. Indeed, it
is one of the most poignant things Morris ever wrote. For all its
atmosphere of etiolated healthiness, Nowhere is a constant source of
anxiety to the Guest. Morris is writing about 'hope', not present
pleasure, which explains why Ellen's farewell words to the Guest are
a suggestion that 'our happiness even would weary you' (p. 197).
That is, even if his hopes could be fulfilled, 'happiness' would still
elude him. Morris is actually less of a hedonist than the more
conservative Ruskin. On the book's last page, the Guest returns to

nineteenth-century England to be 'inexpressibly shocked' by 'a man who looked old' touching his hat to him with 'much servility' (p. 196). 'Hope' is all he is left with, and the faith that his glimpse of Nowhere 'may be called a vision rather than a dream' (p. 197). It is a moving ending, recoiling from one England to imagine another. The guest's journey has been like that of an explorer in a foreign country. Ill prepared, he is reminded at every stage of his 'weak side of not feeling sure of my position in this beautiful new country' (p. 145). What draws him towards Nowhere is precisely this sense of not belonging to it. Nothing could be less complacently sure about what England means. No wonder Morris reprinted Mr Podsnap in the *Commonweal* to show what he was fighting against. By setting his England in the future, Morris was able to guard his reader from the sort of familiar world he would have expected from a realistic novel. The point of his England is that we *shouldn't* recognise it. But this inaccessibility makes it significant, not sentimental. This does not mean that Morris was outside the literary mainstream of his time. *Nowhere* is only unusual in the *degree* to which it infers an imaginary England from a real one. George Eliot looked backwards to similar effect and Hardy's Jude, looking at distant Christminster, does as Morris does – or would, if Hardy would let him. Not many literary Englands are focussed in the present and nowhere else and Morris's is less of an exception that it seems.

When Morris dressed the inhabitants of his Communist Utopia in medieval clothes he showed that he needed nostalgia to help him imagine the future. There was nothing unique in this. He had learnt it from Ruskin as Ruskin had learnt it from the Carlyle of *Past and Present*. All three would have liked to re-locate history (or part of it) in the future. The past served as a tool for rejecting the present as much as to feed nostalgia. If England is really an idea rather than a material fact then it is natural that both responses should be essential for imagining it. Without them, it becomes merely so many square miles charted on a map or a heap of statistics from one of Mr Gradgrind's Blue Books. Morris realised that although the Victorian novelists invited him to think of it in terms of its 'local colour' there was no reason to suppose that that was the *only* way of thinking of it. To demarcate the actual from the imaginary – as hard to do with *Adam Bede* as with *Nowhere* – may falsify both and leave England more problematic still.

In fact, an over-meticulous realism can sometimes shade into

pastoral, or at least into the town-dweller's dream of the country. The
paradox is illustrated by George Eliot herself, in *The Natural History
of German Life*, in a brilliant critique of Holman Hunt's painting *The
Hireling Shepherd*:

> Where, in our picture exhibition, shall we find a group of true peasantry?
> What English artist even attempts to rival in truthfulness such studies of
> popular life as the pictures of Teniers or the ragged boys of Murillo? Even
> one of the greatest painters of the pre-eminently realistic school, while, in his
> picture of 'The Hireling Shepherd', he gave us a landscape of marvellous
> truthfulness, placed a pair of peasants in the foreground who were not much
> more real than the idyllic swains and damsels of our chimney ornaments ...
> English rustics, whose costume seems to indicate that they are meant for
> ploughmen, with exotic features that remind us of a handsome *primo tenore*.
> Rather than such cockney sentimentality as this, as an education for the
> taste and sympathies, we prefer the most crapulous group of boors that
> Teniers ever painted ... The notion that peasants are joyous, that the typical
> moment to represent a man in a smock-frock is when he is cracking a joke
> and showing a row of sound teeth, that cottage matrons are usually buxom,
> and village children necessarily rosy and merry, are prejudices difficult to
> dislodge from the artistic mind, which looks for its subjects into literature
> instead of life. The painter is still under the influence of idyllic literature,
> which has always expressed the imagination of the cultivated and town-
> bred, rather than the truth of rustic life.[15]

This is worth quoting at length because it is still excellent criticism,
both witty and profound, and it is not well known (writers on the
PRB often ignore it, perhaps because it puts them on the spot).
Hunt's painting is a fine one but it is, indeed, very literary. It is
possible to 'read' the whole of it in terms of Milton's 'Lycidas' ('The
hungry sheep look up and are not fed') without forcing the parallels.
George Eliot's brisk demolition of its rural myth is itself enough to
show that a novel like *Silas Marner* proceeds from a quite different
understanding of country life. It has nothing in common with Hunt's
poetical 'chimney ornaments'. And yet, as she notices, his painting is
by no means simply vague and prettified: it is enormously detailed
and (externally) observant and innovative in technique. It turns out
that the more laborious kind of Victorian realism, of which Hunt was
the epitome, could consort quite happily with a blatantly 'town-
bred' picturesque mythology. However much such artists might try
to render reality, their eyes drew a rose-tinted veil over the real
country with its muck and smells. It was this that made George Eliot
so annoyed.

In the famous seventeenth chapter of *Adam Bede* she applied these thoughts about painting to the novel:

It is for this rare, precious quality of truthfulness that I delight in many Dutch paintings, which lofty-minded people despise. I find a source of delicious sympathy in these faithful pictures of monotonous homely existence, which has been the fate of so many more among my fellow-mortals than a life of pomp or of absolute indigence, of tragic sufferings or of world-stirring actions. I turn, without shrinking, from cloud-borne angels, from prophets, sibyls, and heroic warriors, to an old woman bending over her flower-pot, or eating her solitary dinner, while the noonday light...just touches the rim of her spinning wheel.

Her 'idealistic friend', who finds this 'vulgar' and 'low', is sent packing: 'human feeling...does not wait for beauty'. The literary and picturesque accretions of pastoral have to be peeled away to get at the thing itself. The realist must de-mythologise. Yet this programme proved harder to accomplish in practice than in theory. Its spirit is much less documentary than it seems. Words like 'delicious' and 'lovable' are the key ones in it and it is not always easy to distinguish them as completely as the author wants to from those like 'lofty-minded' and 'idealistic' which belong to the opposite camp. Flaubert's *Un Coeur Simple* has a deep compassion but too deep, surely, for reading it to be 'delicious'. In some respects, it would be truer to say that George Eliot replaced a false set of literary models of the countryside with more authentic ones. When she came to create something like The Rainbow Inn in *Silas Marner* she naturally drew freely on her recollections of Scott's rustics and the Shakespeare of Dogberry and Verges. She needed to do so, in order to be faithful to her impressions of rural life. There was no subterfuge in this since both her humanitarianism and her reading were *part* of that life as she saw it. Her 'truthfulness' is English, quite unlike anything French, even in George Sand, because the country in France was a quite different thing with a different history. It is not surprising, then, that it should be so hard to draw any dividing line in *Silas Marner* between where history stops and where the myth of the 'organic community' begins. Perhaps there isn't one? Mrs Leavis has argued persuasively, and with much evidence, that the 'organic community' really was history once.[16] As soon as we begin to talk about George Eliot's 'Englishness' we are back to the premise, whether we see it as radicals or conservatives, that, whenever it has real significance, England is always a country of the mind.

A more modern way of putting this is to say that, since England is forever changing, the notion of *a real England*, must always be a chimera. We have learnt to see it relatively from the novelists, above all from Hardy, who is still taken to be quintessentially 'English' even today. The process was a gradual one and, as a poet at least, he perhaps never abandoned an older way of seeing England. In an early novel like *Far From the Madding Crowd*, social change is contained by locating the action inside a Wessex that seems cut off from the rest of England and self-sufficient. Like earlier pastoral settings, Weatherbury is defined as much by what it excludes as by what it actually is. There is no hint of any England that is not rural. Within these limits, Hardy's historical record of traditional Wessex life can be allowed to shade off towards the mood of the sheep-shearing idyll in *The Winter's Tale*. Again, realism is reinforced through feelings and impressions that do not usually belong with it. James very quickly saw how much the young Hardy owed to George Eliot.[17] Their closeness can be measured by the invitation both extend to nostalgia. But later Hardy is not like this. The world of *Jude the Obscure* is in the grip of accelerated change and fragmentation; it allows no nostalgic backward glances to rural Wessex. If Hardy has not had all the credit he deserves for chronicling this for us it is because so many of us *want* to look back on him with nostalgia. A modern reader ('town-bred'), who thinks that Little Hintock and Marygreen are merely new versions of Weatherbury, therefore reads Hardy through a sort of double nostalgia. But in reality, of course, an English countryman like Gabriel Oak has become a Giles Winterborne, trapped by social circumstance. Hardy may still begin from some traditional myth – Tess is the 'forsaken maid' – but his ballad tales lead into the modern world. One might say that he enacted the programme of *Adam Bede* more rigorously than its author did. Winterborne, in *The Woodlanders*, provides a particularly clear illustration of the deliberate disjunctions of meaning that one finds in Hardy's characters. He stands for the dying class of the life-holder, the independent yeoman whose family has lived on the same spot for generations, passing on a rich body of rural lore. As someone who lives close to nature – the woods – he can appear as a figure of poetry:

He looked and smelt like Autumn's very brother, his face being sunburnt to wheat-colour, his eyes blue as corn-flowers, his sleeves and leggings dyed with fruit stains, his hands clammy with the sweet juice of apples, his hat sprinkled with pips, and everywhere about him that atmosphere of cider which at its first return each season has such an indescribable fascination for those who have been born and bred among the orchards. Her heart rose from its late sadness like a released bough; her senses revelled in the sudden lapse back to Nature unadorned.[18]

This is Hardy's prose at its best and *The Woodlanders* is one of the most poetic of the Wessex Novels. The image of Grace Melbury's heart responding like a 'released bough' when she sees this Autumnal Giles is especially beautiful. In short, this is the Hardy many readers choose to remember. But Hardy is giving us Grace's view of its hero, not necessarily his own. She goes on thinking of him as 'the fruit-god and the wood-god' but, at the end of the novel, instead of representing natural man, we see Giles dying slowly for propriety in the wood. He has lost his house, is unable to marry Grace and, when she leaves her husband, he vacates his hut for her and sleeps outside despite his mortal fever. He sacrifices himself in the body out of love for her, culture and morality repressing 'nature'. (It is the educated Fitzpiers who acts on natural impulse.) So Giles sinks back into his decaying woods, no longer 'sunburnt to wheat-colour':

The look of his face – what had there been about his face which seemed different from its appearance of yore? Was it not thinner, less rich in hue, less like that of ripe Autumn's brother to whom she had formerly compared him? And his voice; she had distinctly noticed a change in tone. And his gait; surely it had been feebler, stiffer, more like the gait of a weary man. (p. 286)

It is an extraordinary scene though it is too fertile in contradictions to come off. At one moment Grace blames herself in almost Lawrentian terms for having 'neglected' Giles 'in the body'; at another, she is idealising 'his freedom from the grosser passions'. Human feelings veer this way and that under the conflicting forces of nature and custom. The only real reality is the dank, decaying wood into which Giles and his kind were born and into which he dies. Yet, as the hints of social Darwinism imply, Hardy also takes his death for a symbol of the decline of a social class that has failed to adapt to modern conditions. Is he then an ideal countryman, 'ripe Autumn's brother', a victim of change, or both at once? What exactly is he a casualty of? The pathos of the scene is of a very complex and unresolved sort. It is far from easy to connect the Giles of the beautiful tree-planting scene at the start of the novel with the Giles who plays out a highly-strung moral drama at the end, dying of consumption. Do the woods reclaim him or has he fallen victim to a half-cultured modern Miss who has been to a provincial finishing school? How far can we still think of him as a poetic figure, a stalwart symbol of English yeomanry? Does Hardy really know what his novel is saying about his and Grace's sexuality? We have more questions than answers. No wonder that the young James Joyce complained that his English predecessors were always 'beating about the bush'.[19]

All one can say with confidence about this flawed but deeply suggestive novel is that Giles Winterborne is not Gabriel Oak, nor Little Hintock Weatherbury, nor – one might add – is England still England. There is nothing in *The Woodlanders*, in contemporary terms, to suggest that Giles is any more 'English' than Fitzpiers is. Indeed, he becomes an anachronism. That is why Grace goes back to her husband after his death – he represents the future. The remarkable thing about the novel is that Hardy can both imagine Giles in depth (he can write marvellously about his work, for example) *and* show us how England has moved on from him and turned him into a myth. These are not conclusions that George Eliot drew from Adam Bede though they may have been latent in him. Unlike her, Hardy took the idea of England in his finest novels and broke it down into the incompatible Englands out of which it had been constituted. That is why he more and more needed to find ways of saying at least two things about it at the same time. How many of his readers, even today, are ready to listen to both is doubtful: the appeal of the Giles who is 'ripe Autumn's brother' remains very strong.

The Woodlanders is the last Hardy novel which still tried to see England as a traditional rural community, albeit a reduced and isolated one. In the Wessex of Tess and Jude this is no longer possible. This is not simply because Hardy was a social historian, interested in change. He rightly called the setting of his books 'Wessex' and not Dorset. More than George Eliot's, they make subtle alterations to England as he knew it in real life. For instance, whereas her novels invariably include some clergyman as a focal point of village life, his either omit the clergy or minimise their role. This was no doubt partly a comment on their dwindling importance and partly a reflection of his own religious views but it was also a way of removing an essential moral and social cement from rural life, a way of de-stabilising it. (Reference to Hardy's own biography soon shows how important someone like the Rev. Horace Moule actually was in it). As a social historian, George Eliot was more accurate in this respect

– any real vicar of Little Hintock would have had far more to say about his parishioners' goings on – but her fidelity to the actual sometimes lacked his instinct for the way the actual was changing. Just as rural England was often taken for an epitome of England in general, though excluding as much as it included, so Hardy's Wessex was a selection from his actual Dorset. In other words, his position had something in common with that of the Morris who wrote *Nowhere*: social reality provided the basis for a selection from which he could generalise. It was not simply a matter of distorting England. Hardy was no longer as sure as writers like Dickens and George Eliot had been as to what England really was. One need only look at the end of *Jude the Obscure* – with Jude and Sue alienated, homeless and ostracised – to see why. It was in precisely their mood of despair that Morris's Guest awoke to find himself in Nowhere. Jude and Sue never get that far but their England is equally putative. Hardy's development from the solid world of *Far From the Madding Crowd* to *Jude* was a drastic and traumatic one: an England which had begun as a reality had become no more than a hypothesis.

It is important that this kind of disorientation was not confined to dreamers and revolutionaries. Richard Jefferies was one of the most down-to-earth writers of the period, the recorder of a particular part of England which he knew as well as Hardy knew his, and yet, like Morris, he chose to explore his feelings about England through a non-realistic fable set in the future. Unlike Morris, however, he had no political ideology to help him explain how his present could become this future and so his *After London* (1884) is simply based on the premise that civilisation has gone backward, a millennium after London has been obliterated in some unspecified disaster. Jefferies makes this fantasy convincing by drawing on the gift for observation that had already made him a fine country writer. His imaginary England has a rich sense of locality that makes Nowhere look rather placeless. The book is admirably exact about the physical texture of life and work in the future; its 'local colour' is substantial, never merely decorative. One notices the difference between the way a farmer like Jefferies felt his environment and Morris's 'Arts and Crafts' attitude to it. David Garnett remarked that Jefferies was unable to imagine how the vast edifice of nineteenth-century civilisation could suddenly disappear but what is really interesting about *After London* is surely the fact that a writer as committed to present realities as Jefferies was should have *wanted* to imagine the dissolution of England at all.[20] He is, after all, just the sort of writer who is usually taken for an exemplar of 'Englishness'. Surely he must have known what England was?

Of course, Jefferies's 'Wild England' is in some ways simply a heightened version of the agricultural depression of the late nineteenth century, most familiar to us from Hardy's *Tess*. But 'Wild England' is also a reversal of present circumstances. As W. J. Keith points out in his book on Jefferies, 'instead of the town overwhelming the country, it is the country that has survived and destroyed the town' so that 'Nature reassumes her sway'.[21] What was hinted at at the end of *Silas Marner*, where Lantern Yard seems to be finally exorcised from Eppie's and Aaron's England, has become a reality. London has somehow disappeared into its own pollution leaving only a poisonous swamp in the middle of the vast lake that now stretches right across the centre of the country. No one can remember how this destruction came about. Thus, when the novel opens, there is a new England there, waiting to be charted. The fact that 'Wild England' is so unlike that of Victoria in its precarious institutions, the crudeness of its culture and its lack of technology is really a smokescreen. Despite its medieval trappings, its world is the present one, an England of social disharmony and religious decline. Its disintegration is confirmed by the fact that those characters who stand for civilised values – Felix, Aurora and Sir Conflans – are marginalised, like dissidents. Felix undertakes his voyage around the great lake because he is an outsider, with no role in society. Only an outsider can chart England truly. Disguising his noble birth, he associates with grooms and begins to see society from their point of view, 'how feebly it was held together by brute force, intrigue, cord, and axe, and woman's flattery' (p. 140). Jefferies is particularly good on class, and the evils of the class system of the 'Relapse into Barbarism' turn out to be only too familiar. The point of translating them into the future is that only there is it possible to imagine any alternative to them. The thought of England as it is would impede any thought of what it might become. But Jefferies's future is itself another Dark Age. Felix's qualification to be a hero is neither strength nor bravery but simply the fact that he knows just enough about the lost arts and sciences to understand how badly in need of them his world is. Unlike the Victorians, the one thing the English of *After London* do know is their own limitations.

After London is not a nostalgic book, though it is in many ways a conservative one. Its landscape is an ambivalent one, both attractive and threatening. If it harks back to the England before the enclosures it is also a world in which agriculture is little more than rudimentary. Nature is beautiful but inhospitable and man can no longer claim to be its master. Those communities it still harbours on its fringes huddle together as much for protection from it as from each other. Yet Jefferies thinks of this 'Wild England' as a salutary antidote to conventional pastoral (rather like Egdon Heath). It is a way of dismantling the received picturesque idea of England in order to get at something more authentic beneath its surface, a process to be repeated by such later writers as Lawrence, John Cowper Powys and Ted Hughes. For Jefferies this does not mean decking out the future in the brightest garments of the past, as it sometimes did for Morris. There is nothing ideal or revivalist about his Middle Ages. The baronial feuding of *After London* suggests no Sir Walter Scott-like romance: it is itself an index of 'barbarism'. For most people in this world, life is 'nasty, brutish and short'. Yet Jefferies still needs to have things both ways, like other novelists. In the end, Felix turns out to be a redoubtable bowman, a sort of futuristic Robin Hood, an aristocrat transformed into a sturdy English yeoman. Jefferies contrives to sum up in him the experience of life as a noble, a plebeian and a king, an even wider range of experience than Morris gave to the heroes of prose romances like *The Well at the World's End*. Felix ends up as the chief of a tribe of shepherds whose task is to conquer the forest without taming its wildness, just as he had navigated the Lake without infringing on its mystery. All this is no mere escape into a fantasy past, even if Felix does at times seem like an advocate of the 'organic community'. What gives him the power to change his 'Wild England' is that he possesses more of the learning of the past than anyone else does. Jefferies hints that his own England already has the means of rectifying its failings in its own hands. That is why *After London*, though it may seem contrived, is neither a dream-like nor a despairing book but an invigorating one. At its heart it has a clear idea of what England ought to be like, neither a pastoral idyll nor an 'Epoch of Rest', but a place of skilful and determined work. What stays longest with us after reading it is not the surface medievalising (two-edged as that is) but the many fine descriptions of real places where people are making real things. This association of rural 'Englishness' with work is at the root of the book's distinction and what makes it uncommon in a positive way. It is also, as I implied, part of its conservativeness. It is as if Jefferies could only go on celebrating the English virtues that Hardy mourned the loss of in his Winterborne by transporting them to a future radically unlike any he could reasonably expect.

After London and *News From Nowhere* mark a limit to how England could be represented in the nineteenth-century novel. Together with *Jude the Obscure*, which came out midway between them, they testify to a need to rewrite England, to turn it inside out and upside down. In that respect, they are precursors of a novel like *Women in Love*. For all their involvement with their own social world, their ambivalent relation to 'realism', they are also *imaginary* Englands and, by that token, *literary* Englands too. But though no writer of the period has shaped, and shapes, our idea of England more than Hardy, his kind of literary version of it was by no means the only kind. Some writers of the time *began* from the premise that England was already, intrinsically, literary. Housman's *A Shropshire Lad* appeared at almost the same time as *Jude*. Yet there is little enough in common between his 'lads' and a lad like Jude or, for that matter, between his elegiac Shropshire and Jefferies's flesh and blood Wiltshire. Housman rarely set foot in his poetic country, preferring to see it from a distance, so that one could say that his Shropshire was *more* literary than real. A more complex example of something similar can be found in Henry James.

James's version of England begins with his earliest stories and is inseparable from his Americanness. (Americans have always been amongst the staunchest believers in England and 'Englishness'). The *donnée* of an early tale like *A Passionate Pilgrim* is that a cultured American already has a rich image of England in his mind's eye long before he first visits the country itself. Pre-Raphaelite paintings, Phiz's illustrations to Dickens, the Picturesque tradition of landscape all prepared him for what to expect even before he saw the real thing. In a way, the 'real thing' was literary and artistic in itself. Its literariness was not simply something imputed to it by culture-starved Americans. The narrator begins by noting this 'latent preparedness of the American mind for even the most delectable features of English life'.[22] The tale itself is a rather finely spun and somewhat too wistful business, about a dying American who thinks he may have a distinct claim on a great English estate, but its sense of place and nationality go much deeper than this suggests. Everything in England strikes Searle, the 'pilgrim', as hauntingly familiar, even the inn where he first stays, which comes straight out of Dickens and Smollett and Boswell and which he has seen 'in dreams' years before. Here is the narrator's response to 'the little village of Hampton Court':

Just the scene around me was the England of my visions. Over against us, amid the deepening bloom of its ordered garden, the dark red palace, with its formal copings and its vacant windows, seemed to tell of a proud and splendid past; the little village nestling between park and palace, around a patch of turfy common, with its tavern of gentility, its ivy-towered church, its parsonage, retained to my modernised fancy the lurking semblance of a feudal hamlet. It was in this dark composite light that I had read all English prose; it was this mild moist air that had blown from the verses of English poets; beneath these broad acres of rain-deepened greenness a thousand honoured dead lay buried. (p. 240)

Searle's pilgrimage ends in Oxford with him pretending to be a remote ancestor who had been a student there. The place seems 'framed to minister to the book-begotten longing for a medium in which one may dream unwaked' but, before he dies, the hero realises that, as an American, he belongs to 'the opposite pole' himself:

Naked come we into a naked world. There is a certain grandeur in the absence of a *mise en scène*, a certain heroic strain in those young imaginations of the West, which find nothing made to their hands, which have to concoct their own mysteries, and raise high into our morning air, with a ringing hammer and nails, the castles in which they dwell. (p. 239)

It is a moot point whether it is the American or the English Searle who eventually dreams most. The very nudity of American civilisation is a spur to the imagination. *A Passionate Pilgrim* may be only an early tale, shot through with clichés, but it is fascinating as a foretaste of the mature James. All through his work, places and characters are introduced as typically 'English' in just the same way, even when they are not being seen through American eyes. A famous example is the first appearance of Lord Warburton, the epitome of his class, in the setting of Gardencourt. It is hard there to draw the line between social observation and a kind of 'dream' that is only a more sophisticated version of Searle's. To say which is not merely to say that American fiction, with its tendency to 'romance', is very different from English. As I have been trying to show, in the later nineteenth century the English novelists themselves came surprisingly close to seeing England in the American way.

One of James's most affectionate portraits of England can be found in another novel of the 1890s, *The Awkward Age*. It is one of his masterpieces, though it has nothing to do with America. At the end of the novel, Nanda Brookenham turns away from a London which James increasingly disliked (just as Morris did) to a more genuine, rural England symbolised by Mr Longdon's house at Beccles in Suffolk. Mr Longdon offers his house to the forlorn heroine who has come 'out' too early, as a refuge from a society in which she is in danger of being corrupted. Mr Longdon is a survival from another age (he had been in love with Nanda's grandmother) and his Suffolk has scarcely changed since Gainsborough's day:

> Beyond the lawn the house was before him: Vanderbank – old, square, red-roofed, well assured of its right to the place it took up in the world. This was a considerable space – in the little world, at least, of Beccles – and the look of possession had everywhere mixed with it, in the forms of old windows and doors, the tone of old red surfaces, the style of old white facings, the age of old high creepers, the long confirmation of time ... the thing was one of those impressions of a particular period that it takes two centuries to produce.[23]

Perhaps only American innocence and culture could find so much poetry in the mere sound of the word 'old'. What makes Mr Longdon particularly English for James is his spotless unworldliness. His England and the London England of Mrs Brookenham and her 'set' won't mix. Nanda has to choose between them and the novel ends when her choice is made. It is as though the great novelist of manners were giving in to the solicitations of pastoral – or it would be if one hadn't known all along how strong the element of 'dream' was in James's realism. But it does not take much imagination to work out that the house in Beccles is really a variant on Lamb House, Rye and the benign Mr Longdon an untravelled version of Henry James himself.

The apt choice of Suffolk for Mr Longdon's house was no accident. James was especially fond of the county and its countryside reminded him of the English tradition of landscape painting. There is an eloquent essay on it in *English Hours* – appropriately entitled 'Old Suffolk' – which sees it as the epitome of everything he thought most 'English'. Among other impressions, it evokes for him the boyhood of David Copperfield. It is a rural England, of course, but one that feels more written about than farmed:

> the very essence of England has a way of presenting itself with completeness in almost any fortuitous combination of rural objects at all, so that, wherever you may be, you get, reduced and simplified, the whole of the scale. The big house and its woods are always at hand; with a 'party' always, in the

intervals of shooting, to bring down to the rustic sports that keep up the tradition of the village green. The russet, low-browed inn, the 'ale-house' of Shakespeare ... The pretty girls, within sight of it, alight from the Marquis's wagonette ... And it is always Hodge and Gaffer that, at bottom, *font les frais* – always the mild children of the glebe on whom, in the last resort, the complex superstructure rests.[24]

Though this refers to a real place, and one James had recently visited, everything is evoked through a haze of nostalgia. Suffolk may be real but it has the extra virtue of not seeming real. James is thankful not to have to mix up England's poetry with its prose. He may see that the picture is a 'complex superstructure' but he has no inkling of the actual divisions within it. He writes as Nanda might have written after a long stay at Beccles. Even the subtlest writers can be emotionally simple at times, simple enough, almost, to call to mind Housman's equally beautiful and vague Shropshire:

> That is the land of lost content,
>   I see it shining plain,
> The happy highways where I went
>   And cannot come again.

Housman, in fact, though simpler, is really more honest than James who was as well-placed as any writer to know how complex the world had become and had less excuse for hymning a poignantly beautiful dead-end. There is a harshness to the lyricism of *A Shropshire Lad* that 'Old Suffolk' lacks, even if Housman never lets one suspect that Shropshire had been the cradle of the Industrial Revolution. His poems mark the point at which rural England, once synonymous with the actuality of the country, has itself turned into an alternative to the actual. There are, of course, other writers in the period for whom it remained as real as it ever was – writers like Jefferies and Sturt – but they underline the point: one never catches them writing about it as if it belonged to the realm of poetry as James does.

  James and Housman do nonetheless remind us that realism and observation are not the only ways of finding out what a country feels like to live in. They at least understand that they are dealing as much with a construction of the mind as an actual phenomenon. Their England, even if it seems thin, is invested with a multiplicity of hopes and fears. In the modern period, when the idea of England has been especially problematic, it seldom omits an element of dream. But dream entails more than just nostalgia and escapism. In Jefferies and Morris it makes possible the juxtaposition of one England against another. James tried to do the same thing himself in a novel like *The Princess Casamassima*, not to propose an ideal England but to elicit the paradoxes and ironies inherent in the one he knew. This hinterland between fact and possibility has been the traditional territory of pastoral. Spenser, for instance, understood very well that a rejection of the actual world could also be a way of acknowledging its power. Writing about faery land did not prevent him from finding a place for contemporary Ireland in his story. As Empson recognised in *Some Versions of Pastoral*, the sort of rejection that entails recognition is integral to pastoral as a form. He develops the point in a brilliant passage on Hardy, noting that tragedy can also have a part in pastoral:

Thomas Hardy is fond of showing us an unusually stupid person subjected to very unusual bad luck, and then a moral is drawn ... that we are all in the same boat as this person, whose story is striking precisely because it is unusual. The effect may be very grand, but to make an otherwise logical reader accept the process must depend on giving him obscure reasons for wishing it so. It is clear at any rate that this grand notion of the inadequacy of life, so various in its means of expression, so reliable as a bass note in the arts, needs to be counted as a possible territory for pastoral.[25]

What Empson says might be applied equally well to the unusual *good* luck that pastoral often celebrates and that is, in ways we have seen, the obverse of a Hardy tragedy. Certainly, the 'territory' he defines is one where a Hardy can sometimes meet up with a Morris. But Empson is also concerned to pin down a particular kind of imaginative sleight of hand and this too has been common amongst writers concerned with imagining a changing England. Thus, pastoral has sometimes helped them to come to terms with things rather than suggesting a way of evading them. The invention of a new England may sometimes help us to accept the one we have.

NOTES

(Place of publication is London unless otherwise stated)

1 *Revaluation* (Penguin, Harmondsworth, 1964), p. 17.
2 *The Lion and the Unicorn: Socialism and the English Genius*, introd. by Bernard Crick (Penguin, Harmondsworth, 1982), p. 54.
3 Her review of *Modern Painters III* can be found in *The Essays of George Eliot*, ed. Thomas Pinney (Routledge and Kegan Paul, 1963), p. 267.
4 See his review of *Middlemarch* in *The House of Fiction: Essays on the Novel by Henry James*, ed. Leon Edel (Mercury Books, 1962).

5 See Arnold's 'Memorial Verses'.

6 The episode occurs in *Modern Painters V*, part ix, chapter 2.

7 Geoffrey Hill has written acutely about George Eliot's mythologising of England in 'Redeeming the Time' in *The Lords of Limit: Essays on Literature and Ideas* (André Deutsch, 1984). (See my chapter 8.)

8 See John Lucas on this in *England and Englishness: Ideas of Nationhood in English Poetry* 1688–1900 (Hogarth Press, 1990), p. 102.

9 *Letters from Edward Thomas to Gordon Bottomley*, ed. with introd. by R. George Thomas (Oxford University Press, 1968), p. 158.

10 *Unto This Last and Other Writings by John Ruskin*, ed. with introd. by Clive Wilmer (Penguin, Harmondsworth, 1985), p. 226.

11 'Dorset', *The Shires, Collected Poems* 1970–1983 (Carcanet, Manchester, 1983), pp. 22–3.

12 Arnold's strictures on Ruskin's eccentricities occur in 'The Function of Academies'.

13 *Our Mutual Friend*, chapter 11.

14 *The Nonesuch Morris*, ed. G. D. H. Cole (New York, 1974), p. 21.

15 'The Natural History of German Life', *Essays of George Eliot*, pp. 268–9.

16 See her very full introduction and notes to the Penguin edition of *Silas Marner* (Harmondsworth, 1967).

17 James's review of *Far From the Madding Crowd* can be found in *The House of Fiction*, ed. Edel, pp. 268–73.

18 *The Woodlanders*, ed. Dale Kramer (Oxford University Press, 1981), p. 193.

19 Richard Ellmann, *James Joyce* (Oxford University Press, 1965), p. 242.

20 David Garnett, introd. to *After London and Amaryllis at the Fair* (Everyman, 1939), p. ix.

21 *Richard Jefferies: A Critical Study* (University of Toronto Press, 1965), p. 122.

22 'A Passionate Pilgrim', *The Complete Tales of Henry James*, ed. Leon Edel (Hart-Davis, 1961), ii, p. 239.

23 *The Awkward Age* (Penguin, Harmondsworth, 1966), p. 245.

24 *English Hours*, ed. with introd. by Alma Louise Lowe (Mercury Books, 1963), pp. 200–1.

25 *Some Versions of Pastoral* (Penguin, Harmondsworth, 1966), *p.* 96.

CHAPTER 2

Edward Thomas: An England of 'holes and corners'

never aiming at what a committee from Great Britain and Ireland might call complete, – I wished to make a book as full of English character and country as an egg is of meat.[1]

Most of the writers discussed in this book shared Thomas's belief that poets and politicians who bang the drum for England simply deflect us from what it really is:

The worst of the poetry being written today is that it is too deliberately, and not inevitably, English. It is for an audience: there is more in it of the shouting of rhetorician, reciter, or politician than of the talk of friends and lovers.[2]

At a time of national crisis a true intimacy of speech was more necessary than ever. People needed to speak to and not *at* each other. England should not turn into a debating chamber. Hence, Thomas's distaste for the public intimacies of Rupert Brooke. Yet his own shyness might have struck earlier poets – Drayton, say, or Milton – as odd and even morbid. Isn't all poetry 'for an audience'? For Thomas, the 'audience' is a snare and a distraction from his 'England', a realm stripped of all urbanity which he thinks of as 'a place of innumerable holes and corners'.[3] Not, that is, an England to be found on any official map.

In our own time, as in 1914–18, the market in patriotism is cornered by sectional interests. The fervour of the press during the 'Falklands War' recalled that of 1914 and was equally remote from the mood of the troops themselves. At such times, the word 'England' is quickly annexed by particular ideologies and a certain kind of art soon follows suit. An Elgar travels the country with rousingly jingoistic concerts and a Brooke is made into a hero.[4] The patriotic becomes the brassy, as do the 'values' from the past that it appeals to.

No doubt such shrill insistence serves today to mask a worrying new subjection to international forces. It may even help to legitimate them, making a hubbub at the gate while they enter by the back door. The patriotic mind is skilled at pulling the wool over its own eyes. This is why the word 'England' becomes so difficult to use honestly, just when one might expect to use it most. This is what Thomas found once war began. The pressure on the word led him to limit it to its private and local senses. For as soon as it was used in its public sense its meaning became tarnished and problematical. The two senses no more coincided than his own 'England' coincided with Brooke's Grantchester.

Sensing this fissure in the idea of England, Thomas understood that it was sometimes best to keep quiet about his country. Unlike the Forster of *Howards End*, he knew that it wasn't enough to write 'England' with a plangent cadence for England itself to be conjured up. The native tradition was harder to continue, harder, surely, than Edna Longley imagines when she sees Thomas as the conduit through which the poetry of Hardy reached Philip Larkin.[5] Such continuities, which it has taken fifty years to recognise, seem more like wishful thinking than traditions. Thomas knew that to express his England meant finding an English speech *of his own*, something the modern world hardly seemed to offer him. In an age of slogans, when so many of the poet's words had been stolen by rhetoricians, the cupboard was bound to look alarmingly bare. How much of what was left for the poet was rich enough to be problematic but sufficiently alive to be more than just a problem?

Such doubts are not peculiar to Thomas but later poets owe it to him to have faced up to them early on, at an unpropitious time. When, in our time, a poet like Tony Harrison explores the contrasting registers of English speech he is drawing on Thomas's legacy. Though Thomas was a Southerner and never used dialect he would have understood Harrison's anger at 'those gentlemen who silenced the men's oath / and killed the language that they swore it in.'[6] The more local language Harrison prefers may seem to rule out any general ideas of 'Englishness' but what other way is there to affirm that English poetry *is* 'English', not just 'written in English'?[7] It was precisely the hegemony of 'Southern English' which made Aurelius in *The Happy-Go-Lucky-Morgans*, Thomas's only novel, say: 'I really did not know before that England was not a shocking fiction of the journalists and politicians.'[8] Such blunt protests recall Dickens. They also indicate that the search for England was never merely nostalgic, despite the Housmans and Elgars. It was also a retrieval operation, a bid to capture some of those 'English' things which most 'English' people had never had.

All this evinces a common feature of modern English writing, what might be called its element of literary devolution. We have 'Northern' novelists and 'Liverpool' poets, voices from Northumberland and Ulster and even East Anglia – writers committed to their region first and their nation second. In the last century a writer like William Barnes was the exception but, since the time of Lawrence (an 'English' novelist from the Midlands), writers like Barnes have become the norm. They fall back on their regional identity for lack of a clear national one. But not out of mere provincialism. Lawrence was no provincial and nor was Basil Bunting, our last link with the heyday of modernism. It was as natural for Bunting to be a European or to explore the poetry of Persia and China as to be a Northumbrian. Similarly, Tony Harrison moves from Leeds to Greece or America. He by-passes London. Likewise Tomlinson, not to mention the obvious regionalists like R. S. Thomas and Norman Nicholson. When Ted Hughes leaves home we are likely to find him in Eastern Europe; Geoffrey Hill worries doggedly at his Midland roots, uncovering their foreignness. And what earlier poet would have looked for England in Hull as Larkin did? Even Betjeman animated only a section of his country, well demarcated by geography and class. The question that arises is not why all these writers find it so hard to imagine England as a whole but whether there is any longer an 'English' mainstream at all. Donald Davie argues eloquently that there is (though he traces it back to Hardy's equally regional 'Wessex') but perhaps it resembles Thomas's England of 'holes and corners' nonetheless?[9] In *Women in Love* Birkin tells Ursula that they will have to live in the 'chinks' between their spreading mass civilisation and this was what Thomas did when he narrowed down his England to 'holes and corners'. Davie's own book, *The Shires* (1974), is surely a celebration of those 'chinks', a poem for every county but none for London or England as a whole. Indeed, London seems a more likely theme for verse to an Australian like Peter Porter than it does to Davie or Hughes or Hill. If there *is* a central 'English' tradition, it will be recognised by what it excludes more than by what it includes. Thomas certainly looks forward, as Edna Longley claims, but it is only too easy to see why he should so often have thought of England in the past tense.

The first great literary regionalists were the 'Lake Poets', the provincial 'Lakers', derided by the more metropolitan Byron for questioning Dryden and Pope. Yet Wordsworth's England is a larger affair than any Thomas could conceive of. Nor does it stop at the borders of Westmorland as Hardy's effectively stopped where 'Wessex' did.[10] Bunting is right to remind us that Wordsworth was a regional writer too but his kind of regionalism provided a means of relating to the whole: it did not marginalise him. There was no hiatus between thinking of his native fells and the thought of his country as a whole. Nor did the Scottish border cut him – or Keats – off from Burns as it tends to cut us off today. As Thomas understood only too well, Wordsworth was one of the last English poets to write good poetry about England *as a state*, a real country and not just a country of the mind. As Coleridge put it:

> There lives nor form nor feeling in my soul
> Unborrowed from my country. O divine
> And beauteous island! thou hast been my sole
> And most magnificent temple, in the which
> I walk with awe.

England is a society, even a 'temple', not just the landscape it has so often been reduced to since. This comes out in the sonnets Wordsworth addressed to its people in the early 1800s. One may dislike these poems but they articulate a national ideal in a way later poets have done. When Thomas himself tries to do the same he only manages to hit the note of rhetoric while missing the accents of prophecy. 'This is no case of petty right or wrong' begins honestly enough but it can only express its feelings for England through second-hand reminiscences of *Henry V*:

> But with the best and meanest Englishmen
> I am one in crying, God save England, lest
> We lose what never slaves and cattle blessed.
> The ages made her that made us from dust:
> She is all we know and live by.[11]

It is more accomplished than better poems by Thomas and more like W. E. Henley than Wordsworth or Blake. It strains for effects which, to them, came spontaneously. To enter Thomas's real England, this public one must be left behind from the start. To him, the thought of England was a lonelier thought than it was to Coleridge and, perhaps for that reason, a less awesome one.

Wordsworth was writing in a tradition of verse about England that went back to Spenser, Drayton and the Shakespeare of the Histories, through Milton to Dryden and Pope, a tradition spacious enough to include minority views without becoming sectarian. By Tennyson's time this consensus was breaking up fast, either into public verse that was *too* public or into private verse that was *too* private. Tennyson wrote both but rarely in the same poem. His descendants – from Thomas himself to Alfred Austin and Sir Henry Newbolt – could only go down one road by ignoring the other. By distancing themselves from the England of Mr Podsnap's boasting, the best of them cut themselves off from part of the public for poetry which Tennyson, for all his divisions, had held together. A poet's public is, of course, a mirror of his nation. In this case, the mirror was broken long before Pound and Eliot appeared and were blamed for making poetry 'difficult'.

When Thomas compiled his anthology *This England* in 1915, he based it on 'a few most English poems like "When icicles hang by the wall".[12] Nearly every one of them had been written before he was born. Among the last writers he felt able to include were also the last great beneficiaries of the public his own generation had lost, Tennyson and Dickens. He found few later versions of 'Englishness' on which he could put his finger with any confidence. As it was, he chose poems about Lincolnshire from Tennyson and Lady Dedlock's 'India ink' view of the same county from *Bleak House*, passages that anticipate the melancholy tinge his own poems give to the English countryside. But what the anthologist passed over was even more revealing. He omitted Thomas Hardy, a writer today's readers often see as the epitome of all things English. Unlike them, or Donald Davie, he was unable to equate 'Wessex' with England – despite being one of the earliest admirers of Hardy's poems and preferring them to his novels. *This England* was part of Thomas's own preparation for writing poetry and no doubt this explains the inclusion in it of two poems of his own under his pen-name of 'Edward Eastaway'. 'Haymaking' and 'The Manor Farm' are beautiful and characteristic (in no way 'prentice work) but they seem startlingly narrow after Wordsworth. Edna Longley finds no break between them and the earlier poems Thomas chose – both poems evoke 'the timeless mystery that is England', she says, but do they?[13] What they evoke is 'a season of bliss unchangeable':

> Awakened from farm and church where it had lain
> Safe under tile and thatch for ages since
> This England, Old already, was called Merry. (TP, p. 49)

Is 'This' the right word? They are complex lines but words like 'safe' and 'unchangeable' suggest that 'England' has been laid down years before, like wine, and that its essence will never change. Yet Thomas knew that it had been changing for at least a century and that few of its inhabitants still located it in 'farm and church', except in dreams. However, as the reviewer of more modern books than virtually any writer of his time, Thomas knew very well that, as he wrote, Englishmen were already studying the *Principia Mathematica*, living in the houses of Voysey and Lutyens and reading the poetry of Ezra Pound. 'England', it seems, had to exclude more than just the brash public world of the patriot. Far from its being 'timeless', even to mention it was to pose a question – one which Thomas had no ready answer to. That is why he wanted to put his anthology, like his 'Haymaking', 'out of the reach of change'.

In one sense, Thomas made his 'choice of life' unusually quickly, both in his early mature writing (*The Woodland Life* was published in the year that he went up to Oxford) and in his decision, soon after graduating, to live in the country. From then on, the books and articles and reviews flowed from him like a river in spate, though whether from fertility or necessity is often hard to tell. Facility was always one of his gifts, whether as a hack-writer or as a poet. Nor was he the doomed hack he often took himself to be in his frequent moods of depression: he succeeded Lionel Johnson as the regular reviewer of the *Daily Chronicle* when only twenty-four. Yet Thomas was one of those rare writers who begin so early and quickly that they never quite have time to find their own voice. Philip Larkin was right to insist (albeit with a betraying flippancy) on the toll taken by this 'savage' hack-work that was the price Thomas paid for bringing up his family in the country.[14] He wrote so much that he had no time to discover where his writing was going. Even more paradoxically, he could be surprisingly slow at coming to terms critically with his own deepest literary influences, despite the fact that he was himself one of the most acute critics of other people's writing in pre-war England. For instance, it took him years (and books) to shed the *fin de siècle*

flavour his prose had acquired at Oxford in the late nineties. Pater's
was a particularly insidious influence, only fully exorcised in his 1913
book on him. It is true that, by then, Thomas was able to write what
is still one of the most penetrating accounts of Pater's style that we
have but, even so, there is a rather too tight-lipped rigour about his
criticism of him that makes one suspect that he was as yet too
uncertain of his ground to learn freely from Pater. Thomas seems to
have developed gradually, without the sudden spurts that characterise greater poets such as Wordsworth, and when his poems did
eventually come to him they still took him partly by surprise.

Why so sensitive a man as Thomas should have been so slow to see
his true vocation remains an enigma, one that even Larkin can't put
down just to the twin fate of being both a professional writer and the
head of a growing family. Nor, I think, should we interpret his career
solely in terms of his complex psychology – though thanks to the
work of William Cooke, R. George Thomas and others we are now
much better placed to do so than his earlier readers were. For part of
Thomas's problem, even before he became a 'man of letters', was
that he was so steeped in literature. This went deeper than the
particular influences which made his writing *literary*. His profound
empathy for the English Romantics, for example, must have meant
that he heard so many voices in his head that it became impossible to
distinguish his own. One of the most attractive qualities of his verse
is that he never pretends to have found out his own mind or know his
own way one whit more than he really does. The open, almost easy-
going tone with which many of his poems begin, receptive to
experience but not trying to button-hole it, was in reality very hard-
won. A part of his finding himself in verse was precisely a matter of *not*
claiming to know, *not* speaking from a fully-fledged literary persona
such as he had had to adopt in his commissioned books and his
reviewing. So often what spoils the early prose Thomas is constantly
having to wear his heart on his sleeve, forever ready to bring out, say,
the approved sort of heady reverence for Oxford architecture or the
appropriately tremulous sensitiveness to describe a beautiful landscape or a new poem. Always having to write as the sensitive,
cultured authority, whether he was or not, made writing more like
impersonation than self-expression. Moreover, the grip of this
manner must have been all the stronger because it combined Paterian
connoisseurship with the ready-to-wear sentiment of Grub Street. No
wonder that when Thomas did begin to speak with his own voice, in

his first poems and in a book like *In Pursuit of Spring*, that voice should have sounded so much more relaxed and so much less anxious to be noticed.

It was perhaps a condition of Thomas's finding himself as a writer that he should first stop seeking for himself. His self-consciousness, by his own admission, was endless and it may, paradoxically, help to explain why it was that, in his mid-thirties, the author of a score of books, with his commitment to the English countryside and English literature long confirmed, it was necessary for an American poet, Robert Frost, to point out to him that he could be an English one. Quite how much this took him by surprise is hard to tell now but, on the face of it, it should not have done. All the writers who had helped to make him the poet he was soon to become had been known to him for many years. The irony was that, like himself, most of them were prose writers: Jefferies, Cobbett, Sturt.[15] In *The Childhood of Edward Thomas*, he gives a vivid picture of his devotion to Jefferies whilst still a schoolboy at St Paul's (his class-mates thought books about gamekeepers distinctly beneath them) but it took him a long time to see that this prose England offered a more living alternative to the poetic England of the Georgians.[16] What writers like Jefferies and Sturt offered him was a literary representation of rural England which knitted it to the present day and the ordinary instead of cutting it off from the real world to drift in some far-off Romantic past. If their England was a shrinking one it was also alive and very tangible. Thomas particularly delighted in Sturt's various accounts of Bettesworth, the 'Surrey labourer' who worked for him as an old man. Praising them in *In Pursuit of Spring*, he singled out precisely those qualities which his own poems are admired for: unobtrusive steadiness, alertness to sensuous impressions, a lively feeling for vernacular English, the sense of a more vivid and less respectable England than that of literary convention. He also drew attention to Bettesworth's fascinating versatility as a worker, the fact that his countryside is a place of labour and never just a back-drop for a garrulous and rather roguish old man. In other words, to someone as saturated as Thomas was in over a century of 'nature poetry', Sturt figured as an underminer of stereotypes: 'in the end comes a picture out of the whole, painfully, dubiously emerging, truthful undoubtedly, subtle, not easy to understand...'[17] In short, Thomas's 'Englishness' would be unthinkable without English literature but it only came to life as his writing ceased to be 'literary'.

It would hardly be an exaggeration to say that writers like Jefferies
and Sturt, with their fidelity to fact and their plain, unpoetical
poetry, helped Thomas to get back beyond Pater and Swinburne to
the writer who counted most in his own verse, the Wordsworth of
'Michael' and 'The Solitary Reaper'.[18] Moreover, unlike Wordsworth, they provided the incentive of having written credibly about
the England he knew best: Surrey and Hampshire and Wiltshire.
That is, far from tempting him to make the local picturesque, they
revealed to him something of the actual social character of the
countryside to which, since his schooldays, he had so often escaped
from the stifling world of London. Jefferies, above all, taught him not
to be bookish about rural England, not to sentimentalise the life and
labour he found there, if he wanted to see nature as it really was: the
lesson was as much social as aesthetic. Not, of course, that Jefferies,
with his Tory background, offered a neutral picture of rural life but
he did provide something better than pastoral. Even *After London*, for
instance, with its romanticised feudalism (the gamekeeper on a
knightly quest?), becomes a powerful mythic exorcism of the late
Victorian preoccupation with money and respectability and class.
Jefferies, like Cobbett and Sturt, speaks for an England under threat
from such forces, an older, yeoman England, one which readily
admits a gamekeeper (or a poacher) into its fellowship but has little
more in common with an industrial 'hand' than the silk-hatted
capitalist he works for. Thus, in *In Pursuit of Spring*, Thomas jokingly
proposes that a statue of Bettesworth should be erected in Sturt's
home town of Farnham, both as a memorial and for the sake of seeing
the shocked expressions of the local bourgeoisie as they looked at it.
Village England, even at the turn of the twentieth century, is less
tainted by the modern class-system than the town is, however
threatened it is by the suburban civilisation of the villa-dwellers so
feared by Sturt and mocked by Forster. In the face of such threats, the
countryside could seem both an opportunity for freedom and, more
ambiguously, a kind of priest-hole. As Thomas said in *The Last Sheaf*:
'who ever met a landowner in a wood?'[19] Not everything is ruled by
class. Thus, just as Sturt talks to Bettesworth as a fellow human being
and not just as master to man, so Thomas, ex-St Paul's and Oxford,
talks without condescension or self-consciousness to a ploughman in
'As the Team's Head-Brass'. Julian Thomas recalled that after his
brother had finished his book on Pater he told him he wanted to write
prose 'as near akin as possible to the talk of a Surrey peasant'.[20] Even

without such testimony, it is not difficult to see how much his command of the vernacular in a poem like 'Lob' owed to Sturt. This is not to say that Thomas's concerns in 'Lob' are simply democratic. The English folklore the poem relies on is pre-democratic. The democrat wants all the citizens of the nation to meet together in one whole, whereas, in modern civilisation, the 'Englishness' Thomas identifies Lob with is an uncertain survival from the past and, therefore, a minority voice: that is why it is so elusive. The social implications of both the poem itself and the vernacular language it celebrates are inevitably ambiguous. Rather than trying to interpret them in terms either of right or left politics I would prefer to point out how much Thomas has in common with a more radical and post-war analysis of the England he had already glimpsed before the war. In *Lady Chatterley's Lover*, rural England also figures as a sort of hidden oasis under threat from the modern world. The England of the wood and the England of the collieries are starkly opposed, no common ground between them. In the final version of the novel the gamekeeper even has two completely distinct kinds of speech, one dialect and the other 'educated', which he switches between, according to whom he is speaking. Lawrence's diagnosis of the plight of the English is, of course, more drastic and more conscious than anything Thomas had to say on the subject. Nevertheless, much of what his novel says is already implicit in Thomas's mature work. It is possible to imagine that, had he too lived through the 1920s, he might have found himself staring into the same impasse that faces Connie and Mellors. This is why it seems more appropriate to think of his verse as contemporary with *The Rainbow* than with the Georgian anthologies or even *Howards End*. In its quieter way, it too had broken with the literariness of the one and the social compromises of the other.

In recent years, Thomas's poetry has been asked to carry a new and heavy load of significance, both as a central link in the native tradition and as an alternative to cosmopolitan modernism. In either case, the emphasis falls on the purity of his 'Englishness'. To most lovers of his poems, this will seem only fitting but, of course, by generalising Thomas's experience, it begs the whole question: how far does Thomas's England correspond to the England in which most English people have lived in this century? We know that in many ways his case was a special and unrepresentative one (for example, he thought of himself as a Welshman as well as an Englishman) so why should we be so ready to let him speak for us?[21] In what ways does his England answer our sense of what we would still like England to be?

Thomas's verse coincided with a watershed in English history when many features of English life were on the point of disappearing for ever. Often, the poems picture it as old and decaying ('The Barn') or inaccessibly remote:

> I would go back again home
> Now. Yet how should I go?
> This is my grief. That land,
> My home, I have never seen.   (TP, p.117)

For all his gift for first-hand observation as a nature writer, Thomas partly saw his England at a remove. He sought to preserve its memory rather as Cecil Sharp was trying to preserve its folk-songs. Like Yeats, with whose poetic career his own offers many parallels, he hoped that reviving the culture of the past might be a means of re-vitalizing that of the present.[22] He could not, of course, translate his 'Englishness' into national political terms as Yeats did with his 'Irishness', nor would he have wanted to if he could. Even in wartime he insisted that 'there is no need to be always blindly shouting like schoolboys at a football match'.[23] Moreover, he was too honest to deceive himself into believing that the England he loved could survive the war in anything but a depleted and marginal form. To him, the image of English commonalty was only clearly visible away from the crowd.

Thomas's alertness to such paradoxes has not prevented later writers from seeing him as an epitome of 'Englishness', rather in the way he himself thought of Izaak Walton. It is a tempting idea and one can even see that some of his poems might seem to invite it (for example, 'Words') but it inevitably tends to distract us from his tough intellectual side and over-emphasises the delicate, sensitive Thomas that moves us in the memoirs and biographies of him. Perhaps it is better to leave the role of being 'forever England' to Brooke? In any case it is misleading to assume that Thomas was as English as Brooke claimed to be. Such claims have more to do with rhetoric than with living traditions. Why see his poems as socio-cultural signposts rather than as writing? To read a good Thomas poem is to follow a live and subtle process of thinking, not to hunger after an abstraction. This is not to deny that many of the poems raise questions about the continuity of English life and, by implication, of English poetry as well. 'Questions' is the operative word. There is no need to take Thomas's version of England for granted. How much did it leave out and what validity did the selection he made have? Was an England which omitted Lord Northcliffe and Baden-Powell, Kitchener and Keir Hardie, Arnold Bennett and Winston Churchill, necessarily more authentic and more alive? Thomas would have distrusted the need to generalise about England and that is implicit in such questions but, in a subtler way, he generalised himself. That is, he defined his own idea of England by deliberately setting it off against all those things in England which he wished were absent from it. To revive one England meant exorcising another. Stan Smith, in one of the few unsentimental books on Thomas, argues that his England was actually a very particular one – southern, pastoral and gently melancholy – which his admirers have conspired to pass off as the country as a whole. His final commitment to it as a soldier strikes Smith as more bitterly tragic than devotees of his 'Englishness' like Andrew Motion can afford to admit. Smith values and enjoys Thomas's poetry at least as much as Motion does, and his account of it is more historically convincing, but he perhaps risks making him seem half responsible for the subterfuges of his admirers. Thomas did not claim to have a hot line to everything truly English. When his poems are wistful, as in 'Home', he makes it quite clear that it is because wistfulness happens to be his particular mood at that moment. It is easy to see why a later poet like Motion, committed to the idea of a native English tradition of modern poetry, should want to harness that wistfulness for purposes of his own but to co-opt Thomas into a myth of 'Englishness' does a disservice to his poetry. The idiom in which it is written – supple, informal, alert – is 'English' in a way that is the reverse of wistful or nostalgic.

It is not hard to see or sympathise with the desire of poets like Motion to present Thomas as representatively 'English'. If he cannot be made to fill such a part, what hope is there that a Larkin can, let alone Larkin's successors? Viewed sceptically, the tradition from Hardy through Thomas to Larkin and his heirs begins to seem like a progressive retreat or exile from some lost England. Of course, this is not the least English thing about it. Nor is the fact that onslaughts like Wyndham Lewis's *Blast* or much of the work of D. H. Lawrence should have had so little effect in denting the clinging fondness that so many modern English writers have felt for England. Not that

Edward Thomas was uncritical himself. He imagined an England *in spite* of his workaday one but he never equated his ideal and his actual England, as Brooke tried to. Indeed, he tried to make his England as real as it was still possible to make it, though he felt bitter about his chances of doing so: 'The countryman is dying out, and when we hear his voice, as in George Bourne's Bettesworth Book, it is more foreign than French. He had long been in decline, and now he sinks before the *Daily Mail* like a savage before pox or whisky. Before it is too late, I hope that the Zoological Society will receive a few pairs at their gardens.'[24] Much of Thomas's writing is elegiac in mood but thinking of 'the days that are no more' never blinded him to change or infected him with the revivalist spirit of so many Victorian writers and artists. Neither did his feeling for England make him insular or suspicious of Europe as Larkin was. As he wrote to Jesse Berridge in the autumn of 1914: 'I am slowly growing into a conscious Englishman.'[25] This is a revealing remark for someone as painfully self-conscious as Thomas was. Every country needs writers to represent it to itself but one wonders if he would have welcomed such a role or thought it too self-important. Perhaps only greater writers – a Chaucer or a Dante – have the energy to chart and define a nation. Nationalism is precisely what his late books, like *The Last Sheaf*, show him shying away from. What he felt for England was not exactly patriotism. 'I do not easily believe in patriotism,' he wrote, 'unless I am in Wales.' Even without this cherished sense of marginality he had no reason to suppose that by representing England he could speak to the nation of Britain. It makes better sense to think of Thomas's 'Englishness' in terms of his achievement of a poetic language capable of drawing on the strength of vernacular English speech. If he had native precedents for this in both Keats and Hopkins it is also a parallel development out of nineteenth-century poetry to that of Pound and Eliot's aspiration to write verse that would be as well written as good prose. Natives and modernists need not be set in opposing camps, any more than Thomas needs to be presented as a little Englander. What was new in the unadorned language of his verse was something he shared with a variety of poets (including Lawrence and the later Yeats) and, if anything, it tended to mark him off from those of his contemporaries who seemed most self-consciously English, the so-called Georgians.

The advantage of a less polarised literary history is that it saves one from trying to make Thomas's poetry out to be more central than it was. For it is intrinsically unconvincing that a slimmish volume of just two years' work could have constituted a bridge over half a century of English poetry, as Motion and Edna Longley maintain. Nor does Thomas's verse need to stand for anything other than itself. In *New Bearings in English Poetry* Leavis presents Thomas as the most distinguished of minor poets ('one cannot say "great" confidently of anything of Thomas's').[26] I would add that, if this is true, the England that was Thomas's main subject was in itself too restricted, despite its seductiveness for English readers, to nourish more than a minor poetry. It left too much of the experience of the age untouched. How different it is from the England of the novelists! There are no steam trains or ocean liners, telephones or suffragettes, garden cities or Labour MPs. Thomas's England was deep but curiously limited, as one sees if one compares his poems with Lawrence's almost exactly contemporary *The Rainbow*. It comes as a shock to realise that the character who comes nearest to Thomas's conscious love of his country is the dutiful Skrebensky. Lawrence guys Skrebensky's naive patriotism though he retains a sneaking sympathy for his attachment to older and simpler certitudes. Thomas, of course, had no wish to belong to a machine as Skrebensky does but he did have a similar need to *belong* and enlistment seems to have had a reassuring effect on him. Perhaps he always harboured a hope that being English might turn out to be a simpler state of mind than he ever found it to be? No wonder so many recent writers have been eager to persuade us that Thomas's version of England was the authentic one. The temptation is to forget that he himself was the first to doubt it – this is where he is unlike Skrebensky – and even to keep it at arm's length. As he wrote in a letter of 1900: 'After all, Wales is good for me. In spite of my accidentally cockney nativity, the air here seems to hold in some virtue essential to my well-being, and I always feel, in the profoundest sense, at home.'[27] It is quite plausible to see Wales rather than England as the lost 'home' he was always in search of.

Thomas thought of this feeling for 'home' as a private rather than a public thing. Writing of W. E. Henley's patriotism he commented: 'In print men become capable of anything. The bards and the journalists say extraordinary things. I suppose they do it to encourage the others. They feel that they are addressing the world; they are intoxicated with the social sense. But it is a curious thing that they do not talk like this in private ...'[28] Thomas felt England most deeply when he could bring together in his mind the openness of its landscapes with his sense of privacy. The privileged moments in his poetry are often those when the world seems to be shut out. In 'The Unknown Bird', for example,the bird he listens to is as secret and solitary as himself:

> Three lovely notes he whistled, too soft to be heard
> If others sang; but others never sang
> In the great beech-wood all that May and June.
> No one saw him: I alone could hear him
> Though many listened.   (TP, p. 85)

One of the things Thomas's poetry offers is an assurance that it is still possible to establish an intimacy with nature. The strength of this appeal ought not to be under-estimated. How many weekenders still sally forth to his rural England for relief from the one in which they work? How much do we still think of it as 'home', despite our 'social sense'? Yet if Thomas voiced a dream held in common by many English people in this century, he never pretended that his dream was an easily accessible one. His elusive 'wild England' was no mere happy hunting ground for the suburban middle classes from which he came. If it supplied an alternative to the city, rather as the suburban garden offered compensation for the grind of 'the office', it was also a place of labour itself – as in 'As the Team's Head-Brass'. Yet Thomas's countryside leaves out much of the real England of Thomas's day. The part is made to stand for the whole. Sometimes his England reminds one of William Morris's Nowhere, after the revolution. He was, perhaps, virtually the last English writer who could imagine England as the country without the town and make the picture credible. Even then, as W. J. Keith notes, he was the first important English country writer to be born in London. In other words, he was well placed to know what a tightrope he was walking to his 'Manor Farm'. In Orwell's *Coming Up for Air*, a novel written twenty years after Thomas wrote his poems, George Bowling decides to re-visit the rural England of his pre-war boyhood and finds that it has been obliterated by migrants from the cities in search of rural seclusion: '... doesn't it make you puke sometimes to see what they're doing to England, with their bird-baths and their plaster gnomes, and their pixies and tin cans, where the beechwoods used to be?'[29] As Bowling is forced to admit, the past is a closed door: 'What's the good of trying to revisit the scenes of your boyhood? They don't exist. Coming up for air! But there isn't any air' (pp. 215–16). Certainly

Thomas himself did find 'air' in the countryside – more than Orwell could – but perhaps he found less of it than we sometimes like to think?

To describe Thomas's partial, private England as an 'organic community' would be misleading. He did not chronicle rural society and culture in the way that *Change in the Village* did. Nor did he see the English village as central to the English way of life. Books like *The South Country* and *In Pursuit of Spring* as often as not avoid the villages Thomas finds on his way. The famous anthology piece 'Adlestrop' is not so much about a village as about its arresting name and what can be imagined of the village from the name, *without* visiting it. The typical Thomas poem takes place either outside human settlement or in very small communities tucked away from the world, like the pub in 'Up in the Wind'. In this respect, he differs from his mentor Jefferies who, in Thomas's own words, was 'one of the great Londoners', a man who found in London 'the exuberance and carelessness of Nature herself.'[30] But nowhere can Thomas's country be said to include or even imply the town: there is nothing for it to be organically connected to. In this it differs from such landmarks of the tradition to which Thomas seems to belong as 'Michael' and *Silas Marner*. The countryside of 'Haymaking' is like Hardy's Wessex without the metropolitan interlopers. Because there is less interaction between town and country than in Hardy or George Eliot there is also less emphasis on work. Thomas does write about rural poverty ('Man and Dog') and labour (though his haymakers are resting in the shade) but not with the passionate exactness with which Hardy describes Winterbourne and Marty South planting trees. We rarely find that sort of *shared* meaning in the rural life Thomas writes about.

In other words, Thomas did not come to his England from a position sufficiently *inside and of it* to think of it as more than special and local. He was reticent when it came to investing it with any significance beyond itself (as later readers have been tempted to do). This becomes clear if we compare it with the rural world of a writer like T. F. Powys, whose entire life was spent in the country. Powys's world is a deliberately small one but it is also a bigger one than Thomas's and humanly far more exact. Powys used the Dorset villages he lived in as grist for ironic and realistic allegories that go far beyond a preoccupation with England in their scope but, inci- dentally, reveal a great deal about it on their documentary side.[31] But novels like *Unclay* and *Mr Weston's Good Wine* are too steeped in

England to be self-conscious about their 'Englishness'. Powys preferred to see his world *sub specie aeternitatis* rather than as the expression of a particular historical moment. One consequence of this was that he had no interest in idealising it. Sometimes – as in *Mr Tasker's Gods* – he finds in it a violence and cruelty that it would be hard to match in any of his contemporaries. But if he never writes about village life in a protective spirit he does depict it as if it were in a time capsule which the twentieth century has somehow passed by. It is as if he needed to reduce his England to these limited proportions in order not to be side-tracked by its particularities. Though Thomas is a very different sort of writer from Powys, in many respects one can discover a similar strategy in his poems. The nature they celebrate embodies something permanent in the human feelings that are drawn to it. In both writers, the life of the spirit is implicitly marginal, like the rural world itself. They both remind us that any less local versions of England than theirs become too problematic to stand for life itself.

Thomas found a marvellously real England in his Steep but to look for it there also had its cost. Nativeness has drawbacks, just as being cosmopolitan has, and England is not necessarily best seen only from deep within itself. Thomas's problem was that he had to exclude half of England from England before he could feel at home in it. The fact that, so long after his death, it is still so easy to think of our own 'Englishness' in his terms should give us pause. Whatever it says about him, it certainly tells us a lot about ourselves. Among other things, it tells us that in order to believe in our 'Englishness' we need some sort of myth and Thomas's career is as congenial a myth as any that are available. This is why I have taken this indirect route to get to his poetry. There is a thick undergrowth of myth to be cut through before one can read the poems without trying to turn them into some elixir of 'Englishness'. It is no easy matter to restore to them their innate modesty, their avoidance of all grand gestures.

It is not difficult to see the England of Thomas's poems as a retreat from the modern world though there are few precise signs of retreat in it. He seldom feels the need to get London out of his system as Wordsworth did. Nor do the moments of illumination in his poetry have a human or partially human occasion as consistently as they do in Wordsworth. Often, they centre on birdsong, heard in solitude, as in 'March', where the thrushes strive to unpack their 'unwilling hoard of song' before night falls:

So they could keep off silence
And night, they cared not what they sang or screamed;
Whether 'twas hoarse or sweet or fierce or soft;
And to me all was sweet: they could do no wrong.
Something they knew – I also, while they sang
And after. Not till night had half its stars
And never a cloud, was I aware of silence
Rich with all that riot of songs, a silence
Saying that Spring returns, perhaps tomorrow.   (TP, p.17)[32]

The thrushes' song is happily untranslatable into human terms, too beautiful to be understood. The poet's pleasure in it is full but undiscriminating; he makes no attempt to put the 'something' the birds 'knew' into words. His 'impulse from a vernal wood' is valued not for what it tells him about 'man' but for what it discloses in the wood itself. The final line of the poem is characteristic of the way Thomas will seem to draw laconically back from the brink of some revelation which just eludes him. The verse leads one to expect a rhetorical flourish after 'Spring returns', only to subside into tentativeness. The same hiatus occurs in 'Something they knew – I also' where it looks, for a moment, as if we are going to learn what they 'knew'. Thomas constantly regulates the emotional experiences his poems explore, as if he were wary of taking them for granted. He never pretends to know his England more than he actually did or to be as close to it as the poets he most admired had been. Writing to Gordon Bottomley in 1906, for instance, he described his *The Heart of England* as 'Borrow & Jefferies sans testicles & guts'.[33] It might be said that he felt the lack of that physical awareness of his world which Lawrence was trying to recover. But the fact that Lawrence's way of seeking it was more intuitive and passional than his own does not inevitably make Thomas 'sans testicles & guts'. He habitually ran his own writing down. We only miss his physical side (embodied in his love and energy for walking) if we dwell too exclusively on his resigned, melancholy side, the Thomas who was like the aspens of his own poem:

Whatever wind blows, while they and I have leaves
We cannot other than an aspen be
That ceaselessly, unreasonably grieves,
Or so men think who like a different tree.   (TP, p. 233)

The music of the wind blowing sadly through the leaves is quintessential Thomas but not the whole man or poet. He too could

'like a different tree' and was less given up to grieving than he
sometimes made out. Ezra Pound, for instance, was too brusquely
American to see the capacity for joy and wonder in him, his
intellectual elasticity, or to see much more than what he called his
lack of 'vinegar'.[34] What Thomas also possessed (notably, in his four
perplexed, probing reviews of Pound's own verse) was a quality of
intellectual toughness and suppleness. This is what marked him out
from the Georgian contemporaries he reviewed so astutely. Without
it, with only his delicate feeling for nature and his aspen-like pathos,
he would have been a virtual Georgian himself. It was his intelligence,
at least as much as his sensibility, which prompted him to look to the
vernacular for a more direct and sinewy poetic language – just as
Hopkins and Yeats and Lawrence did. This is what makes him a
modern rather than a late Romantic poet: his poems are vehicles for
exploration, not decoration. Thomas did not need Frost to alert him
to the intellectual implications of plain writing; nearly everything he
wrote, however rhapsodic or Paterian, had a question mark and a
problem at the back of it. Otherwise, Thomas the modern poet would
never have emerged so clearly out of that sub-Romantic cocoon in
which he wrote *The Heart of England, A Literary Pilgrim in England* and
all the rest. He might have gone on helplessly oscillating between the
clashing influences of Jefferies and Pater, Sturt and Shelley, forever.
As it is, his most typical way of looking at nature is by walking deeper
and deeper into it, through a searching that is itself a metaphor for
thought. This is most true of his finest poems. It is no wonder that
Leavis, whose own work was so committed to a heuristic process of
thought, should have seen Thomas's strengths as a poet so clearly and
so soon.[35] To look at the poems themselves is, therefore, partly to try
to rescue Thomas from his admirers and even from himself, from
what has by now become the largest and most attractive ghetto in
English poetry, the domain of the 'nature poet'. He is more than a
'nature poet' and neither his art nor his England belongs only there.

   Thomas's tentativeness is not, of course, merely the product of
modern *Angst*. He can be self-conscious in a refreshingly direct way
and his doubt always hovers on the edge of wonder. Question marks
are positive signs in his poetry; they give his thought a shape of its
own, in a subtle, winding syntax that works through and across the
conventional metrical form of his verse. The way a lilt of rhyme keeps
creeping into his poems is an index of his ability to combine thought
movements with song. Though he sought and needed a plain style, he

was too much an heir of the nineteenth century to rest content with a style that was merely plain. A relatively simple early poem which illustrates these qualities is 'The Signpost', which sums up a favourite thought of the travel books: 'where to next?' At first its mood is sombre, recalling his friend Frost's most famous poem:[36]

> I read the sign. Which way shall I go?
> A voice says: You would not have doubted so
> At twenty. Another voice gentle with scorn
> Says: At twenty you wished you had never been born. (TP, p. 23)

By dint of such questions the mood of the poem changes and introspection gives way to vivacity. This is not the only time that Thomas's commitment to the vernacular enables him to introduce the rhythms of light verse into a poem that most of his contemporaries would have treated more solemnly. His verse never settles into a manner. In fact, the ending of *The Signpost* makes the distinction between 'light' and 'serious' verse seem artificial:

> if there be a flaw in that heaven
> 'Twill be freedom to wish, and your wish may be
> To be here or anywhere talking to me,
> No matter what the weather, on earth.
> At any age between death and birth,
> To see what day or night can be,
> The sun and the frost, the land and the sea,
> Summer, Autumn, Winter, Spring,
> With a poor man of any sort, down to a king,
> Standing upright out in the air
> Wondering where he shall journey, O where? (TP, pp. 24–5)

The lyrical 'Summer, Autumn, Winter, Spring' recalls 'Tinker, Tailor, Soldier, Sailor', as 'king' in the next line confirms. The humour is English in the way that Puck is: the landscape feeling includes humour just as it includes more obviously poetic sentiments. In this respect, 'The Signpost', though unassuming, points us to something of Thomas's range as a poet, from the spontaneous charm of his occasional verses to his children and his wife, Helen, in one direction, to the graver questioning of 'Old Man' in the other. In approaching the last-named poem, then, it needs to be said that both of these directions are part of what 'Englishness' was to Thomas.

While I would not argue much with the received view of 'Old Man' as Thomas's finest poem (assuming there *is* just one) it only

represents one major strand in his work. There are things in 'Lob'
which are not yet present in 'Old Man' for, astonishingly, it was one
of the earliest poems Thomas wrote. That said, it clearly takes poems
like 'The Signpost' (or the 'Home' poems or 'The Manor Farm' and
'Haymaking') much further in the direction of a human profundity.
The poem is too familiar to analyse in detail but it insists on being
noticed because it provides the richest illustration of the epis-
temological bent of Thomas's poetry. This is not to imply that it is
either dry or unimaginative. Searching thought, in Thomas, is a
means of releasing deep emotion and that is so here in the thought
about time and memory and childhood (all good Wordsworthian
themes). In writers like Henry Newbolt and Kipling, the thought of
England is often little more than a brazen assumption. Thomas is
different because his England is never just an actual thing, a fact: it
is partly hidden in time and only visible through memory. There can
therefore be no slogans such as more imperialist writers rely on. The
search *for* poetic experience often becomes the poetic experience
itself. This means that Thomas's verse may move more inevitably as
well as less stridently than, say, Kipling's and that it moves at a less
conscious level. The thoughts don't come off the peg. This is true of
any good Thomas poem but in 'Old Man' the attempt to plumb the
'dark, backward and abysm of time' derives a peculiar power from
the marked negative charge of the language. A great many of the
subtlest and most crucial words are of this sort: 'no', 'not', 'nothing'
or, rubbing against them, 'perhaps', 'only', 'in vain' and 'never'.
The knowing in question is inseparable from the recognition of what
cannot be known, the 'avenue, dark, nameless, without end' of the
last line. This may sound arid but it is actually a positive starting-
place for Thomas's meditation, an emptying of the mind not unlike
the mystic's, which makes creation possible.[37] The negatives are a
way of facing the elusiveness of words (as well as of memories) and
accepting the need to worry at them for meaning. In the process, the
concern with knowledge becomes a way of getting to the larger,
Shakespearian resonances of the poem's theme. Even in a poem of
this complexity Thomas is still in search of that 'pure thrush word',
a language beyond the snares of ordinary words:

> Even to one that knows it well, the names
> Half decorate, half perplex, the thing it is:
> At least, what that is clings not to the names
> In spite of time. And yet I like the names.   (TP, p. 19)

The power of language is bound up with its inadequacy and it is precisely this which gives it the possibility of alerting us to something beyond itself. The supple rhythms of the poem, flowing and halting by turns, induce a similar sense of meanings that come and go, defying us to pin them down.

Is 'Old Man' also a poem about England? One thing that suggests it may be is the fact that, English as the scene and situation are, England itself is not mentioned. For, as we know from the *This England* anthology and the essay on England in *The Last Sheaf*, Thomas thought the name redundant if the feeling of England were present. 'When icicles hang by the wall', his prime instance of 'Englishness', makes no mention of England either. This is a line worth pursuing if we want to distinguish Thomas's England from Kipling's or Elgar's. The name 'England' *is* mentioned in other Thomas poems ('The Manor Farm' and 'Haymaking' being the most obvious) and it is worth noting that 'Old Man' is different from them. I would prefer to say that it shows Thomas going further and deeper than the thought of England alone could or did ever take him. Its feeling of time and mortality is no more tied to place than it is in a poem like 'That time of year thou may'st in me behold'. Thomas knew that names – whether of England or 'Old Man' – had limits in a way that his more patriotic contemporaries did not. His poem probes something unconscious, below language, even though Thomas portrays himself as the classic adult (in Blake as in Freud) forbidding the child to venture there:

> Not a word she says;
> And I can only wonder how much hereafter
> She will remember, with that bitter scent,
> Of garden rows, and ancient damson-trees
> Topping a hedge, a bent path to a door,
> A low thick bush beside the door, and me
> Forbidding her to pick. (TP, p. 19)

The poet's feelings put him in touch with an unspoken reservoir of feeling in the child. But it is the bitterness and growing darkness behind the landscape that matter, not the fact that the poem takes place in a cottage-garden in the south of England.

'Old Man' is too disquieting a poem for criticism to pretend that it is as parochial as the early 'nature' books. It clearly isn't. Thomas wrote it when Proust was about half-way through *A la Recherche du*

Temps Perdu and both its similarities and differences from the novel are striking and significant. Proust may be the greater writer but it is Thomas's distinction to take up the same theme as he does and then find notes in it which Proust only seldom sounds himself. Time and memory are more tragic in Thomas, less available for Bergsonian recuperation than in Proust. Thomas understands the notion of *temps perdu* very well but there is little prospect in his poem of any *temps retrouvé*. In Thomas the negatives just go on twisting and doubling back on themselves so that, even when they do arrive at an unequivocal statement, what they speak of is ignorance and darkness:

> I have mislaid the key. I sniff the spray
> And think of nothing; I see and I hear nothing;
> Yet seem, too, to be listening, lying in wait
> For what I should, yet never can, remember:
> No garden appears, no path, no hoar-green bush
> Of Lad's Love, or Old Man, no child beside,
> Neither father nor mother, nor any playmate;
> Only an avenue, dark, nameless, without end.   (TP, p. 21)

This describes what has *not* been seen but the negative experience now has far greater depth than at the start of the poem. The poem's equivocal desire both to confront and to transcend actuality, the positive negatives by which it responds to the 'hoar-green feathery herb' and is prompted by its scent to a deeply human sense of time, all this is more complex than any other single Thomas poem. Not that 'Old Man' is untypical. It is not – its refusal to think in terms of a direct statement and 'names' that are really received ideas is to be found in all Thomas's poetry. For instance, in the beautiful but much simpler 'Adlestrop' (chosen by Larkin for his Oxford book), the same concern with naming determines the nature of the emotion. 'Adlestrop' may seem more obviously 'English' than 'Old Man' (it may be *only* English) but it too has its nameless penumbra surrounding it ('only the name / And the willows, willow-herb, and grass') to enrich its more accessible Cotswold 'Englishness'. What 'Old Man' show us is that, in Thomas, England is always ringed round by such a penumbra and it is precisely that which makes it a richer thought in him than in any other poet of his generation.

Thomas complained bitterly about the 'dead rhythm of my prose' in his last years but it was never the same deadness that he diagnosed so unerringly in Pater, the mannered syntax and the too conscious

cult of the 'single' word. The movement of the mature Thomas is
fluent and alive where the prose of *Marius the Epicurean* is congealed
and marmoreal. Likewise a Thomas poem is born out of a counter-
point between its ostensible rhythm and a second (spoken) rhythm
that runs against it, across the line-endings. Hence his fondness for
internal rhyme and for introducing rhymes into blank verse. A quite
simple poem which is made complex by the way it hinges on two
musics to find its form is 'Interval'. Any verse would show this but
here is its ending:

> It smokes aloft
> Unwavering:
> It hunches soft
> Under storm's wing.
>
> It has no care
> For gleam or gloom:
> It stays there
> While I shall roam.
>
> Die and forget
> The hill of trees,
> The gleam, the wet,
> This roaring peace. (TP, pp. 39–41)

This final effect (the half rhyme, the change of key) carries the
hallmark of Thomas the poet: technique is the midwife of emotion. It
is also, of course, a reminder of how much he owed to Hardy and, in
particular, to what Donald Davie has defined as Hardy's 'virtuosity'
as a poet.[38] Take his Hardyesque treatment of the Hardyesque
subject of rain in 'After Rain'. It is no less a Thomas poem because
it confesses its *provenance*. The magical moment when rain that has
stopped begins again is evoked not by mere description but through
the pattering sounds of the verse itself:

> What hangs from the myriad branches down there
> So hard and bare
> Is twelve yellow apples lovely to see
> On one crab-tree,
> And on each twig of every tree in the dell
> Uncountable
> Crystals both dark and bright of the rain
> That begins again. (TP, p. 37)

Something in this might be called 'Georgian' (the apples suggest de
la Mare) but not the fusion of a lyrical fluidity within a controlled

structure of sense. The plain style includes the poetic. The poem's
sound determines what we see. It was moments like this, encapsu-
lating English weather, which Thomas valued for the sense of
'Englishness' they distilled. The fact that England is not mentioned
confirms the point – where else could we be? The poem is as English
as 'When icicles hang' (even though *Love's Labour's Lost* is set in
Navarre!) Things can be evoked without being named. As early as
his book on Jefferies (1908), Thomas had praised his master for
writing with 'a natural fineness and richness and a carelessness, too,
like the blackbird's singing'.[39] That is how he wanted to write
himself, the sort of note he wanted to hear below all his more
conscious words.

A quite different poem which also draws on this speech in things
unspoken is 'The Other', a long semi-allegory which echoes Dante's
and Herbert's theme of the spiritual journey. Thomas pursues his
own *Doppelgänger*, so intent on his 'unseen moving goal' that 'I quite
forgot I could forget'. The hint of Poe is relevant if uncharacteristic,
reminding us of the tormented, self-conscious side of Thomas which
the poem explores. The 'other' continues to elude the poet (rather as
Lob will) like the double of William Wilson in Poe. At one point he
even turns on him and pushes him back. Nonetheless, the poet's
picture of his 'melancholy' is by no means *just* out of Poe or
Dostoievsky. At its peak, Thomas brings birds into his poetry here
too, as in 'Adlestrop':

> A dog barked on a hidden rise;
> A marshbird whistled high unseen;
> The latest waking blackbird's cries
> Perished upon the silence keen.
> The last light filled a narrow firth
> Among the clouds. I stood serene,
> And with a solemn quiet mirth,
> An old inhabitant of earth.   (TP, p. 31)

Another magical transformation brought about by birdsong. The
prevalent ghostly introspection of the poem gives way to a solid sense
of belonging in nature. Such moments of oneness with the earth are
vital in Thomas. So too is the 'silence' which accompanies them and
which the poetry feels its way towards. 'The Other' is not, of course,
as fine as 'Old Man' but neither is it as different in kind as its
groping, Kafkaesque portentousness makes it seem. Its modern
feeling, gnawing away at life as at a bone, reminds us that by putting

Thomas in a purely native tradition, as a bridge between Hardy and Larkin, one plays down his affinities with the Modernists, many and obvious as they are. His self-consciousness was clearly as intrinsic to his verse as his spontaneity or his feeling for nature. Not for nothing did he claim that *Hamlet* had been written expressly for him.[40] The final mood of 'The Other' could hardly be more Hamlet-like if it tried:

> He goes: I follow: no release
> Until he ceases. Then I also shall cease. (TP, p. 33)

The soliloquies are clearly behind this. As Leavis saw, the essence of Thomas is not so much 'nature' as an effort of self-discovery: 'the outward scene is accessory to an inner theatre'.[41] Hence, Thomas's 'distinctly modern sensibility'. This, then, is the stage on which to bring forward his most famous accounts of 'Englishness'. It is richly problematic, half magic and music, half epistemology and introspection. We may not like it, preferring to see him by the light of 'Clare and Cowper, Morland and Crome', but it is surely the only light we can see 'The Manor Farm' by and see it honestly. The alternative is to exchange his real intuition of England for a simpler, more nostalgic substitute.

Despite his concern with naming the nameless, some of Thomas's most famous poems are more explicit. 'The Manor Farm' begins with the probing regard of 'Old Man' but soon becomes more simply realistic:

> The rock-like mud unfroze a little and rills
> Ran and sparkled down each side of the road
> Under the catkins wagging in the hedge. (TP, p. 49)

A slow unbroken camera shot. Later, 'three cart-horses' come into focus, 'swishing their tails / Against a fly, a solitary fly.' All these prosaic things are more definite than the 'hoar-green feathery herb' yet the poem reaches beyond them to name England as 'Old Man' won't. It is named, as in a diapason, as if it were emerging out of the mud of the opening. Significantly, in the final moment of uplift, Thomas chooses to express it by a cliché:

> But 'twas not Winter –
> Rather a season of bliss unchangeable
> Awakened from farm and church where it had lain
> Safe under tile and thatch for ages since
> This England, Old already, was called Merry. (TP, p. 49)

Thomas liked this cliché because it went back to Robert of Gloucester's chronicle in the Middle Ages. Part of his nostalgia was for the phrase itself, which acts as a password to that past. The feeling is simpler, less bitter than in 'Old Man'. Yet the very fusion of the plain and the poetical is a way of redeeming the cliché. The lines are more self-conscious than they seem; the cliché becomes indelibly actual. It resembles what Wordsworth does with the sheep and the old stone wall in *The Prelude*, except that Thomas seeks to reassure rather than to transfigure: there is nothing Wordsworthian about 'bliss unchangeable'. In fact, that last word undercuts both the realism of the poem and its implicit metaphysic. This pastoral of 'Merrie England' looses any link Thomas still has with the idea of the 'organic community'. 'The Manor Farm' offers a kind of plenitude to the consumer who comes upon it but the civilisation it embodies seems thin after *Adam Bede* or *Change in the Village*. Work is either excluded or finished, superseded by 'bliss'. It is a farm too rare for farm-work, reminding us that, in Raymond Williams's phrase, men like Thomas '*came to* the country'.[42] Their countryside was a picture, their England beautiful because of its proximity to myth. Williams is surprisingly hard on Thomas, possibly because he sees him as a threat to his own idea of the country (and as a lapsed Welshman to boot):

a traditional and surviving rural England was scribbled over and almost hidden from sight by what is really a suburban and half-educated scrawl.[43]

One doubts whether more authentic rural antecedents give anyone the right to condescend to Thomas like this. The mud is still there, as well as the myth, and the farm, though a conservative image, is also a concrete one. Nor is it as easily accessible to the day-tripper as Williams implies: the essence of the place is that it is hidden, though probably only someone from the town would be struck by its beauty. Thomas makes it quite plain that it has been miraculously preserved.

'Haymaking' draws on a similar, even more well-worn, image of England: the England of English landscape painting. Perhaps only a few of its readers will know how to make hay (just as most readers of *Far From the Madding Crowd* know nothing about sheep) but it is less a poem about work than one about the sensuous ease of having stopped working:

> In the field sloping down,
> Park-like, to where its willows showed the brook,

Haymakers rested. The tosser lay forsook
Out in the sun; and the long waggon stood
Without its team; it seemed it never would
Move from the shadow of that single yew.   (TP, p. 225)

It is the English landscape of the collective memory but with a
humdrum, worsted beauty. Thomas makes no mention of Turner or
Gainsborough, nor even of Constable who might have fitted in here,
but he conscripts all the plainest poets and painters to swell his
chorus:

And all were silent. All was old,
This morning time, with a great age untold,
Older than Clare and Cowper, Morland and Crome. (TP, p. 226)

These names are a guarantee that the poem will find its poetry in
its details. Even the honorific use of the word 'old' (satisfyingly
threadbare?) seems less Romantic in their proximity. Thomas begins
rather portentously, like Owen ('After night's thunder far away had
rolled'), but his customary lightness soon takes over. With every
observation, he appears like someone biting a coin to test that the
poetry is true:

The smooth white empty road was lightly strewn
With leaves – the holly's Autumn falls in June –
And fir cones standing stiff up in the heat.   (TP, p. 225)

As in Marvell, the pastoral is aphoristic as well as instinct with
feeling. The place is actual – at another season one could almost
imagine being bored there. Even so, and despite the strong
suggestions of work in the mention of Morland and Crome, the scene
is really Virgilian. (Thomas regularly read Virgil at the end of a day's
reviewing). We are far above the world of organic communities and
agricultural revolutions, 'Under the heavens that know not what
years be'. Workaday England is transformed:

The men, the beasts, the trees, the implements
Uttered even what they will in times far hence –
All of us gone out of the reach of change –
Immortal in a picture of an old grange.   (TP, p. 226)

This 'picture' both is, and is not, England. It is impossible not to
succumb to the pleasantly inert, after-dinner feeling of spiritual well-
being but equally impossible to confound the nostalgic idea behind it

with the real England in which Thomas was living and writing. It is as if England could only be preserved for poetry by keeping it in the past. It could be as 'old' as you liked as long as it wasn't *new*. In other words, 'home' becomes where one no longer is, a beautiful exile 'out of the reach of change'.

For all their popularity, 'The Manor Farm' and 'Haymaking' do not represent Thomas's deepest vision of England. A closer extension of the mood of 'Old Man' is found in 'The Combe', a poem short enough to quote in full:

> The Combe was ever dark, ancient and dark.
> Its mouth is topped with bramble, thorn and briar;
> And no one scrambles over the sliding chalk
> By beech and yew and perishing juniper
> Down the half precipices of its sides, with roots
> And rabbit holes for steps. The sun of Winter,
> The moon of Summer, and all the singing birds
> Except the missel-thrush that loves juniper,
> Are quite shut out. But far more ancient and dark
> The Combe looks since they killed the badger there,
> Dug him out and gave him to the hounds,
> That most ancient Briton of English beasts.   (TP, p. 226)

This is the 'south country' filtered through the rugged landscapes of *King Lear*, Egdon Heath without the operatics. Yet the scene is close to home: Thomas knew well the combes at Steep and Selborne. The verse has more vigour and (as in the first line) broods on its own energy. The landscape grows to a moment of symbolic disclosure that has nothing of a 'picture' about it. Instead of peace, there is a pungent feeling of mortality and violence like a flashback to the 'wild England' of Jefferies and Borrow. This England is more problematic but also more alive. The badger is a 'Briton'. As Michael Kirkham says, the poem sets a 'recent vein of Englishness' against the 'primordial darkness' of the combe.[44] The past seldom goes as far back as the primitive in Thomas. We are left with a problem, not a resolution, the jarring tension of an England within England. There is nothing here 'safe under tile and thatch'. The feeling is nearer Ted Hughes than the long Georgian summer.

The poem which is most successful at combining this sense of darkness with the 'Englishness' of 'Haymaking' is 'As the Team's Head-Brass'. It was written in response to the war and also, more subtly, to those Hardy Poems like 'In Time of the Breaking of

Nations' which registered the impact of war on rural life. Like
Hardy, Thomas watches a 'maid and her wight' but his lovers,
though they too ignore the war, are more fragile, less immemorial
than Hardy's. While the poet talks about war with the ploughman as
he narrows 'a yellow square of charlock', they slip into the wood.
Their unchanging love-making is only implied in the Dantesque
colloquy that ensues:

> 'I could spare an arm. I shouldn't want to lose
> A leg. If I should lose my head, why, so,
> I should want nothing more'...'Have many gone
> From here?' 'Yes.' 'Many lost?' 'Yes, a good few.
> Only two teams work on the farm this year.
> One of my mates is dead. The second day
> In France they killed him. It was back in March,
> The very night of the blizzard, too. Now if
> He had stayed here we should have moved that tree.'
> 'And I should not have sat here. Everything
> Would have been different.'   (TP, pp. 325-7)

This verse is more dramatic than 'The Manor Farm'. There is none
of that poem's static peace; the rhythms of the land are broken by the
thoughts of war. (Hardy was too much the ironist to capture such
sadness.) But this England is dislocated, not lost. The speakers still
have time to think out their plight and, at the end, 'The lovers come
out of the wood again'. War has not changed them but neither are
they incompatible with its tragedies. England may not be 'Merrie'
but the rural is strong enough not to need to fend off the tragic.
Mortality has its rightful place in the pastoral. The final picture is
again an echo of Hardy's poem:

> The horses started and for the last time
> I watched the clouds crumble and topple over
> After the ploughshare and the stumbling team.   (TP, p. 327)

This, in its way, is also immemorial but it is too deep for 'bliss
unchangeable'. It is an England one can belong to rather than one to
pine for. Few modern poets have written as simply as this, with as fine
an ear for prose, and few poets – as in the way the idea of 'crumbling'
links earth and sky – have found a plain style of such emotional
power.

Thomas never severed his links with the Georgians, even though
Marsh left him out of his anthologies, and no poet of the period could

give a more heart-stopping sense of England than he did in poems like
'Adlestrop' and 'Tears'. He knew how to let emotion have its way.
A sudden access of beauty, doubled with a sense of transience, is
typical of his more poignant versions of England. But he knew the
'young countrymen' of 'Tears' were displaced in their uniforms and
that England was really much less of a pageant for the patriot than
'Tears' makes out. Some of his loveliest lyrics seem beautiful only for
beauty's sake. 'Adlestrop', praised by John Bayley for its essential
'Englishness',[45] is the obvious example:

> And for that minute a blackbird sang
> Close by, and round him, mistier,
> Farther and farther, all the birds
> Of Oxfordshire and Gloucestershire.　　　　　(TP, p. 185)

There is something fanciful about this glimpse of England. It lacks
the solidity of the ending of 'As the Team's Head-Brass'. But Thomas
did not need to keep England on the fringe of his consciousness, like
hidden birdsong. He knew the train would leave Adlestrop and its
alluring mistiness behind. One would never find a phrase like 'No
whit less lovely fair' in 'The Combe'. 'Adlestrop' is a poem which
never quite gets away from the realm of poetry, a modern poem by a
writer who grew up in the nineties. That is why it is an anthology
piece.

　　Long before *The Sacred Wood*, poets from Swinburne to the
Georgians were drawn to dramatic verse and this is so of Thomas's
best rural poems too. His model was probably the Wordsworth of
'Resolution and Independence' rather than Webster. In a poem like
'Man and Dog', one hears an authentic rural voice whose roughness
is muffled in 'Adlestrop'. An old day-labourer, needy but content,
travels the country for work. He is out of the leech-gatherer by one of
Hardy's peasants:

> Then he went on against the north-east wind –
> Straight but lame, leaning on a staff new-skinned,
> Carrying a brolly, flag-basket, and old coat, –
> Towards Alton, ten miles off. And he had not
> Done less from Chilgrove where he pulled up docks. (TP, p. 93)

He is indubitably English, but ageing, weather-beaten and plebeian.
Like Sturt's Bettesworth, he has been all over the country, from
'Southampton to Newcastle-on-Tyne', as well as in the army.
Poverty and hardship are the rule – enough to put all the birds of

Adlestrop to flight. His England is neither lyrical nor atmospheric yet it is in his voice that Thomas can turn from the countryside to the war:

> 'Many a man sleeps worse tonight
> Than I shall.' 'In the trenches.' 'Yes, that's right.
> But they'll be out of that – I hope they be –
> This weather, marching after the enemy.'   (TP, p. 95)

This is a voice in which Thomas could not only speak about England but speak to other Englishmen too. He clearly needed it to prevent his England from seeming beautiful but tame. In the peasant's wake came a train of paupers and gypsies (wanderers like Thomas himself) who make no appearance in the poems of Housman or Brooke. (One recalls his kindness to W. H. Davies, the 'super-tramp'). All this was not so much a departure from late nineteenth-century tradition as a return to an older one. 'Man and Dog' evokes *The Ruined Cottage* and Crabbe rather than the second-generation Romantics at the back of 'Adlestrop'. In its new, 'wild England' one can hear gypsy music and the earthy folk-songs that Thomas, like his friend Cecil Sharp, preferred to Beethoven. Tattered and unlovely, its darkness like 'an underworld of death' ('Gypsies'), this England could be transformed by song. Its wildness reminds us that England is not merely a fugitive essence pursued by wandering poets athirst for beauty. The poem has some of the same recoil from suburbia as 'Haymaking' and it adds a salutary tartness to the sweetness of that way of imaging England. Most importantly, it was out of it that Thomas was able to create a third version of his country in 'Lob'.

Like Whitman, Thomas is a poet of the open road, but one who likes to get off the beaten track. In *The South Country* he prefers a downland church to Winchester Cathedral. On the road he meets other travellers, as in 'Wind and Mist'; a walk to Thomas was like a quest. Paths gave him a metaphor for knowing:

> the path that looks
> As if it led on to some legendary
> Or fancied place where men have wished to go
> And stay; till, sudden, it ends where the wood ends. (TP, p. 145)

One has the feeling, as in *Alastor*, that where the path ends so may knowledge. Nature may throw one back on the self, 'Alone in all the world, marooned alone'. The journey is as likely to end in solipsism

as in 'the consecration and the poet's dream'. England is where
Thomas goes *to*, not where he arrives *at*. It is on this sort of road that
he sets out after Lob.

'Lob' opens with the poet 'in search of something chance would
never bring'. (TP, p. 159). He cannot count on calling up any fixed
meaning for the landscape, any biddable spirit of England. This is no
Puck of Pook's Hill, however influenced it may be by Kipling's book.
'Lob' is about the perceptions that elude us as well as those we know
we know. Its affirmations arise out of a bedrock of doubt. In
Wordsworth's phrase, 'we see by glimpses'. This is why Thomas
begins by clutching at names rather than things. The poem tries to
pluck an identity out of the air and give it a 'local habitation and a
name'. Shakespeare's Puck is its presiding spirit, always one step
ahead of us. Sometimes Thomas is left with nothing but names,
confused in his memory in empty resonance, no more than a simple
map to the real countryside:

> To turn back then and seek him, where was the use?
> There were three Manningfords, – Abbots, Bohun, and Bruce:
> And whether Alton, not Manningford, it was
> My memory could not decide, because
> There was both Alton Barnes and Alton Priors.   (TP, p. 160)

When the poet returns years later for news of his 'ancient', the same
confusion persists among those he questions about him:

> One man I asked about him roared
> At my description: ' 'Tis old Bottlesford
> He means, Bill.' But another said: 'Of course,
> It was Jack Button up at the White Horse.
> He's dead, sir, these three years.' This lasted till
> A girl proposed Walker of Walker's Hill   (TP, p. 160)

The poet is embarked on a particularly baffling paper-chase, not a
full-blooded communion with nature. The spirit of England is not
above playing pranks. The 'squire's son', later revealed to be an
avatar of Lob, accuses the girl of 'roguery'. England is a home for
mischief – its elusiveness is more than just a way of being wistful. The
vernacular itself, as Thomas uses it, is playful.

Thomas sees Lob's England as out of bounds, an enemy to
convention. As Stan Smith remarks, it lacks the 'fortified' and tidy
feeling of *The South Country* where the countryside has become owned
and enclosed: 'Lob's appeal is that he refuses to accept such

enclosures'.[46] He insists on his birthright and takes whichever path he pleases:

> His home is where he was free.
> Everybody has met one such man as he.
> Does he keep clear old paths that no one uses
> But once a life-time when he loves or muses?
> He is English as this gate, these flowers, this mire. (TP, p. 161)

Even so, the squire's son refuses to give him one name. He may be present but not everyone can recognise him. His is a homely mystery but he has the ubiquity of a fairy, popping up everywhere:

> And when at eight years old Lob-lie-by-the-fire
> Came in my books, this was the man I saw.
> He has been in England as long as dove and daw,
> Calling the wild cherry tree the merry tree,
> The rose campion Bridget-in-her-bravery;
> And in a tender mood he, as I guess,
> Christened one flower Love-in-idleness... (TP, p. 161)

Like Puck, Lob brings the countryside to life by naming it. He is a master of etymologies, able to interpret local place-names and to teach the blackbirds to sing in English. But if he is a sprite he is also a kind of antiquarian, akin to Cecil Sharp or even Sturt. For though Lob stands for our need to know the place we inhabit, he also stands for Thomas himself, and for a generation of English writers and musicians committed to the belief that to know England was the beginning of self-knowledge.[47] His 'Englishness' may be earthy ('Mother Dunch's buttocks' proved too much for Thomas's first editor) but it is also very much of the mind, self-conscious like any other sort of virtuosity. It only comes to life when he finds words for his landscape and humanises it. Lob's England is very different from Hardy's Egdon Heath and Salisbury Plain. The truly English thing about it is the language it finds to express itself in. Lob seems invisible but he has 'thirteen hundred names for a fool' (TP, p. 163). His favourite form is the proverb or saying, language shared in common by all its speakers, for example 'She had a face as long as a wet week' (TP, p. 163). Self-consciousness does not preclude companionship. Thomas himself describes 'social intercourse' as 'only an intense form of solitude'[48] but he enjoyed meeting other travellers when he went on walks: like Lob, he could be sociable in that situation without having to make any ties. Thus, 'Lob' is one of the most social poems in the language, worthy to set beside Jonson and Pope, despite the fact that it is also a poem about Thomas himself. Lob figures as a good object, something to seek for, both on the levels of fantasy and of fact. But he should never be completely confounded with Puck. There is something of Bottom in him too, the Bottom who sees a 'most rare vision'. If he can trick a giant into making the Wrekin Hill with his spade he never escapes into a fairy-tale: his poetry is balanced by his proverbs. It is prior to art though art comes out of it, something to breathe in like the air that flows in us like blood. In just this way, the poem says, do we possess our language. In this respect, Lob is within the reach of all of us and is better represented by a 'squire's son' who recalls Jefferies than by Puck or Percy Shelley.

'Lob' concludes with an extraordinary bravura passage which rings the changes on Lob's other name of Jack. It is a cadenza one would not have predicted from the author of poems like 'As the Team's Head-Brass'. Yet it is also at this point that history enters explicitly into the poem. Until now the only history in it has been the speech of Shakespeare as it has been assimilated from the language of the folk. Now, folklore, which is pre-historical, gives way to images of English history which bring us up to the present day. It is only at this point that the poet identifies the 'squire's son' as an emanation of Lob himself:

> 'Do you believe Jack dead before his hour?
> Or that his name is Walker, or Bottlesford,
> Or Button, a mere clown, or squire, or lord?
> The man you saw, – Lob-lie-by-the-fire, Jack Cade
> Jack Smith, Jack Moon, poor Jack of every trade,
> Young Jack, or old Jack, or Jack what-d'ye-call,
> Jack-in-the-hedge, or Robin-run-by-the-wall,
> Robin Hood, Ragged Robin, lazy Bob,
> One of the lords of No Man's Land, good Lob, –
> Although he was seen dying at Waterloo,
> Hastings, Agincourt, and Sedgemoor, too, –
> Lives yet. He never will admit he is dead
> Till millers cease to grind men's bones for bread,
> Not till our weathercock crows once again
> And I remove my house out of the lane
> On to the road.' With this he disappeared
> In hazel and thorn tangled with old-man's-beard.
> But one glance of his back, as there he stood,
> Choosing his way, proved him of old Jack's blood,
> Young Jack perhaps, and now a Wiltshireman
> As he has oft been since his days began.   (TP, p. 167)

The lines are full of a delight in words, words as a way to identify, but they are also full of conjecture and improvisation. Other Thomas poems are more measured and the references to the war in them are moving. This is Thomas in his Hamlet mood, full of Miching Mallecho. Lob is no four-square Wordsworthian solitary: his name changes too fast for us to keep up with him. No sooner pinned down than he dwindles to a 'glimpse of his back'. The poem is a great celebration of England and the English language but, even at the end, it is England partly seen from outside rather than from within. England figures as a way of life that we look back on.

In the end, 'Lob' is more of a *tour de force* than the poems where Thomas is sure of what he grasps and has no call to spruce it up. The influence of Kipling – and, for that matter, of Shakespeare – is not wholly assimilated.[49] What redeems it and distinguishes it from other exponents of 'Englishness', is that it is honest enough not to pretend to some privileged vision of England. That would be impossible. There is no such static spirit in the first place, however many myths there may be, because England always lies just ahead of us, waiting to be discovered. The poem is too subtle and too light to give us the option of falling back on words like 'nation' and 'race' to explain everything. We end simply in Wiltshire, with particular places and things, reminded of the battles still to come in Flanders. If Lob is a spirit he is also a common soldier, at most a yeoman like Jefferies or a 'squire's son'. But it is wrong to fix him to one class only, even though Thomas's own sympathies are clear: his 'English words' are classless. 'Englishness' is a name for learning to use them. It is the most fitting politics for a poet. Thomas would surely have disliked being considered as a fount of essential 'Englishness', as if he were bigger than his own material.

Whether 'This England' was really Thomas's lost home or not, this is not the note to end on. He knew that his way of writing out his England was a limited one, best fitted to a time of decline which was forced to retrench back to its spiritual reserves. Spenser or Milton would not have been so private. Could Gloriana have been distilled into a 'pure thrush word'? When Thomas essays the tone of his precursors he loses the touch and tone of 'Lob'. In 'This is no Petty Case of Right or Wrong', for instance, he writes less movingly about the war the more he places it in the centre of the stage. We have plangent chauvinism instead of the lightness and fellowship of 'Lob'. This was the price Thomas paid for never having given the social and political England of his time an adequate place in his verse. His England was narrow as well as deep: what was private in it held little commerce with what was public. To that extent it was marginal.

But the thought of England should not be the final one. In some of his last poems Thomas points to something deeper still that had been implicit all the time. 'Lights Out' and 'Out in the Dark' focus on the nameless darkness that invades a poem like 'The Combe', a realm of death that tingles with life, in which nationality, even of the birds, is superseded. In these poems, the self too is at last in abeyance before the unknown:

> Out in the dark over the snow
> The fallow fawns invisible go
> With the fallow doe;
> And the winds blow
> Fast as the stars are slow.
>
> Stealthily the dark haunts round
> And, when a lamp goes, without sound
> At a swifter bound
> Than the swiftest hound,
> Arrives, and all else is drowned.   (TP, p. 375)

It is his lightness of tone as he yields to the power of darkness that guarantees Thomas's seriousness, his avoidance of gesturing. His own 'universe of sight' (TP, p. 375) never ignores the non-human. In so far as England also belonged there, beyond words, he evoked it as few writers have done; in so far as it could be named and labelled he hardly touched it. It is from this division in the English psyche that later writers have had to begin, for, if Thomas left England more beautiful when he died, he also left it more problematic. It was a fraught but fertile legacy.

NOTES

(Place of publication is London unless otherwise stated)

1 *A Language Not to be Betrayed: Selected Prose of Edward Thomas*, selected and introduced by Edna Longley (Carcanet, Manchester, 1981), p. 222.
2 *Ibid.*, p. 281. *N. B.* this does not reflect everything Thomas had to say about Brooke.
3 'England' from *The Last Sheaf*, *ibid.*, p. 227.
4 For Elgar in wartime see Jeremy Crump, 'The Identity of English Music: The Reception of Elgar 1898–1935', *Englishness: Politics and*

Culture 1880–1920, eds. Robert Colls and Philip Dodd (Croom Helm, 1986), pp. 164–90.

5 See her *Poetry Between the Wars* (Bloodaxe Books, Newcastle, 1988).

6 'National Trust', *Selected Poems* (Penguin, Harmondsworth, 1984), p. 121.

7 See Andrew Motion's *The Poetry of Edward Thomas* (Routledge and Kegan Paul, 1980) though it invests too heavily in the sentimental view of Thomas.

8 *Language*, p. 221. Relevant here is Geoffrey Hill's essay on Ivor Gurney, *Essays in Criticism*, vol. 34, no. 2 (1984), 97–128.

9 *Thomas Hardy and British Poetry* (Routledge and Kegan Paul, 1979), chapters 1 and 2.

10 The only way Hardy could write about the nation was to have George III come to Casterbridge in *The Trumpet Major*.

11 *The Collected Poems of Edward Thomas*, ed. R. George Thomas (Clarendon Press, Oxford, 1978), p. 257 (given hereafter as TP).

12 *Language*, p. 221.

13 Edward Thomas, *Poems and Last Poems*, ed. Edna Longley (Dent, 1973), p. 173.

14 'Grub Village', *Required Writing: Miscellaneous Pieces* 1955–1982 (Faber, 1983), pp. 188–90.

15 To these prose writers one should add Wordsworth and Crabbe, whose verse, like Thomas's own, also had the strength of prose.

16 *The Childhood of Edward Thomas*, preface by Roland Gant (Faber, 1983), p. 142.

17 *In Pursuit of Spring*, introd. by P. J. Kavanagh (Wildwood House, 1981), p. 85.

18 See *Letters from Edward Thomas to Gordon Bottomley*, ed. with introd. by R. George Thomas (Oxford University Press, 1968), p. 102.

19 *Language*, p. 225.

20 *Childhood*, p. 6.

21 William Cooke, *Edward Thomas: A Critical Biography* (Faber, 1970) quotes Thomas as saying he only felt like a 'patriot' in Wales (p. 190).

22 See Longley, *Poetry Between the Wars*, chapters 1 and 2.

23 *Language*, p. 229.

24 Quoted by Cooke, *Edward Thomas*, p. 126.

25 *The Letters of Edward Thomas to Jesse Berridge*, with a memoir by Jesse Berridge, ed. with introd. by Anthony Berridge (Enitharmon Press, 1983), p. 74.

26 *New Bearings in English Poetry* (Chatto and Windus, 1961), p. 72.

27 Quoted by Stan Smith in *Edward Thomas* (Faber, 1986), p. 15.

28 *Language*, p. 222.

29 *Coming Up for Air*, (Penguin, Harmondsworth, 1962), p. 215.

30 Edward Thomas, *Richard Jefferies, His Life and Work* (Hutchinson, 1909), p. 127.

31 See Judith Stinton's *Chaldon Herring: The Powys Circle in a Dorset Village* (The Boydell Press, Woodbridge, 1988).

32 Longley (*Poems and Last Poems*) gives 'Stained with all that hour's songs'.

33 *Letters to Bottomley*, p. 107.

34 Cooke, *Edward Thomas*, p. 189.

35 *New Bearings*, pp. 68–73.

36 See *Complete Poems of Rupert Brooke* (Holt, Rinehart and Winston, New York, 1964), p. 131.

37 For Thomas's interest in mysticism see Berridge, *Thomas to Berridge*, pp. 88–9.

38 *Thomas Hardy*, chapter 1.

39 *Richard Jefferies*, p. 188.

40 See Cooke, *Edward Thomas*, p. 68.

41 *New Bearings*, p. 69.

42 *The Country and the City* (Chatto and Windus, 1973), p. 256.

43 *Ibid.*, p. 258.

44 *The Imagination of Edward Thomas* (Cambridge University Press, 1986), p. 122. See his interesting section on 'The Passing of England', pp. 120–9.

45 'English Equivocations', *Poetry Review*, vol. 76, no. 1/2 (June, 1986), 4.

46 Cooke, *Edward Thomas*, p. 30.

47 It makes a good deal of sense to think of Thomas's poetry in the context of the great revival of English folk-song in the period.

48 *Letters to Bottomley, p.* 53.

49 For a thorough and suggestive account of Kipling's treatment of 'Englishness' see Sarah Wintle's introduction to the Penguin edition of *Puck of Pook's Hill* (Harmondsworth, 1987).

CHAPTER 3

Forster and Lawrence: Exiles in the homeland

Forster has had a good press because, for many years, he offered intellectuals the image of England they wanted. Lawrence, who included some of the same Liberal faith in his make up, offended them by doing the opposite. The kind of character satirised in *Women in Love* – Hermione or Sir Joshua – usually wins Forster's cautious sympathy. This is one reason why Forster was more influential on the Auden generation than Lawrence was. It may also explain why Forster has been persistently pardoned for precisely the fault which has most damaged Lawrence's reputation as a novelist: the tendency to make first-person intrusions into his fictions. Some intrusions are more intrusive than others. It is one thing to be interrupted by one of one's own kind – genial, modest and urbane – but another to be on the end of a tirade that is both impolite and disturbingly *ad hominem*. Who could object to a narrator as insinuating as Forster? As Virginia Woolf said, he has 'a vision which he is determined that we shall see' but he reminds us of it very gently: 'we are tapped on the shoulder'.[1] Perhaps it has only been since his death, now that his 'charm' is more distant, that it has become clear that the task he sets the reader of his novels is to establish exactly what that 'vision' was. Is it still one we can share in?

Forster's early version of England was very much Matthew Arnold's, fifty years on. *The Longest Journey*, for instance, pits two distinct Englands, each claiming to represent the whole country, against each other: the public school ethos of Mr Pembroke's Sawston (to which Rickie finally capitulates) and a Wiltshire which Stephen Wonham presides over as a sort of Tony Lumpkin-cum-earth god. The clash of apostles of Culture and Philistines rumbles all through the book (it begins in chapter 1 with a picture of Rickie in the company of friends who are every inch Cambridge Apostles and acolytes of G. E. Moore). However, this Sawston-Cambridge divide is not so neatly expressed in class terms as it will be in *Howards End*. Stephen Wonham, perhaps the central figure of the novel, is neither a gentleman nor a member of the lower middle classes like Leonard Bast. Hence his pathos: it is unclear whether England really belongs to him or whether there is a place for him in it any more. It is into this dilemma that Rickie Elliott, who writes rather Forsterian stories about the countryside, goes down from Cambridge in wide-eyed pursuit of England, only to find himself unable to choose between the two Englands on offer. His Arnoldian faith hesitates. 'England is immense', he tells Mr Pembroke, especially for 'its literature', but one England seems to exclude another.[2] In this predicament, all his Cambridge culture can offer him to fall back on is an uneasy detachment from any feeling of community. This is not surprising because England is also small: the alternatives it provides tend to miss out most of its working population.

It is at this point that Forster's comic distinctions begin to be blurred by his penchant for poeticality. Stephen, who turns out to be Rickie's illegitimate half-brother, is 'English' in the way Rickie would like to be but is unable to. When Agnes, Rickie's wife, tries to have Stephen shipped off to the colonies he has the sort of gut-reaction that Cambridge lacks:

But he burst into an odd passion: he would sooner starve than leave England. 'Why?' she asked. 'Are you in love?' He picked up a lump of the chalk – they were by the arbour – and made no answer. The vicar murmured, 'It is not like going abroad – Greater Britain – blood is thicker than water – .' A lump of chalk broke her drawing-room window on the Saturday.
Thus Stephen left Wiltshire, half blackguard, half-martyr. Do not brand him as a socialist. He had no quarrel with society. (p. 244)

And Forster sends him off to Sawston to break more windows. It might seem like a very cosy world in which a Stephen Wonham does nothing more than behave like Just William but that is not the point, as the author's advice shows. Stephen is really a patriot and his offending lump of chalk an emblem of his closeness to the land: 'class distinctions were trivial things to him'. Such closeness, in a novel written by a former Apostle, tends to be rather conjectural – Stephen isn't exactly a farmer because that would imply too definite a niche in society – but neither is he quite as natural as he seems. For all his horse riding and his sleeping out at night, he lives off either Mrs

Failing or off Elliott money. He owes his natural life to the bourgeois world. Poetry may make this more appealing but it hardly alters the fact that he is having his cake and eating it too. Forster needs to make him innocent to exonerate him from the charge of bad faith. He may be outside the pale of one England, heaving missiles through its windows, but he is not as near to the other as he thinks. His vaunted 'Englishness' looks increasingly like a picturesque disguise. Stephen really stands for the life of the body, which is as far from Cambridge as from Sawston. His Wiltshire is a refuge for the novel's submerged eroticism, a way of passing off sexual feeling as nature-worship. Whether Stephen's physical emotions are directed at horses or girls is secondary: the crucial fact is that Rickie is excluded from them by his lameness. His blood relationship to Stephen underlines their unlikeness from each other. Yet Stephen is more of a symbol than a character. The novel imagines the body without imagining the sense of touch. As in *A Passage to India*, this is where the smoke-screen goes up. Two smoke-screens in fact, for if Stephen is never clear sexually, despite the way Forster dwells on his virility, so too he leaves us confused about his social meaning. Is he as easy to buy off as the ending says?

I would agree with Lionel Trilling that 'privacy for Forster is never a personal provincialism'.[3] The Characters of *The Longest Journey* have their meaning only in relation to England as a whole. As Rickie himself says, 'I never cared a straw for England until I cared for Englishmen.' (p. 174) But this does not mean that one has to take Forster's intention for what he actually realises. It is precisely the nature of his characters' relation to England that is uncertain. Trilling also claims that *The Longest Journey* is his 'most passionate book'[4] and this too is to take the word for the deed. In fact, 'passion' makes its exit early on with the death (or liquidation?) of Gerald. As Rickie tells Agnes, Gerald's erstwhile fiancée, 'Never forget that your greatest thing is over' (p. 80). This does not stop Forster from using love as a way of doctoring his sense of England but it does get something intractable out of the way. We can then see that, if Rickie is unable to choose which England to belong to, so is Forster. Is Wiltshire an alternative to Sawston or a consummation of Cambridge? Is it really England that it represents at all? The poetic descriptions of it have the effect of brushing it under the carpet. One distrusts the novel's tendency to present it as a sort of extension of Stephen's personality. So Rickie, like Arnold, finds himself stuck 'between two worlds'. Finally, he takes the easy option of Sawston, just as his creator takes the easy option of killing him off. When we finish the novel we still aren't sure where 'the longest journey' was to. If England *was* its destination all we know is that several trains go there but all by different routes at different times and someone has made off with the timetable.

The link between Forster's 'liberal humanism' and his idea of England was by no means unique. Something comparable is found in the Edward Thomas who believed in free love, disliked Christianity and Imperialism and sent his children to Bedales. However, in both men it was often the conservative feeling within liberal ideas which had the strongest pull. Neither Howards End, nor The Manor Farm strike very democratic chords. But when the Thomases, like the Lawrences and the Murrys, withdrew to inexpensive inland villages they did not think of themselves as re-locating their advanced ideas within traditional Tory territory. No more does Margaret Schlegel wonder what Miss Avery would think of the books she moves to Howards End. Even Lawrence betrays no unease that Birkin should marry on the strength of his private income. Yet for all the reader knows, it might have been invested in Gerald's coal mines.[5] It was a period when a radical hat could be worn at a conservative angle. Of course, a writer like Thomas also found something resistant in the countryside to test his liberalism but it is doubtful whether Forster ever had that experience: the country tended to bring out his Georgian side. He does not always pass the test of honesty that Thomas's poems suggest, nor is his countryside exactly the same one. The salient fact about Howards End is that it is *owned* and we know to whom it belongs, whereas the Manor Farm simply belongs to England.

An obvious way to define twentieth-century 'Englishness' is in terms of power and empire yet, since the days of William Watson and Kipling, this version of it has never figured as prominently in literature as it has in politics. The political mainstream has often seemed no more than a cultural tributary. It is a peculiarly English split and one that Forster was very conscious of. He at least realised that other Englands existed than those of which he knew himself. Hence the curiously conjectural character of the Wilcoxes and their business world in *Howards End*. The novel must have originated in its author's need to enlarge his understanding of what England was. The problem it begins from is whether the Wilcoxes and the intellectual

Schlegels can ever learn to 'connect'. Because we tend to see this problem through Schlegel eyes we are inevitably made hyper-conscious of how wide the rift between the two families is. In its turn, this tends to divert our attention away from the fact that what is at issue is only a schism *within* the middle classes, leaving the gulf between the middle and the working classes untouched. (Even if the Wilcoxes and Schlegels got on like a house on fire, England would still be a divided society.) Forster is not sanguine but he does believe – or hope – that a connection between them is still possible and he arranges his plot in order to enable either side to see that it needs the other. This is why *Howards End* is not simply a dream of England but also a remarkably prophetic novel. It's hypothetical character is its strength. It is also its weakness. How can it chronicle the 'strange death of liberal England' and still uphold the liberal values it reveals to be so vulnerable? Is 'liberal humanism' equipped for the job it sets itself? All that one can say, looking back, is that it has proved far more resilient than might have been expected, for *Howards End* remains a less dated picture of England than it has any right to be.

I would put this down to the fact that Forster is so anxious to 'connect' with his reader, to make sure he or she is reading the signs in the right way. He seldom trusts his imagination to work on its own, without explanation. There is a delightful moment at the end of T. F. Powys's *Mr Weston's Good Wine* when Mr Weston tells Mr Gunter the Sexton, who enjoys the quite false reputation of being the Folly Down Casanova, that 'you only live to be talked about'. Mr Gunter has his reply at the ready: 'No woon about here do want to die', he says, 'an' what else be life for but to make talk?'[6] The culture Powys describes is still an oral one and, whatever its theme, the talk is always interesting. It counts for more in the way the story is told – or tells itself – than description does. The novel unfolds out of it and any narrative comment about that talk is kept to a minimum. Because each character's talk is so precisely caught, his or her identity comes to us with complete clarity. Powys's people are often odd but there is nothing putative about them. The difference from Forster (who is less naturally a novelist) is striking. Forster's people also live to talk but they leave a very different impression. The narrator himself can never stop introducing and glossing and paraphrasing what they say as if he were really composing one of Charles Lamb's essays. Some of the characters, particularly the ones Forster is less sure of, look more like debating topics than flesh and blood. This can even be true of his 'symbols', like the Marabar Caves in *A Passage to India*, which can become overcast with discussion. It is as if the story-teller had cast a spell on himself which prevented him from distinguishing his novel from his own thought on it. Some of the most interesting Forster characters, like Stephen Wonham, only elude this talk by seeming unexplained. At other times the novelist seems to be chattering in the dark. If time were to stop in a Forster novel, as it does in *Mr Weston's Good Wine*, the ticking of the clock would at once be taken over by the ticking of the narrator himself. There are times in *Howards End* when one begins to think that England itself has been reduced to mere talk. Yet somewhere inside it there is a very fine novel indeed, if only the author would leave it alone.

Here is an example of the sweetly reasonable way the narrator talks about falling in love (Helen Schlegel and Paul Wilcox have just had their momentous kiss):

But the poetry of that kiss, the wonder of it, the magic that there was in life for hours after it – who can describe that? It is so easy for an Englishman to sneer at these chance collisions of human beings. To the insular cynic and the insular moralist they offer an equal opportunity. It is so easy to talk of 'passing emotion', and to forget how vivid the emotion was ere it passed. Our impulse to sneer, to forget, is at root a good one. We recognize that emotion is not enough, and that men and women are personalities capable of sustained relations, not mere opportunities for an electrical discharge. Yet we rate the impulse too highly. We do not admit that by collisions of this trivial sort the doors of heaven may be shaken open. To Helen, at all events, her life was to bring nothing more intense than the embrace of this boy who played no part in it.[7]

There are yards of writing like this in *Howards End*, more sensible than any agony aunt, and at the root of it is Forster's undogmatic 'liberal humanism', ever anxious to tip the reader's imagination in the right direction. But even though he can't resist crossing his 't's' the commentary somehow has the effect of making it harder to imagine what has happened to Helen and Paul. Its sage, confiding tone is not commensurate with the explosiveness of their situation. Even in recognising the extremes of passion the novel seems to want to hold them in check. It is as if one of the narrators functions were to propose a kind of educated consensus as to how to live. Indeed, *Howards End* might be seen not only as an attempt to suggest how the English should live but also as offering a model of which English people are the most truly English. Of course, it does this in the most urbane and ingratiating way.

The pre-war England in which *Howards End* is set sometimes seems like an unusually coherent culture whose divisions feel like little more than cracks in the smooth social surface. As Peter Widdowson says, with the benefit of hindsight, 'there is no "liberal crisis" before the Great War for Forster or for most other liberal humanists.'[8] Perhaps he was less easily taken in than this suggests but he certainly came to look back on the period with a fond regret, envying its innocence of the shocks that lay in store for it. One of his reasons for not publishing *Maurice* in his own lifetime, apart from its homosexual subject, was that it belonged to an age whose time had passed: 'it belongs to an England where it was still possible to get lost. It belongs to the last moment of the greenwood. *The Longest Journey* belongs there too, and has similarities of atmosphere. Our greenwood ended catastrophically and inevitably.'[9] What this neglects to ask is whether the seeds of this catastrophe may not have existed within the 'greenwood' itself. The notion that the home counties picturesque of early Forster, with those rather arch references to 'Pan', might have coincided with the 'wild England' of Borrow and Jefferies is an incongruous one. The romantic associations of the word 'greenwood' suggest more a place for long summer holidays than one where people have to work for a living. There is little in Forster to suggest that he saw many charms in living in the 'greenwood' as the poor do, without dividends. Even Stephen Wonham's nature-worship is subsidised. The real danger to the 'greenwood' came when the unsubsidised many began to go there for the recreation that had previously been open only to the subsidised few. Forster raises this issue in *Howards End*, in the shape of Leonard Bast, but without being able to resolve it. One condition for the novel's 'happy ending', with Margaret safely installed in Mrs Wilcox's house, is that Leonard must first be got out of the way. This possessiveness about the countryside is not uncommon in Forster. In a letter written in 1918, for example, he admits to being 'prejudiced beyond all explanation against the poetry, prose, personality, and papa of Edward Thomas'.[10] This might seem surprising, given how much common ground the two writers had, but it is presumably a response to his feeling that Thomas's country books were helping to make the countryside more accessible to suburbia. Writing later, in 'The Challenge of Our Time', Forster finds himself unable 'to equate the problem' of the social need for new towns with the destruction of the countryside caused by them: 'I cannot free myself from the conviction that something irreplaceable has been destroyed, and that a little piece of England has died as surely as if a bomb had hit it. I wonder what compensation there is in the world of the spirit, for the destruction of the life here, the life of tradition.'[11] The irony is that, in creating a democratic environment fit for English people to live in, England is unwittingly conniving at the destruction of the liberal values it thinks it is upholding. Forster is clearer about what England should be than he is about which English people deserve to inhabit it. In this respect, *Howards End*, for all its enlightenment, remains trapped in the contradictions of the Edwardian age.

Howards End is above all else a novel about inheritance. Who deserves to inherit the England that Mrs Wilcox passes on from the past? Does anyone? In theory, Forster believes that England should be a common possession. In practice, the real inheritance the book describes turns out to be a personal one from Mrs Wilcox to Margaret Schlegel. It is striking how many people are excluded from it. Howards End has no meaning when seen from London or even from the Hertfordshire new towns. Nor to the Basts, because they would not know how to appreciate it. What is more, the Wilcoxes themselves are spiritually (and in Charles's case, physically) ineligible to inherit the house. In other words, the whole range of the middle class seems unfitted to preserve the traditions the house represents. Its only true inheritors are Miss Avery, a rather eccentric descendant of the old yeomanry, and Margaret herself, a liberal intellectual who is backed with new money. Howards End, the epitome of rural England, will be saved, if at all, by a half-German successor of the Clapham Sect. (Forster enjoys having a dig at nationalism even when he is being patriotic.) His liberalism founders on the same reef as *The Longest Journey*: Margaret Schlegel is also Mrs Wilcox and it will be Wilcox money that keeps Howards End in good repair. Mr Podsnap is harder to budge than we thought. A novel committed to toleration and democracy has to settle for a conclusion which, however expedient, can guarantee neither. The Schlegel/Wilcox compromise, which so many readers since Lawrence have jibbed at, is an index of how near Forster thinks England is to falling apart. Coalitions are unavoidable in times of crisis. The personal, Schlegel way of life can only be identified with the idea of England with the help of the far-fetched ending (it symbolically castrates Mr Wilcox) and a good deal of rather wispy prose poetry. All the weight of the final meaning is put on Margaret, even though she had been in search of something larger than herself on which to rest the weight of her own personal life. England adds up to not much more than a light in her mind's eye. Whether this is meant to suggest its tenuousness or her insight is a moot point. Either way, the England Forster celebrates at the end of the novel seems only to become visible because so much of England has had to be excluded from it.

Not surprisingly, *Howards End* has always rankled with those readers who have never been in a position either to marry into or do a deal with Mr Wilcox's class. Lawrence respected Forster as a satirist of that England and therefore saw no occasion for him carefully to remove his own darts. But when he admonished him with the words 'Business is no good' he was in a sense only saying what Forster himself had already said.[12] In most of his fiction it is the Wilcox/Podsnap kind of 'Englishness' which has least hope of being saved. And yet it is very characteristic of Forster to undercut his own negatives, just as he undercuts his positives. Only two damns for the bourgeoisie to go with his 'two cheers for democracy'. It is precisely this that makes him so different from the Lawrence who dreamed of leaving England for a new, ideal community of free spirits called Rananim.[13] In Forster's England, it was still just possible to be saved. For Lawrence, salvation lay rather in extricating oneself from England as it was. The obligation to 'connect' with the likes of Mr Wilcox inevitably struck the creator of Birkin and Paul Morel as nothing less than a Trojan Horse, designed to subdue genuine individuals to the mass of meek ones who were fast inheriting the twentieth century. Of course, Lawrence says 'Only connect' too – especially after his last visit to England in the late 1920s – but, in order to do so, his earlier books had to begin by saying, in effect, 'Only disconnect'. That said, and making what allowance one chooses for Forster's greater timidity or gentility (or irony), his sceptical liberal humanism is closer to Lawrence's work than meets the eye. He may not have the same vividness and intensity (who has?) but he made fiction out of a closely related sense of the pathos of England and its need to resolve oppositions in itself which, in practice, were splitting it farther apart. That is not, of course, what *Howards End* wants to say (save in the melodramatic execution of Leonard Bast by Charles Wilcox) but it is surely what it fears. We know this from *Maurice* where those divided by class and convention only 'connect' in what Forster calls 'the greenwood', outside of society or in some last vestige of traditional England. *Maurice* is, to my mind, Forster's most poignant book – the one where the dangers and pleasures of trying to 'connect' still feel acutely painful. The fact that it constructs its image of a true England on the basis of its aversion to the real one is no accident. In their various ways, setting one English time or place against another, that is what *News From Nowhere* and *After London* and the last part of *Jude the Obscure* do too. England is best defined against England. And nowhere is that process of definition that distinguishes *Maurice* from the more wishful Edwardian England of *Howards End* more central or more like an opened wound than in the three versions of *Lady Chatterley's Lover*, the first in particular. This is not as much of a paradox as it may seem. Though Forster stands for 'personal relations' and Lawrence for a kind of relationship he considers deeper than the purely personal, Forster thinks of 'personal relations' along broadly 'Bloomsbury' lines – that is, as part of a finer living that is beyond society in the aggregate. In this respect, the 'civilised' loves and friendships of Russell Square and the passionate interludes in the keeper's cottage in Wragby Wood have something in common (even though in his novel Lawrence put those characters he based on 'Bloomsbury' on Sir Clifford's side of the fence). In fact, this odd parallel would have squared with Lawrence's own experience of the English class system and the way each class tended to be a little England fenced off from the rest of England, a sect or an enclave even down to the sub-class of the working class which went 'down pit'. Many of the communities he lived in during this time in England were, so to speak, Englands within England: Eastwood with its non-Conformist Chapel, Nottingham University (endowed by Jesse Boot and surrounded by his more commercial enterprises), his school in Croydon, Garsington, Zennor, the Café Royal and so on. Rananim was implicit in these micro-cultures as much as Forster's 'greenwood' was implicit in 'Bloomsbury' or pre-suburban Weybridge. In both writers, we find more social versions of Edward Thomas's England of 'innumerable holes and corners'. In this century writers have usually been happier in seeing England *in petto* than in seeing it whole. This even goes for Kipling or Belloc, not to speak of Walter De la Mare or Housman. One could make a quite good case for saying that the modern writer who seeks to depict England needs to be a regionalist, a Basil Bunting or a Norman Nicholson, rather than a metropolitan. Perhaps that was part of the advantage Lawrence had over Forster? Nonetheless, the sense of a whole community rather than of a small community within a larger one has been almost as rare as big ('three-decker') novels have been. In this sense the novels of Ivy Compton Burnett are as *regional* as those of, say, Lewis Grassic Gibbon – if not more so. To come back to Forster, then, with this in mind, is to notice that, beginning from similarly limited parts of England – Surrey, Cambridge, Sawston etc. – and brilliantly pinpointing their peculiar limitedness, Forster proceeded in *Howards End* to try to evoke the spirit of England as a whole. But did 'England as a whole' still exist? Had it done since Tennyson had given it artificial respiration at the time of the Crimean War? If so, had it survived *The Shropshire Lad* ('those blue remembered hills')? One way of seeing the last part of *Howards End* is as a sort of subtler anticipation of Rupert Brooke. For Margaret and the by now tame Mr Wilcox also end up in a poetic, secluded spot that is 'forever England', surrounded by another England that is to all intents and purposes a 'foreign field'. Of course, Forster's ending is more qualified and less indulgent than this implies but the novel is still one of those where it is best to 'trust the tale, not the teller'. And since Forster's death we have also been able to trust *Maurice*. The penultimate scene of that novel, where Maurice and his lover play together in Clive's cricket match, pretending to go along with the hierarchical occasion but actually retreating into a world of their own, makes it sharply and poignantly clear that the Englands Forster tries to marry in *Howards End* actually pull asunder with the force of their own motion. I don't think that this is simply because Maurice is a homosexual and therefore condemned to live outside the pale. It is more crucial that we should believe in his and Alec's love, *despite* their class differences, as we do in Connie's and her gamekeeper's.[14] Nowhere does Forster imagine any love lived within the pale of society as having such intensity – not in Rickie Elliott or even the decent but oddly lukewarm Fielding or in the chaste sexiness of George Emerson and Lucy Honeychurch. Above all, not in Margaret and her Mr Wilcox. If we refuse to believe in the social hopes and possibilities their marriage symbolises this is not because it is socially improbable – far from it, many businessmen like to have 'cultured' wives, but because it is so difficult to believe that there is anything happening between them emotionally. If this was partly Forster's sceptical point, he can hardly have meant to suggest, as his ending does, that there is no spark there at all, that, judged by the

standard of *Maurice* or *Lady Chatterley*, they simply *don't connect at all*.
Yet despite this, the book's ending is cautiously optimistic in its hope
for England's future. Such hope based on such emptiness is surely
significant. There is a certain logic in the fact that a novel committed
to a more democratic and liberal England should make it so hard for
us to tell the difference between connecting and failing to connect.
Even if that was part of Forster's 'message' one wonders if he saw it
himself at the end. Or was there still a Helen Schlegel in him? –
bolting in disgust to Germany like Maurice to his 'greenwood'. It
isn't 'only' a matter of connecting, as Forster knew only too well in
real life, but of *where* the connecting is done and with whom. If
Maurice's 'greenwood' is (or was) 'England' then it seems unlikely
that Howards End can be too. It is at the cross-roads of this choice
that most of Forster's novels stop.

In *The Common Pursuit* F. R. Leavis rather surprisingly excludes
Howards End from his general praise of Forster as the sort of liberal
humanist whose values were especially pertinent to the England of
the 1930s. Not only did he find its 'poeticality' on the theme of
'Englishness' obscurantist; he also detected in it an unmistakable
whiff of *mauvaise foi*.[15] Though he respected Forster's piously liberal
hopes for the conversion (or pacification) of Mr Wilcox, he wanted
no truck with Mr Wilcox's England himself. Forster was an appeaser
even when his own imagination ruled out appeasement (for instance,
once we learn how Mr Wilcox has treated the Basts). The moral that
Leavis, like Lawrence at much the same time, drew from the war and
its aftermath was that the modern (Wilcox) world had to be met with
its own intransigence. This does not simply mean that he and
Lawrence make less allowance for inevitable human weaknesses like
Mr Wilcox's fling with Jacky Bast: Forster, though often astringent
about the Wilcoxes, ends his novel not just with tolerance but with
emollience. It was this soft centre that Leavis disliked the novel for.
He thought its ostensibly humanist fine feeling shaded into a betrayal:
'We are driven to protest, not so much against the unreality [of
Margaret's marriage] in itself, as against the perversity of intention it
expresses: the effect is of a kind of *trahison des clercs*.'[16] Yet this
criticism is less damning than it sounds. The key word in it is 'effect',
as Leavis wanted to keep it deliberately unclear whether Forster had
betrayed his own values or had simply *appeared* to betray them. This
equivocation surely fits the case like a glove? Forster might well have
retorted to Leavis that a union between the Schlegels and the

Wilcoxes was something that *ought* to have been possible. What else than such a union (with the Basts thrown in) was the idea of England itself for most of his contemporaries? The idea that the marriage is a 'trahison des clercs' is in many ways virtually a 'Bloomsbury' one. One can imagine Duncan Grant or Clive Bell looking down on a Wilcox/Schlegel England as on a house they didn't visit, people with whom they didn't have those magical 'personal relations'. Elsewhere, of course, Forster knew this very well – witness his famous remarks about having the courage to put his friend before his country. It is at least to Forster's credit that, in *Howards End*, for all its faults, he can still be seen as one of the last English novelists to have tried to go on thinking of England as a whole. For this is the other meaning of the final (mis)alliance: no one can conceive of England as a country if they can only imagine it through the eyes of just one of its parties. Leavis's real objection was not that Forster tried to do this (so, in a way, did George Eliot and Dickens) but that he failed to see it was no longer possible.

Leavis's critique of *Howards End* is actually more nuanced than I have so far allowed:

The perversity, of course, has its explanation and is not so bad as it looks. In Margaret the author expresses his sense of the inadequacy of the culture she stands for – its lack of relation to the forces shaping the world and its practical impotence. Its weaknesses, dependent as it is on an economic security it cannot provide, are embodied in the quixotic Helen…The novelist's intention in making Margaret marry Mr Wilcox is not, after all, obscure. One can only comment that, in letting his intention satisfy itself so, he unintentionally makes his cause look even more desperate than it need: intelligence and sensitiveness such as *Howards End* at its finest represents need not be so frustrated by innocence and inexperience as the unrealities of the book suggest.[17]

This is interestingly near to a Marxist diagnosis of liberal culture and its twin failure (exemplified in Forster himself) to realise the worlds either of business or the Basts. Forster would not, for example, have known enough about the twentieth century to write a book like *Culture and Environment*: with merely his polarity of Wilcoxes and Schlegels 'there could hardly have been civilization' in the first place.[18] Nonetheless, a novel that begins like a celebration of liberal values turns into a critique of their ineffectualness. The more embroiled Margaret becomes in her husband's world, the more she seems compromised by it. Yet such well-meant compromises need to be distinguished from vulgar bad faith. To try to live through self-contradictions like Margaret's is, for Forster, to have a hope of being saved: it is those who know only certainties – the Mr Pembrokes, the Charles Wilcoxes and the Callenders – that his novels consign to darkness. The fact that Margaret's initial idea of England seems to slip through her fingers just as she tries to grasp it matters less than the fact that she approaches it through questions and problems and not by clutching for answers. Like Edward Thomas, she looks up at the signpost, 'Wondering where he shall journey, oh where?' If *Howards End* is still such a well-known novel, despite its shortcomings, this is to a considerable degree because its drama sums up so well that crucial moment when English people began to realise, almost like Monsieur Jourdain talking prose, that it was possible to grow up in England, to live and work there, and yet not know what England actually was.

Perhaps Forster's real motive for wanting to 'connect' his different Englands was that, more than either Margaret or her husband, he was unsure which of them he belonged to himself. Nor could he ever convince himself that the new democratic England could be adequate compensation for the England it had supplanted. To settle for an England in which the custodian of *Howards End* has to depend for finance on a member of precisely that class most likely to sell it off or knock it down (rather as if the National Trust were to be sponsored by a conglomerate of jerry-builders) shows that Forster knew just how tight a corner he was in. It is under the pressure of this thought that the novel backs away into poetical obfuscation. Leavis puts his finger on this in the passage which describes England as 'alive, throbbing through all her estuaries'. The Elgarian *frisson* of such moments distracts us from the real question of whom 'this England' really belongs to, 'those who have moulded her ... or to those who have added nothing to her power, but have somehow seen her, *seen the whole island at once*'.[19] The poetry glosses over just those connections the novel pretends to be making. As Leavis notes, 'Mr Forster's "poetic" communication isn't all at this level of poeticality (which, had there been real grasp behind his intention, Mr Forster would have seen to be Wilcox rather than Schlegel), but it nevertheless lapses into such exaltations quite easily.'[20] It is really the Wilcoxes who have most need of the 'greenwood' since they have lost it most irrevocably. (This is why Maurice is a public schoolboy and a businessman). Margaret herself has less need of nostalgia (or stockbroker Tudorbethan), having more real inklings of the 'elder race' to whom she looks back 'with disquietude'. She understands why the 'country which we visit at week-ends was really a home to it'.[21] Yet when Forster goes on to say, 'In these English farms, if anywhere, one might see life steadily and see it whole' we can't help feeling that it is late in the day to wax Arnoldian, just as we feel the farms themselves to be much less real than the ones Sturt and Jefferies wrote about. There is something slightly suburban and even genteel about Margaret's country. Fortunately, she does not sentimentalise it. She knows that her desire to 'connect' is no guarantee of connecting and may even make it harder. Mr Wilcox probably feels more at home in Hertfordshire than she does. Yet Forster at least deserves the credit for having glimpsed that England may be too deep to categorise and too hidden to be willed into being as soon as it is summoned. When he tells us that Margaret could not 'even break loose from culture' (p. 147) he does not simply mean that she never severs her ties to the city (why should she?) but that the real England may lie deeper than liberal culture has imagined: what he had hoped might be complementary worlds actually turn out to occupy different strata altogether. Though Margaret prefers her England to be quiet and 'meditative' it is something more ancient and intractable that she finally catches sight of – just as Stephen Wonham did in Wiltshire.

What makes Forster's descriptions of England less rhapsodic than at first appears is the prosaic settings he gives them (as if the poetry were hedging its bets). Usually, it is Helen, not Margaret, who pretends to live in an England that is like a Shelleyan never-never land, though there are a few moments – such as the opening of chapter nineteen – when the author tilts towards that view too:

If one wanted to show a foreigner England, perhaps the wisest course would be to take him to the final section of the Purbeck Hills, and stand him on their summit, a few miles to the east of Corfe. Then system after system of our island would roll together under his feet. Beneath him is the valley of the Frome, and all the wild lands that come tossing down from Dorchester, black and gold, to mirror their gorse in the expanses of Poole. The valley of the Stour is beyond. (p. 164)

And so on – to Salisbury Plain and the 'glorious downs of Central England'. 'Suburbia' may loom in Bournemouth but 'the cliffs of Freshwater it shall never touch'. The Wight floats forward, 'a fragment of England ... to greet the foreigner', 'Chalk of our chalk, turf of our turf, epitome of what will follow' and, as the 'reason fails' at the sight, 'the imagination swells... and encircles England'. (pp. 164–5) Anyone who knows this marvellous landscape will forgive Forster for getting carried away – though that won't of itself explain what the passage has to do with Hertfordshire and Howards End. Perhaps the real point, beneath the poetics, is that 'culture' is merely an abstraction without a keen sense of the place it has grown from. It has to be defined locally, in terms of the land itself, as well as more metaphysically. Even the landscape of chapter nineteen is not so much 'the whole island at once' as a 'fragment' and a noticeably Hardyesque one at that: a geographical synecdoche whose parts hint at some further whole, 'chalk of our chalk, turf of our turf'. These liturgical cadences cannot disguise the fact that this is no vision of plenitude but merely a foretaste of it, promising more than it can disclose. And Forster keeps his lyrical side in check by presenting the whole view through the prosaic German eyes of Frieda Mosebach who observes discriminatingly that Dorset's hills are 'more swelling ... than in Pomerania'. (p. 165)

It seems, from all this, that England's beauty will only be preserved if not too many people come to live in it. The hordes from Bournemouth must be kept under control if England is to be saved from the English. There could even be too many of the *right* people for its beauty to go round. So Margaret reflects in the Avery farmhouse ('over which the touch of art nouveau had fallen' (p. 265)): it is only when cloistered in the countryside that she can see England 'whole, group in one vision its transitoriness and its eternal youth, connect – connect without bitterness until all men were brothers'. (p. 266) The only proviso is that not 'all men' can be allowed in, brothers or not. In the scene that follows Miss Avery's vulgar niece beats a retreat and Margaret finds that the old woman has re-furnished Howards End with her own furniture. It seems that England has become exclusive, a kind of home for Matthew Arnold's 'aliens' to see life 'steadily' in. The question which this solution evades is, what could a liberal like Margaret do to maintain such an inheritance? Would she simply live *off* it – not unlike the middle classes who are poised to invade Dorset? Margaret may have 'seen' England but she is not one of those who 'mould' it. Hers is a country of the mind, divorced from action; it seems a thin and high-falutin exchange for the England of Cobbett or Jefferies.

The more weight Forster tries to put on Mrs Wilcox's house, therefore, the more it begins to seem like a picturesque backdrop to

Margaret's contemplations, a countryside cultivated as if by magic without visible cultivators, no longer a place to work but a place to dream. It is as new an England, despite its old clothes, as a Surrey stockbroker's. In comparison with other home counties writers like Sturt or Thomas it seems lacking in roughness of texture and dirt – not a workplace but a beautiful view. Its active life is *over*. Probably this is what Forster half wanted to imply; he never pretends that his Hertfordshire is an 'organic community' (in some respects it constitutes a base for an élite, rather like a Cambridge college). Its world of old retainers guiding new owners, keeping the masses at bay, is a place for beautiful inaction. Margaret lives for what comes 'through' it – 'the notion of "through" persisted' (p. 202) – but she does not really live *in* it. She is its spiritual consumer. It is less a place than a medium. Who but an Edwardian liberal would have thought it possible to symbolise a land which had seen so much history through a Ruth Wilcox as perpetuated in a Schlegel? Forster gives only a reduced version of Henry Wilcox at the end but the final picture of Hertfordshire, though more subtle, is just as reduced itself. As someone who grew up in that county I find it quite clear that most of its natives would be *persona non grata* at Howards End, save as servants. Forster may close with a vision of local farmworkers as England's 'hope' ('men had been up since dawn') but his hope is hardly full-blooded, even if the 'clodhopper' and the 'board-school prig' may once more 'throw back to a nobler stock, and breed yeoman' (p. 320). Anyone who knows the Hertfordshire of more recent times – present-day Hatfield and Watford and even St Albans, a county to drive through or round by the fastest route available – can add up the price we have paid since Forster's day for those liberal dreams of rural England. We may still make our Sunday excursions there but Margaret's refuge at Howards End did not come cheap. It left the rest of England at her husband's mercy.

Forster was soon busy with *Maurice* after completing *Howards End*. It is a more personal book, written for a private audience. Forster saw it as a way of getting something out of his system before going on to more public themes. This was naive of him, to judge by the account in Firbank's biography, but also candid. One can judge the profundity of the vaunted 'personal relationships' of *Howards End* by comparing them with Maurice's. (There is little sexual emotion in the earlier book save for Helen's sexual charity to Leonard Bast). *Maurice* is also a comment on Forster's inability to invest his faith in

the England he actually knew. The Cambridge represented by
Maurice's friend Clive is distinctly less rosy than that of *The Longest
Journey*. One surmises that the England of *Howards End* is a shade
sentimental because the author only half believed in it. He told his
friend Florence Barger when *Maurice* was almost finished that it could
not be published 'until my death or England's'.[22] Yet there was a
sense in which *Maurice* was written *for* England, as well as for 'the
happy few'. When it finally came out, after Forster's death, the
England it described was arguably dead too. Part of what had died
was Howards End itself – that time-honoured bucolic gentility.
Maurice could not have appeared in an England in which Howards
End was still central. There was no place for it in Margaret Schlegel's
dream. Its hero would have been an outsider there, like Helen. This
does not mean that *Maurice* is the finer novel – I find it cruder but
more moving – but that Forster manages to write more frankly in it
and dress his emotions up less. Critics ought not to be surprised by
how little fiction he wrote after it. It was already clear that the
England of *Howards End* would never take him further than the
threshold of the modern world.

One of the paradoxes of Lawrence's work was that he was
passionately English and yet, to develop, he increasingly needed to
write *against* England and, in the end, to live in exile from it. He
described himself, in a letter written in 1922 to Lady Cynthia
Asquith, as 'English in the teeth of all the world, even in the teeth of
England.' And, he added, 'How England deliberately undermines
England.'[23] He wrote, that is, with the constant sense of coming at
the end of a long tradition which, with the advent of war, had begun
to break up, leaving nothing of comparable value in its place. Had he
lived in more confident times, Lawrence might have been a
conventional patriot. As it was, his acute sense of England's decline
exacerbated his feeling that, having moved from the industrial
working class to the world of letters, there was no natural place for
him in the England of his day. He left without finding another. The
reception of his writing paralleled this experience in an especially
bitter way. Few writers have written as directly for their countrymen
and yet as early as 1915, one finds him telling his agent, J. B. Pinker,
that ' *The Rainbow* is the end of my writing for England. I will try to
change my public. '[24] There was no going back on this. (An equivalent
to it in his novels is Birkin's and Ursula's decision at the end of *Women*

in Love to resign from their jobs.) Before we try to identify Lawrence with the England of Cossethay and the Marsh Farm, we therefore have to recognise that his later work assumed no specific English public such as we can still feel ourselves to be continuous with. Many critics have stressed the traditional sources of his art but, for him, the tradition was broken for good. This is what makes him a 'modern' where Forster or Thomas or the Georgians are not. To the author of *England, My England*, 'Englishness' was something the English could no longer be relied upon to understand.

Lawrence's early novels can be read as attempts to chronicle this dying England. To read *Sons and Lovers* now is like looking through an old photograph album. We have this sense of looking back because, as he wrote the novel, Lawrence was looking back himself. Not that the novel became enmeshed in nostalgia. *Sons and Lovers* is such a vivid book that one easily forgets how painfully it was written, in several drafts and with several false starts. Lawrence could only complete it once he had *left* England, with Frieda. It was finished not in Nottinghamshire but, of all places, on Lake Garda. Even then, detached by expatriation, its author began to fear that English audiences would not understand what he had written. Heinemann, his publisher, declined one manuscript on the grounds that 'its want of reticence makes it unfit, I fear, altogether for publication in England as things are ...'.[25] Prim though he was, Heinemann could see that *Sons and Lovers* was more than just a naturalistic account of working-class life. Lawrence had diagnosed the condition of England as a whole in it, not just that of Paul Morel. Nowadays, it leaves an impression of lyricism and spontaneity in most readers' minds but it is important to remember its more Zolaesque qualities too. Often it sags under a weight of nineteenth-century gloom. Frieda, for one, felt oppressed by its 'House of Atreus' feeling.[26] It is the work of a writer who had been at school during the heyday of Ibsen and Thomas Hardy. There is more of the *Zeitgeist* in it than there is in Lawrence's mature novels. Most of the characters for most of the time feel trapped rather than liberated by their experiences. Take this description from chapter 10 of Nottingham as seen by Paul and Clara from the castle. Everyone is frustrated and stuck:

The little, interesting diversity of shapes had vanished from the scene; all that remained was a vast, dark matrix of sorrow and tragedy, the same in all the houses and the river-flats and the people and the birds; they were only shapen differently. And now that the forms seemed to have melted away, there remained the mass from which all the landscape was composed, a dark mass of struggle and pain. The factory, the girls, his mother, the large, uplifted church, the thicket of the town, merged into one atmosphere – dark, brooding, and sorrowful, every bit.[27]

This is how the city appears in a novel where people only find freedom outside it – at Willey Farm or by the sea in Lincolnshire – but the gloom lies inside Paul too. Indeed, he wallows in it. That is the only outlet this amorphous England offers him. If his love-life seems so intense that is because he has to put all his eggs in that one basket: the life of work is so thin in comparison. Paul's mind moves between this social alienation and the loss of his mother, a double homelessness. Separation from her confirms his separation from the world in which she is trapped. If he feels a sense of liberation at the end of the novel, as he moves 'towards the faintly humming, glowing town',[28] that is because he feels liberated at *not belonging any more*. The book is an exorcism of England as it is. This is why Lawrence had to go abroad, both to finish it and to come to terms with the death of his mother. There was a parallel release to be won. In a sense, his mother was a symbol of England to him: he felt the same need to escape from both. Already, we can see the Lawrence whose most powerful images of self-development and social growth would be expressed as occurring *outside* society, the Lawrence who created Birkin and Ursula and was so fired by novels like *The Scarlet Letter* and *Jude the Obscure*. Many years later, in 1926, when he returned to Nottinghamshire, he wrote (in 'Return to Bestwood') that 'I feel more alien, perhaps, in my home place than anywhere else in the world'.[29] As *Sons and Lovers* shows, he came to feel 'alien' and exiled in England even before he left it.

Because he grew up in midland mining countryside, Lawrence never thought of the English landscape as offering a retreat from the present, a buffer against England as it was, as his southern contemporaries did. The scarred country of the coalfields had a different pathos from Housman's Shropshire or Thomas's Hampshire, a pathos which implied rather than hid its social meanings. This saved him from the usual association of 'Englishness' with a declining rural way of life. Nor did he confuse England with southern England as Belloc had done. Like Sturt, but more painfully, he refused to tear himself away from the drama of England's defacement in the hope of finding refuge in some England of the mind. He knew that the past could not be an alternative to the present: hence, his sceptical view of revivalist attempts to bring it back, like the Arts and Crafts Movement or the craze for English folklore which he used to place the hero of *England, My England*. Hence, too, his rare ability to evoke the pathos of modern England without succumbing to nostalgia for some 'land of lost content'. But already in 1915, in a letter to Lady Asquith written from the pacifist stronghold of Garsington, there is a distinct feeling of mourning in the way he thinks of his country:

When I drive across this country, with autumn falling and rustling to pieces, I am so sad, for my country, for this great wave of civilisation, 2000 years, which is now collapsing, that it is hard to live. So much beauty and pathos of old things passing away and no new things coming: this house – it is England – my God, it breaks my soul – their England, these shafted windows, the elm-trees, the blue distance – the past, the great past, crumbling down, breaking down, not under the force of the coming birds, but under the weight of many exhausted lovely yellow leaves, that drift over the lawn, and over the pond, like the soldiers, passing away, into winter and the darkness of winter – no, I can't bear it. For the winter stretches ahead, where all vision is lost and all memory dies out.[30]

'Englishness' is a kind of phantom presence here, opposed in spirit to the England that is coming to replace it. A drastic lack of continuity, underlined by the war, condemns this older England to a purely inward existence. As Lawrence was to conclude, soon after these years of war-time tension, in a letter written from Taormina in 1922, the English had to 'withdraw from the world, away towards the inner cities that *are* real, only to return later, when one is quiet and sure'.[31] Such quietness no longer existed in England: the wood in *Lady Chatterley's Lover* is only an oasis, not a way of life. Nor did Lawrence simply want the 'old things' back. He knew that they were part of the problem and that 'new things' were needed in their place.

In *The Rainbow*, Lawrence still kept one foot in the England of Cossethay and Hardy whilst trying to straddle the divide in consciousness made by the Great War. Whereas most writers opted for one world or the other, he juxtaposed an afterglow of the England of *Adam Bede* with images of modern industrialism. In this way the human cost of recent history could be measured. The people who seem most modern, like Winifred Inger and the younger Tom Brangwen, turn out to be spiritually dead, whereas Ursula, with her potential for spiritual growth, is forced to detach herself more and more from her society in order to go on growing. It was during the war years that Lawrence became increasingly possessed by what he called Rananim, his dream of a community of free spirits who could live on the fringe of society with genuine commonalty, in contrast to its false belief in the masses. It could be said that this idea, often associated with Lawrence's post-war globe-trotting and books like *The Plumed Serpent*, was already implicit in the picture of Paul's estrangement at the end of *Sons and Lovers*. Rananim was an ideal, alternative England, analogous to the more backward-looking ideal of the 'organic community' but with the emphasis on reconstruction rather than nostalgia. Even in exile, without any clear English audience, Lawrence could go on writing about England's future by projecting it on to Italians or Mexican Indians. It was no longer necessary to locate England only *in* England. After *Sons and Lovers*, until *Lady Chatterley*, he never limited his fiction to naturalistic pictures of England in the present. *The Rainbow* may start out like a re-run of George Eliot and Hardy but the lives of its characters are not socially determined as theirs are, as if by a kind of fate. Lawrence's work has a very different precedent in the fiction of William Morris, particularly in *News From Nowhere*, a Utopian dream-vision which both predicts and enacts the death of the Victorian realistic novel. We tend ourselves to put that novel in a separate box, outside the mainstream, but Morris's prestige was great during Lawrence's formative years. I don't think it is an accident that – as I shall shortly show – there should be a clear reference to his Utopia in one of the most crucial dialogues of *Women in Love*.

In earlier Lawrence there are still glimpses of the 'old wild England' evoked by Borrow and Jefferies: in the farming country of *The Rainbow* or even the 'savage' heathland of *England, My England*. But this England was dwindling fast and, by the time of Lawrence's return home in 1926, it seemed boxed into a corner, in Connie Chatterley's and the gamekeeper's retreat in the wood, its silence punctuated by the sirens from the colliery, its flowers – like their eroticism – a frail exception to the general grime, a kind of voluntary internal exile almost as remote as Taos. After the novels set in the New World there is an acute lack of space, both physical and spiritual. The wood is an oddly Georgian impasse to return to. It recalls the empty house in which Hardy's Tess and her Angel spend a few idyllic days prior to her arrest and execution. Lawrence still believed that 'the most living clue of life is in us Englishmen' but he more and more saw the danger of its being 'quenched'.[32] In the *Lady*

Chatterley novels even 'the spirit of place' has become vulnerable, a fragile hiatus in the surrounding materialism, temporarily immune to the deadening effect of actual English culture. It can only be a vision, not a social reality like the mines. Small wonder that sex takes on such unprecedented centrality.

At the end of *Women in Love*, Birkin and Ursula still have somewhere to go but this is much less true of the *Lady Chatterley* novels. Even in the first one, the gamekeeper, Parkin, is dismissed and goes to work in Sheffield as a lorry driver, doomed to be a foot soldier in the class war. In his *Study of Thomas Hardy*, Lawrence had complained that Hardy constantly evaded the real 'tragedy' of his novels by having his characters brought down by the secondary agency of social convention. Places like Egdon Heath were really far more potent to them than mere social laws were but Hardy founded their struggle on the latter and not the former. In *Lady Chatterley* this predicament has been so exacerbated that both worlds seem smaller: the wood is merely an oasis or refuge, without impact on society, whilst industrial England has taken over the whole country. The wood is like a trap. Nevertheless, it *is* England as the rest of England is not, rather as Forster's 'greenwood' also is. For Lawrence never identified his 'England' with the 'nation' as a political unit. He came to think of it in increasingly visionary ways, transforming the usual regressive nostalgia with which his contemporaries thought of it. There are many indications in his late work of this interest in the visionary. In his essay 'Making Pictures', for instance, he records a debt to Blake and Samuel Palmer, who depicted an England prompted by their vision, in precisely the sort of context where Edward Thomas relied on more realistic painters and writers like 'Clare and Cobbett, Morland and Crome'.[33] This is why *The Rainbow* has a greater range than those Thomas poems which might be felt to fit within its ethos. Unlike Lawrence, Thomas had no means of imagining any future for England. This was presumably one reason why he joined up in 1915. The past eluded him because the present did too. There are no grounds, so far as I know, for suggesting that Lawrence had Thomas in mind when he created Egbert, a 'born rose', as the hero of *England, My England*. Egbert is sensitive, cultured and doomed to live off England's past in ignorance of its present. Like Thomas, he and his family live a rural life, close to the soil and to English folklore, in a cottage in Hampshire. There are enough parallels with Thomas for us to draw them even if Lawrence, who seems to have liked Thomas, did not. Egbert is not a writer but, like Thomas, he does join up and, eventually, die. From being 'caught out of the world'[34] in the countryside, he chooses annihilation in a modern war. Yet, like Thomas, he feels no 'hatred' of Germans, no nationalism. He even has Thomas's melancholy. Of course, Egbert is satirised (for his 'Arts and Crafts' enthusiasms) and whether or not Thomas was intended in him is not really important. What is, is that Lawrence could never be seen as an Egbert himself. The satire shows how anxious he was to get that sort of 'Englishness' out of his system. Revivalism was beside the point, as well as being too obviously 'southern'.

Lawrence was not against the war as his war-time collaborator Bertrand Russell was but he was certainly not fit for it like Thomas. No doubt he had once shared in the working-class patriotism which had thrilled to W. E. Henley's 'Take and break us: we are yours / England my own!' before he satirised it. But the Lawrence who proclaimed 'I am English and my Englishness is my very being'[35] had little time for the patriotism of the Great War volunteers. In *The Rainbow*, written at the time Thomas was deciding to enlist, he makes Ursula attack her lover Skrebensky for wanting to fight for King and Country in the Boer War. Her attack clearly has the author's backing:

'I hate soldiers, they are stiff and wooden. What do you fight for, really?'
  'I would fight for the nation.'
  'For all that, you aren't the nation. What would you do for yourself?'
  'I belong to the nation and must do my duty by the nation.'
  'But when it didn't need your services in particular – when there *is* no fighting? What would you say then?'
  He was irritated.
  'I would do what everybody else does.'
  'What?'
  'Nothing. I would be in readiness for when I was needed.'
  The answer came in exasperation.
  'It seems to me,' she answered, 'as if you weren't anybody there, where you are. Are you anybody really? You seem like nothing to me.'[36]

For Ursula, the 'nation' can no longer express the individual: instead of offering him some consummation, it simply diminishes him to 'nothing'. Skrebensky the soldier betrays his own emotional truth for the sake of a cliché, a mere convention. It is not that Ursula is being unpatriotic but that she refuses to pretend to have feelings like her lover's, feelings that spring only from duty. The 'nation' is an abstraction and only the individual is living and tangible. Where Lawrence differs from earlier novelists is in putting the lovers' debate in such dualistic terms. No compromise between them is possible. Yet, in opposite ways, they are *both* arguing a case for the importance of their 'Englishness'. What narrows their options so much is that Lawrence (and Ursula) appear to believe that any true 'Englishness' will inevitably run counter to the 'nation' and ought therefore to have no truck with it. A quality usually thought of as cultural and social in origin is thus felt capable of growth only in opposition to the culture from which it has been born. Not surprisingly, this passage was one of those which led to *The Rainbow* being suppressed. It writes off so much of what society (and, surely, the English novel of the nineteenth century) stood for. Ursula, having grown beyond her own social world, sees very little space in any other. Like many Lawrence characters, she has no ties and yet no room in which to move. Society offers her not a series of opportunities, as it did to David Copperfield or even the characters of George Eliot, but a series of obstacles and barriers.

This impasse is the problem *The Rainbow* passes on to *Women in Love*. How do we live when the 'nation' and 'Englishness' no longer move in the same direction? It is not a question that the novelist could hope to answer by charting English society as it was, as his predecessors had done. That might point out the problem but not its solution. Birkin and Ursula know precisely what they want to leave but they only have a tentative idea of where they want to go. This is why Birkin borrows the language of William Morris to put his point more clearly:

'Where will you wander to?' she asked.

'I don't know. I feel as if I would just meet you and we'd set off – just towards the distance.'

'But where can one go?' she asked anxiously. 'After all, there *is* only the world, and none of it is very distant.'

'Still,' he said, 'I should like to go with you – nowhere. It would be rather wandering just to nowhere. That's the place to get to – nowhere. One wants to wander away from the world's somewheres, into our own nowhere.'

Still she meditated.

'You see, my love,' she said, 'I'm so afraid that while we are only people, we've got to take the world that's given – because there isn't any other.'[37]

If the 'world's somewheres' seem unreal, 'nowhere' is the logical place to go to, even if it means trying to develop one's 'Englishness' outside of England. 'Nowhere' is not unreal just because it has no locality, any more than Morris's 'Nowhere' is: it has reality in the mind. Like Morris, Lawrence has to qualify his vision to express it at all – he needs Ursula's scepticism to bring Birkin down to earth – but he does not use workaday reality as a measure of it. The tension within his vision is not between the real and the ideal but between the probable and the possible. It is, one might say, more the sort of tension he found in the 'classic American novel' than in any of his European predecessors.

Before they go abroad Birkin and Ursula visit a street market where they buy a chair: 'When I see that clear, beautiful chair,' [Birkin says] 'and I think of England – it had living thoughts to unfold even then. And now, we can only fish among the rubbish-heaps for the remnants of their old expression' (p. 355). For all its beauty, it is the past itself that is stifling England from growing. The past takes up nearly all the available room. They decide to give the chair away after all, to an ordinary young couple who are combing the market for things to set up home with. Watching them go off with the chair, Birkin and Ursula realise that they are the 'meek' who will 'inherit the earth':

> 'Are they going to inherit the earth?' she said.
> 'Yes – they.'
> 'Then what are we going to do?' she asked. 'We're not like them – are we? We're not the meek?'
> 'No. We've got to live in the chinks they leave us.'
> 'How horrible!' cried Ursula. 'I don't want to live in chinks.'
> 'Don't worry,' he said. 'They are the children of men, they like market places and street corners best. That leaves plenty of chinks.'
> 'All the world,' she said.
> 'Ah, no – but some room.' (p. 361)

Lawrence is under no illusions about these 'chinks'. He knows how small the modern world is. Birkin and Ursula do not have the option of a Gauguin-like retreat from it into a world of their own. There are no peasants in Brittany any more and even the west of Ireland will hardly outlive J. M. Synge. The unknown has been reduced to a few bolt-holes. Even in New Mexico, Lawrence was to find the march of American culture unstoppable and the native Indians as vulnerable as his own 'wild England' had been. Words like 'nowhere' and 'chinks' suggest restriction as well as openness. England smothers its children, whose love for it is 'like the love for an aged parent who suffers horribly from a complication of diseases, for which there is no hope' (p. 395). Gudrun, glad to be out of it, asks Birkin if there is any hope for it?

'Any hope of England's becoming real? God knows. It's a great actual unreality now, an aggregation into unreality. It might be real if there were no Englishmen.'
    'You think the English will have to disappear?' persisted Gudrun...
    'Well – what else is in front of them but disappearance? They've got to disappear from their own special brand of Englishness, anyhow.' (p. 395)

To see why Lawrence was unique one has only to think how many of his contemporaries devoted themselves to preserving just the 'special brand of Englishness' he was fighting to cast off. Yet neither Birkin nor Lawrence are iconoclasts. Their very need to renew and replace their received 'Englishness' is a measure of how English they are. But England is no longer a fixed, immutable entity. Like all human things, it grows and dies and it has to change to stay alive. In *Women in Love*, however, the 'Englishness' of the four main characters is changing faster than the 'nation' is.

Lawrence's version of 'Englishness' is best seen as a kind of emergency self in a period of social fragmentation. It is doomed to being English without England and at the expense of England. 'England' was no longer *in* England in any case. But Lawrence did not see this as simply the consequence of industrialism. The present predicament also reflected the limitations of the old rural England and its corresponding failure to embody itself in the city and in civic ideals. The cult of 'home' (refused by Birkin and Ursula) has prevented the English from thinking beyond the social horizons of the village:

As a matter of fact, till 1800 the English people were strictly a rural people – very rural. England has had towns for centuries, but they have never been real towns, only clusters of village streets. Never the real *urbs*. The English character has failed to develop the real urban side of a man, the civic side. Siena is a bit of a place, but it is a real city, with citizens intimately connected with the city. Nottingham is a vast place sprawling towards a million, and it is nothing more than an amorphous agglomeration. There is no Nottingham, in the sense that there is Siena.[38]

Already, before Lawrence's day, English history has involved change without real organic continuity. This is why Birkin and Ursula cannot expect to find any stimulus to growth in their actual England.

The whole transition from a rural to an urban society has been bungled so that, in effect, history has been reduced to the blind superimposing of one England upon another. Hence, cities like Nottingham and the amorphous post-war England of *Lady Chatterley's Lover*:

England my England! but which is *my* England? The stately homes of England make good photographs and create the illusion of a connection with the Elizabethans. The handsome old halls are there, from the days of Queen Anne and Tom Jones. But smuts fall and blacken on the drab stucco, that has long ceased to be golden. And one by one, like the stately homes, the Georgian halls are going...

This is history. One England blots out another. The mines had made the halls wealthy. Now they were blotting them out, as they had already blotted out the cottages. The industrial England blots out the agricultural England. One meaning blots out another. The new England blots out the old England. And the continuity is not organic, but mechanical.[39]

When a people's history isolates it from its past, social ideals either have to be put even further back in the past (as with Carlyle) or projected into the future, 'away from the world's somewheres'. Thus, on his travels, Lawrence sometimes celebrated the kind of village world that had gone forever in England (Tuscan peasants, Hopi Indians) and sometimes, as in *The Plumed Serpent*, imagined visionary versions of Rananim. Either way, he could not disguise the fact that such solutions were *faute de mieux*. They did nothing to make Nottingham tolerable. The exotic material of his later writings too often seems like a surrogate for experiences whose real roots lie in England. Neither 'nowhere' nor the 'chinks' in 'the world's somewheres' gave full scope to his social genius. This explains why he never put so much of himself into any novel after *Women in Love*. But did he lose touch with his real subject-matter in rejecting England? To assume that he did is to forget that he felt that England had betrayed itself and not that he himself had betrayed England. The one thing he took with him to Mexico was his 'Englishness'. Yet this hardly alters the fact that, though England's greatest writer from the working class, he should have needed to develop in such a radically different direction from the class he came from. All of which makes *Lady Chatterley's Lover* (all three versions of it) crucial to defining how he understood his own 'Englishness'.

Among other things, *Lady Chatterley's Lover* is Lawrence's dismayed recognition of what had happened to England since he had left it after the war. Its social world is unnaturally small and closed, quite without the possibilities still open to the characters of the earlier novels. The classes seem locked in unvaryingly predictable responses to life. As an exile Lawrence had not thought of himself as exiled from his own 'Englishness' but, on returning to England, he suspected that that was the fate of many English people who had stayed at home. He could still write from Ceylon in 1922 that, 'the most living clue of life is in us Englishmen is England, and the great mistake we make is in not uniting together in the strength of this real living clue ... ' Making such a claim, Lawrence was affirming that his own 'Englishness' could be preserved in a state of physical and spiritual exile from England *as it was*. Where the *Lady Chatterley* novels sharpen this perception is by locating this exile, not in Ceylon or Mexico, but in the heart of England itself. The contrast between the fugitive England of the wood where the lovers meet and the England of the collieries becomes starker with each version of the novel. When the colliery sirens disturb the lovers in the wood they seem like alarums from a foreign country. It is as if England is no longer one single, coherent entity any more. Half of English humanness has to be hidden from the other half – the sexual from the social – as if people were afraid to admit themselves to themselves. The novel is as much about the way the divisions between the classes prevent English people from feeling any sense of community with each other as it is about sexual love. The two possibilities seem almost mutually exclusive. For instance, this moment in the first version of the novel:

'Folks like you,' he said, 'is more like the moon than this world.'
'But my world is the real world. Tevershall isn't real. They aren't real, all of them. Only the moon is real, and you and me. Say I'm real to you!'
She clung to him in supplication.
He stroked his arm down her tense, chill back, and the silky, cool sense of beauty, the beauty of *her*, took away his worldly consciousness for a while.
'Tha'rt real an' nowt else is,' he said.
'Yes! The moon! And the flowers! And you!' she insisted. 'The wood is real. The sky is real. Only people aren't real.'
'Maybe!' he said. 'Maybe they aren't!'[40]

There is a pathos in this missing from Birkin's more confident talk about 'nowhere'. Parkin and Connie are more afraid of 'people' than bent on defying them. They are desperately trying to persuade each other that the outside worlds they belong to don't matter. It is as if, once in the wood, they cannot even afford to admit to themselves the existence of the world outside the wood. What this means, at least in the first version of the novel, is that they can only bring a part of themselves to their love-making. She remains a 'Lady' to him and he is always a worker to her and on that level they fail to communicate as they do sexually. Their recourse is therefore to pretend that the world of class distinctions (Tevershall, England) is simply unreal. Yet the very fact that the wood belongs to Sir Clifford, who also owns the collieries, tells the reader that 'people' are more 'real' than they choose to believe.

As lost mother and ransacked home, England had seemed steeped in pathos to Lawrence since the Great War, brooding on its own ruins. For all its social and industrial changes, the England of Wragby Hall is governed by its past. Everybody's social role is predetermined by class. It therefore seems as if, when people behave spontaneously in Lawrence, the most natural thing for them to do is to avoid other people, as Connie and Parkin would like to do. Even the English landscape itself is felt to be most beautiful when English people are absent from it. Thus Birkin dreams wishfully of a 'world without people' (*Women in Love*, p. 127), in the scene after Hermione hits him with a paper-weight, and, at Gerald's water-party, the Brangwen sisters instinctively ask for a boat in order to get across to an island on the lake, away from all the other guests. As Raymond Williams says, *Women in Love* is about 'the experience of loss: a loss of ... the experience of community'.[41] By *Lady Chatterley's Lover*, that sense of 'loss' has become even more difficult to escape from. Connie and the gamekeeper cannot shut out the world as Birkin and Ursula do – indeed, each represents a part of that world and its class system to the other. The wood serves only as a makeshift refuge, somewhere where they are not so much free as at bay. It may seem like the polar opposite of the idea of England as 'the nation', subscribed to by Skrebensky, but it is also an opposite to more traditional ideas of rural England, like Constable's or Cobbett's, in which human work still cemented a bond between man and nature. In Tevershall, work is a pollutant and even the gamekeeper's labour – raising pheasants for the gentry to kill – seems meaningless. His position holds no future for him and its only real attraction is its solitariness. There is no place for work in the 'nowhere' the lovers mean to go to, no scope for community other than that between themselves. In Lawrence, establishing one relationship nearly always means breaking off another. This is not to say that the theme of his novels is merely an *égoisme à deux* but that they insist on the extreme difficulty of making relationships at all, given the odds against their being made. Connie and the gamekeeper are underdogs and outlaws. There is never any chance of their love finding its place *within* the community.

Not that Lawrence's characters find it easy to opt out of society. Exiles carry their country with them. Although Birkin and Ursula take the 'old Imperial road' south at the end of *Women in Love* they have to retrace their steps back to England to bury Gerald. The past proves harder to shake off than they supposed. The dichotomy between free spirits and the country they leave turns out to be less cut-and-dried than it seemed. The same is true of tales like *The Princess* and *The Woman Who Rode Away*, which contrast the civilised with the primitive: they rarely go as far in the direction of the 'Dark Gods' as one expects them to. Lawrence's fiction is better described as dialectic than as dualistic. However sick the society of *Lady Chatterley's Lover* may seem, the novel never suggests that the notion of society is in itself sick. There is always tension between the desire to reject civilisation and the wish to regenerate it. Thus, the lovers can never put off their social selves or forget their class differences. Much more than the nonchalant Ursula and Birkin, they are stuck with the problems and contradictions of their social position. Whereas Birkin's private income makes things easier for him and Ursula, Connie's constitutes an obstacle to her and the gamekeeper. It is not possible to ignore one's class even if, like Connie, one wants to.

This unpalatable realism is most prominent in the first version of *Lady Chatterley's Lover*, the one which, in my view, describes the lovers' predicament most honestly and movingly. Lawrence makes no attempt to make the problems they face one whit less intractable than they are. One never feels, for example, that their sexual compatibility will make their social incompatibility unimportant, as one does in the novel's final version. Parkin (the gamekeeper had not yet acquired the more stylish name of Mellors) is quite uneducated, unlike his successor, and never speaks anything but dialect. It is possible to think of him as an unusual man and still feel that he is bound by his class. Often, he is depicted as coarse, pig-headed and even stupid and Connie frankly admits to herself that too much of his conversation would bore her. Lawrence is quick to see the thousand and one little words and gestures by which class estranges them. He does this most strikingly by means of social comedy (something in short supply in the final version), by not being afraid to bring out what is ludicrous in the situation. At one point Connie suddenly has an appalled vision of Parkin eating bloaters:

Why this passion, which meant more than the rest of her life to her? – Ah, if she could be in the cottage with him now, just lighting the lamp! Perhaps they would have – she tried to think of something really common – bloaters, yes, bloaters for supper, grilled bloaters. The house simply reeked of grilled bloaters. And he sat with his elbows on the table, in his shirt-sleeves, and picked bits of bloater bones away with his fingers. And drops of tea hung on his fierce moustache. And he said:

'These 'ere bloaters is that salty, they're nowt but brine. Pour us another cup o' tea, leass.' (*First Lady Chatterley*, pp. 63–4)

Connie is laughing at herself as well as at Parkin; her laughter is a way of facing the facts. She realises that 'if they lived together they would humiliate one another' and she also knows that, being in 'another world of culture than his' she could never simply give that 'culture' up for him, nor he his for her (p. 64). She is still powerfully drawn to the Chatterley world she belongs to. There is no danger that Parkin will be idealised as Mellors is.

The strength of *The First Lady Chatterley* is that Lawrence never allows his faith in the lovers' 'tenderness' to persuade him that it will override their differences. Sexual fulfilment, important as it is, is only a part of a full human fulfilment. The novel's theme is as much the limitations of sexual love as that sexual love can be a panacea for social ills. This comes out poignantly in a highly comic scene which is absent from the last version of the novel. Parkin is living with a friend and his family at Blagby Street, Sheffield (he is working at a steel-works) and Connie is invited to tea. The whole scene is an excruciating series of *faux pas*, both by Connie and her hosts, starting from the moment she knocks at the front door, not realising that she should have gone to the back. Neither she nor Parkin pretends that they are any less alien to each other than they actually are. At one point in the meal Bill Tewson, the host, wonders whether his own feelings and those of Sir Clifford are 'so very different'. Connie can't help answering truthfully:

Were his feelings the same as Clifford's? Good God, no!

'Yes!' she said in her soft, composed voice.

'Eh?' he started. 'Yes?'

'Yes!' she repeated.

He stared at her with those bright, grey, intense eyes for some moments as his tension slackened.

'You mean to say there *is* a difference between my feelings and those of a man like Sir Clifford? You mean to say there is?'

'Yes!'

'There *is*? And a big difference? Big enough to matter?

'Yes.'

He sat slowly back in his chair, his face very pale and as if bewildered. Then he quickly rubbed his forehead and ruffled his hair so that it stood on end. Then he gave a queer, quick, deep little laugh as he looked round, half-rueful, half-roguish, at Parkin.

'It's what tha towd me, lad!' he said.

Parkin did not answer. He suddenly seemed to Constance such a furtive bird.

'What did you tell him?' she asked softly.

'Me!' He looked her in the eye. 'I towd him folks like us an' folks like you an' Sir Clifford wasn't in the same world an' never would be.'

'But have you found me in a very different world from the world you are in?' she said.

'Ay!' he answered, pushing a cake into his mouth, and speaking as he chewed. 'Different as owt can be.' (p. 173)

Parkin is under no illusions about how divided English society is, so much so that, while in Sheffield, he becomes a Communist, putting another barrier between himself and Connie. It is with this gulf between the lovers' social and sexual lives that *The First Lady Chatterley* ends. Lawrence could see no resolution to the problem. The lovers symbolise an England completely split asunder and lost.

The one thing that is clear at the end of the novel is that Connie and Parkin can never go back to Wragby Wood, though their love is associated with it. They have no place of their own any more, as if they were stateless. It seems to be part of Lawrence's intention to make all their possible homes – together or apart – look provisional and rootless, as if the only England they had to live in were an England of the mind. The England of Sheffield and the collieries is unthinkable and the England of the wood seems lost for ever. Yet each of them stands for something that is a fundamental part of England. The tragedy is that the only way they can understand each other's different kind of 'Englishness' is by setting themselves apart from England. No wonder Lawrence said, in 'Return to Bestwood', 'I feel a doom over the country, and a shadow of despair over the hearts of men, which leaves me no rest.'[42] Few versions of England have been so bleak.

NOTES

(Place of publication is London unless otherwise stated)

1 Quoted by Peter Widdowson, *E. M. Forster's 'Howards End': Fiction as History* (Sussex University Press, Brighton, 1977), p. 93.
2 *The Longest Journey* (Penguin, Harmondsworth, 1960), p. 51.
3 Lionel Trilling, *E. M. Forster: A Study* (Hogarth Press, 1967), p. 30.
4 *Ibid.*, p. 67.
5 Where Lawrence's northern working-class background comes out is in his much harsher attitude to *rentier* intellectuals like Egbert in *England, My England* and Rico in *St Mawr*.
6 *Mr Weston's Good Wine* (Chatto and Windus, 1960), p. 261.
7 *Howards End* (Edward Arnold, Abinger Edition, 1973), pp. 22–3.
8 Widdowson, '*Howards End*', p. 38.
9 'Postscript' to *Maurice*, introd. by P. N. Furbank with Forster's own 'Terminal Note' (Edward Arnold, 1971), p. 240.
10 *Selected Letters of E. M. Forster 1879–1920*, eds. Mary Lago and P. N. Furbank (Collins, 1983), I, p. 184.
11 *Two Cheers for Democracy* (Edward Arnold, 1951), pp. 67–8.
12 *The Letters of D. H. Lawrence*, (Cambridge University Press, 1987), IV, p. 301.
13 George Zytaruk, *The Quest for Rananim: D. H. Lawrence's Letters to S. S. Koteliansky 1914–1930* (McGill-Queen's, Montreal, 1970).
14 One thing that Forster liked to imagine happening in the 'greenwood' was that the class system would break down. Furbank's biography is fascinating on his relations with his working-class lovers. The parallel with the wood in *Lady Chatterley's Lover* is striking.
15 *The Common Pursuit* (Penguin, Harmondsworth, 1962), p. 271.
16 *Ibid.*, p. 269.
17 *Ibid.*, pp. 269–70.
18 *Ibid.*, p. 270.
19 *Howards End*, p. 172.
20 *Common Pursuit*, p. 271.
21 *Howards End*, p. 266.
22 *Selected Letters*, p. 259
23 *The Letters of D. H. Lawrence*, eds. George J. Zytaruk and James Boulton, IV, p. 234.
24 *The Letters of D. H. Lawrence*, II, (Cambridge University Press, 1981), p. 619.
25 *Ibid.*, p. 525.
26 In *D. H. Lawrence: A Composite Biography* ed. Edward Nehls, 3 vols. (University of Wisconsin Press, Madison, 1957), I (1885–1919), p. 182.
27 *Sons and Lovers* (Penguin, Harmondsworth, 1948), p. 333.
28 *Ibid.*, p. 511.

29 *Phoenix II: Unpublished and Other Prose Works by D. H. Lawrence*, eds. Warren Roberts and Harry T. Moore (Heinemann, 1968), p. 257.
30 *The Letters of D. H. Lawrence*, II, pp. 431–2.
31 *Ibid.*, IV, p. 175.
32 *Ibid.*, IV, p. 219.
33 *Phoenix II*, pp. 602–7.
34 *England, My England*, ed. Bruce Steele (Cambridge University Press, 1990), p. 14.
35 *The Letters of D. H. Lawrence*, II, p. 414.
36 *The Rainbow* (Penguin, Harmondsworth, 1949), p. 311.
37 *Women in Love*, eds. David Farmer, Lindeth Vasey and John Worthen (Cambridge University Press, 1987), p. 315.
38 'Nottingham and the Mining Countryside', *Phoenix: The Posthumous Papers of D. H. Lawrence*, ed. Edward D.McDonald (Heinemann, 1936), p. 139.
39 *Lady Chatterley's Lover* (Penguin, Harmondsworth, 1960), pp. 162–3.
40 *The First Lady Chatterley*, with a foreword by Frieda (Heinemann, 1972), pp. 155–6.
41 *The English Novel: From Dickens to Lawrence* (Paladin, 1974), p. 147.
42 *Phoenix II*, p. 264.

CHAPTER 4

Late witness: George Sturt and village England

> Few things uplift me so much as do suggestions that sometimes
> come, of England spreading out before and all around me.[1]

This sense, which *came* to Sturt, seems to have reached Leavis mainly
through literature, through the talk of Mrs Poyser in *Adam Bede* for
instance:

> George Eliot had grown up in a community in which that traditional art of
> speech flourished – the popular, generally cultivated art of speech that
> made the English language that made Shakespeare possible.[2]

Yet though Leavis regards this language as the indispensable source
of 'English Literature' he no longer regards it as an active constituent
of English life. To understand the changes this implies one needs to
turn to his response to Sturt, at the beginning of his critical career.
There, in *Culture and Environment*, Sturt figures as a guarantee that
what has since been lost once really existed. His name comes up with
Bunyan's *Pilgrim's Progress*, 'the supreme expression of the old English
people':

> this great book, which is so much more than Bunyan's, will, together with
> (say) *Change in the Village, The Wheelwright's Shop* and the other works of
> George 'Bourne' (or Sturt) ... serve to bring home to the doubting that the
> English people did once have a culture.[3]

Sturt, in other words, served partly as an intermediary with the past.

Accounts of Leavis often mention Sturt's influence on his early
work but they usually leave matters there. My argument will be that
that influence was a more fruitful one than has commonly been
recognised and that it is best understood through the unusual
complexity with which both writers, at their best, invest the notion of
'Englishness'. This will perhaps seem off-putting. Though it is
fashionable nowadays to dissect the idea of 'Englishness', as if we
were in a position to perform an autopsy on it, it is not an idea with

which we readily sympathise. Twentieth-century English culture has not found it easy to think of itself as 'English' in the traditional way. How far have what for Sturt and George Eliot were still certitudes become merely assumptions or conjectures for us? Of course, for both Leavis and Sturt the word 'English' was almost as problematical as it was necessary. Writing about them, one has to be on one's guard against taking its meaning for granted. It is neither purely descriptive nor simply an occasion for the sort of emotional-patriotic throb that leader-writers and politicians invite. Indeed, it is a word that has inspired so much nonsense from such sources that not everyone will agree that it is still capable of serious meaning. Though we still use it with surprising confidence, recent history hardly permits us to make assumptions about what it actually is. Sturt himself, writing *before* the Great War, already needed to distinguish it from precisely those ideas that are still loosely associated with it: '"The Empire", or "The Nation", or "Prosperity", or any abstraction of that kind' (sj, ii, p. 580). He can only define 'Englishness' by reference to what he regards as a false, majority view of it:

'Englishness' is the most precious thing we know in England, and ... instead of wasting and misusing it, and leaving all sorts of obstacles in its way (Poverty, Land Laws, etc. etc. etc.) we ought to be cherishing it. We want more, not less of it; and of better quality.
 We also want a better name for it than 'Englishness'. (sj, ii, p. 580)

In much the same way, Leavis too came increasingly to speak against his present England in order to speak on behalf of the English culture inherited from the past. He assumed that the two were discontinuous and incompatible. In itself, there was nothing new in this – Goldsmith's 'Deserted Village' had long been a favourite anthology piece – but there *was* a new anguish in the modern sense of dislocation. It did not, for instance, take the form of idealising the past as Goldsmith had. Leavis had no time for nostalgia, even of the bitter kind one finds in Carlyle. The indulgence in rhetoric – as in Pugin's famous antitheses of past and present in his *Contrasts* (1836) – had become a luxury. Things had gone too far for mere regret and lamentation. Like Sturt, Leavis had no truck with 'William-Morrisian' revivalism, much as both admired Morris as a man.[4] Sturt was much less pessimistic about his present but he too never pretended that the past was still available for imaginative escapes of the sort made by Borrow and Arnold's Scholar Gypsy. For both

writers, the thought of England was more likely to be disquieting
than uplifting or seductive. It was bound to be so. The memory of the
past brought them inescapably back to their deracinated present, the
only England they still had. Whether they could still call it 'English',
in anything like the old sense of the word, became one of their central
problems. For there was no 'Rananim' for them and they knew it.
One of the things Sturt suggested to Leavis, in the disillusioned
aftermath of the war, was, in fact, the prospect of an alternative way
of thinking about England that nonetheless refused any dreams of
escapism. It is by no means clear that the later D. H. Lawrence could
offer him as much. For, like Sturt, Leavis felt himself to belong to
England in a way that Lawrence, at least after the banning of *The
Rainbow*, did not. He saw no 'world elsewhere' for himself, nowhere
else from which to say what he wanted to say.

Recent readers of Leavis, especially those on the left, have been quick
to dub his belief in 'the educated minority' as a form of 'élitism'. His
preoccupation with the function of the university strikes them as
culturally divisive in the degree of authority it claims for a very
limited group of people. Even his emphasis on 'great' literature is
now frequently taken to betray the fact that he stands for an exclusive
canon of 'high culture' rather than for any 'Englishness' that is more
broadly based. Superficially, such criticisms are hard to gainsay –
nowadays any appeal to 'the people' can have the force to silence
doubts that appeals to the Bible had in the past – but Leavis would
probably have found them naively optimistic. Is there still a more
broadly based 'Englishness' to appeal to in the first place? Moreover,
the view that wants to cast Leavis as a reactionary has an interest in
obscuring some of the most typical features of his cultural stance. It
is not, for instance, obvious why a high-brow élitist should have
admired Sturt's Bettesworth books so much, nor why he should have
appealed to 'the English people' (though not rhetorically) in the
course of a critical essay on *Adam Bede*. In fact, Leavis constantly
made such appeals over the heads of the cultural establishment. That
has been one source of the uneasy attraction that Marxists have so
often felt for him. It is easy – and convenient – nowadays to forget
how much of his career was spent in attacking the (to him) pernicious
influence of the 'élites' which ran 'Bloomsbury' and The British
Council, the Sunday papers and the academic world. In books like
The Great Tradition and *D. H. Lawrence: Novelist* his own value-

judgements are specifically urged in opposition to the conventional taste embodied in such institutions. He maintained, with growing bitterness, that such opinion-shaping élites had betrayed their responsibility to uphold critical standards: the clerisy was itself one of the sources of England's cultural ill-health. Now that his own influence has extended so widely, and *The Great Tradition* has itself become a source of received opinions in English departments all over the world, this is easily forgotten. The modern reader is likely to skip the parts of Leavis's books which indulge in internecine fighting with his contemporaries. We have other things to do than to get hot under the collar about E. M. W. Tillyard and Lord David Cecil. Nevertheless, if we do not want Leavis to be misrepresented as some voice of the cultural establishment, we have to remember the fierce atmosphere of polemics in which he lived and thought. It may have harmed him but he would be inconceivable without it.

What was unusual about the élite that Leavis fostered through *Scrutiny* was that it enjoyed no institutional status or official influence. It was run on a shoestring and it had none of that self-assurance (with overtones of class superiority) that others besides Leavis have associated with 'Bloomsbury'. To the older generation in Cambridge, from which many 'Bloomsberries' had come, the Scrutineers were rather *petit-bourgeois*, not quite scholars and gentlemen.[5] They thought of themselves more as scourges of cultural paternalism than as handing down cultural values from on high. The fragmentation of the public into the 'high-brow' and the 'low-brow' seemed to them a symptom of sickness, not a remedy for it. Nonetheless, the 'educated minority' they hoped to represent did constitute a kind of élite, despite their hostility to the other minorities of the age. How is one to account for the apparent self-contradiction that this discrepancy between principle and practice resulted in?

The first point to make is that an editorial chair at Cambridge was never the comfortable vantage-point that a Bloomsbury drawing-room afforded. Leavis only regarded the 'educated minority' as a desperate expedient for combating modern conditions, not as an ideally necessary element in *any* healthy culture. He saw even more positive minorities, in the eighteenth century for example, as intrinsic signs of a gradual fragmenting of the 'reading public'. There is not so much in his work about the maintaining of critical standards in the age of Shakespeare and Donne. In a sense, critical standards are something a culture needs consciously to remind itself of when it begins to lose instinctive touch with its own roots. Leavis saw the George Eliot of *Silas Marner*, for example, as consciously re-creating values which in Shakespeare and Bunyan had been felt spontaneously. His own position, therefore, was that of someone forced to argue, from the viewpoint of a minority, for values which originally had not been minority values at all. Rather than seeing it as an *élite* it is perhaps better to think of *Scrutiny* as a last-ditch defence of what had once been 'popular' but had been so eroded that it was now virtually lost. Its contributors were, in fact, a kind of remnant, a minority *faute de mieux*, like Matthew Arnold's 'aliens', but in a much tighter corner. If they were not an élite what else *could* they be? They must have felt more like a band of irregular guerillas come down from the hills to make forays into a culture that preferred to think them off-the-point. It was not a position from which they were likely to argue that great literature was itself necessarily the exclusive creation of small social minorities, working on the fringes of the national life. Indeed, that was precisely the sort of thing of which they complained in modern literature when they compared it with that of the past. It was not for nothing that Leavis came to think so highly of Dickens in his later years and to see his work as the last breath of a genuinely popular culture, stretching back to Shakespeare. It had, after all, always been one of the justifications of 'English' as a discipline that it could alert its students to such roots. The failure to do that in conventional higher education was precisely, he thought, what had produced a phenomenon like 'Bloomsbury' in the first place, as it had characterised the divisive and patrician influence of the 'Classics', which 'English' aspired to replace. This, and not more spleen, is the point of all his many attacks on the condescending treatment which 'Bloomsbury', and Eliot in particular, gave to Lawrence. He himself believed deeply that there was a sense in which the culture that the young Lawrence grew up in at Eastwood was richer than that which nurtured the Apostles. His élitism was clearly a very strange thing.

Though he was otherwise deeply indebted to Eliot's notion of 'tradition', Leavis never thought of English culture in the predominantly literary terms that Eliot himself did. His interest in *The Wheelwright's Shop* is just one sign of his concern with the non-literary roots from which that culture had drawn its strength. The fact that his own work was mainly in literary criticism tends to obscure this, until one sees that it has to take that form because, Leavis believed from the start, it was only through literature that those roots were still accessible at all to modern England. Thus, he knew quite clearly that his own struggle for culture had necessarily to be fought from a tighter corner than the one Matthew Arnold had stood in. Only the English language itself still embodied a living sense of continuity. Furthermore, it was through popular tradition, as much as through literature, that the significance of the language could be grasped. To do so was not easy – in the 'Machine Age', it could no longer be done by listening to 'the people' themselves. Sturt's world was gone and 'the decisive use of words' had moved to 'advertising, journalism, best-sellers' and so on. It was this move that made the literary tradition so vital:

For if language tends to be debased instead of invigorated by contemporary use, then it is to literature alone, where its subtlest and finest use is preserved, that we can look with any hope of keeping in touch with our spiritual tradition – with the 'picked experience of ages'. But the literary tradition is alive only so long as there is a tradition of taste, kept alive by the educated (who are not to be identified with any social class); such a tradition – the 'picked experience of ages' – as constitutes a surer taste than any individual can pretend to. True, it is only in individuals that tradition lives; it is you and I who make judgments and exhibit taste; just as it is George Cook who handles the tools. But 'in watching Cook putting a wheel together I was watching practically the skill of England, the experience of ages': just so a good critic, or a cultivated person of sure judgment, is exhibiting more than merely individual taste.[6]

The idea attempts to cut across the divisions made by class. The word 'taste', with its Augustan resonances, is coupled with the 'skill' of Sturt's workman, George Cook. Leavis completes the point by quoting Sturt's claim in *Change in the Village* that his father and grandfather 'knew "England" in a more intimate way'.[7] The 'minority' thus becomes the conscious refuge of an 'Englishness' which in former times had been the reverse of exclusive. Its mission is to remember things which, except in imagination, it can no longer be. The traditional culture is knowable only through books – *The Pilgrim's Progress, Silas Marner, The Rainbow* – rather than through direct living.

When Leavis spoke of what he called 'the living language' he always opposed it to the work of writers whose art was more hieratic and catered for the 'happy few', writers like Milton and Flaubert and Joyce. When he and Denys Thompson chose to set the England of

Sturt against the England of the mass media they were not setting themselves against democracy as such (Leavis's fine essay on Bentham and Mill is one sign of that). Literature could not in the end be made out of other literature without a price being exacted. Leavis still made the same point forty years later, in *Nor Shall My Sword*, and he still brought in Sturt to make it:

I didn't thirty years ago point to the state of affairs, the relation between cultural values (or – shall I say? – human significances) and economic fact, documented in *The Wheelwright's Shop* – which I've hardly mentioned these thirty years – as something we should aim at recovering; but as something finally gone. That relation was an essential condition of the kind of achievement of the higher culture (spiritual, intellectual, humane) that is represented by Shakespeare's works. Such a relation, for any world we can foresee, is gone.[8]

The bleakness, if not the tone, of this was there in the 1930s. So too, perhaps surprisingly, was a good deal of common ground with what, in a way, was anti-Arnoldian in Sturt's thought, the suspicion that 'for modern people, art supplies the place that was filled by tradition in the case of the Folk' (sJ, II, p. 596). Though the name 'English' had become the name of an academic discipline in his time, Leavis went on reminding his readers that the 'Englishness' to which it referred was something much larger than this specialised usage seemed to imply. The language of a literature like English is at its best a 'currency of criteria and valuations collaboratively determined', an 'accepting participation' in a way of living.[9] When Sturt himself wrote of modern culture as a 'hot-house thing' (sJ, I, p. 153), self-conscious and artificial, he was anticipating Leavis, as if castigating 'Bloomsbury' in milder tones. If there was any real difference between them it was, in fact, that Sturt was much readier than Leavis to admit to being part of this artificial culture himself. As always, he had a keen sense of what he was implicated in.

Sturt's books about the old village economy came out during the period of Edwardian Imperialism and Great War patriotism, the period of Lord Curzon and Kipling, Brooke's 'Grantchester' and Elgar's wartime concerts. Their reception was favourable but they must often have fallen on deaf ears.[10] His own feelings for England were very little coloured by the sort of sentimental bumptiousness so common among his contemporaries; he leaned more towards the Johnsonian view of the patriot. His distinction, in fact, was to perceive an 'Englishness' which lay deeper in English life than the clamant public versions of the idea that prevailed. Though he could be wistful about the past (and knew it), he never pandered to the fashionable nostalgic view of rural England that could be so enervating in Georgian poetry and that was the stock-in-trade of a painter like Sir Alfred Munnings. *Change in the Village* states unequivocally that 'there are never any signs in the valley of that almost festive temper, that glad relish of life, which, if we may believe the poets, used to characterise the English village of old times'.[11] Brooke still wanted to characterise 'his' village in that way and even Edward Thomas, in his prose works, is not quite free from the same sort of sentiment. In place of this myth of modern ('hot-house') culture, Sturt relied on his gift for patiently exact observation, a gift which, significantly, he shared with men like his Bettesworth. The originality of his approach lay in its refusal to try to project literature on to rural life. Sturt read the poets in a very different way from his contemporaries, a way in which it is hard to read them now. He put the England out of which they had come first. This comes out quite clearly from a *Journals* entry on Wordsworth which he made in 1917:

how little all this literary stuff appeals to me. I am not interested, like the critics, in singling out this or that famous writer – Chaucer, Wordsworth, Browning – and studying his work, as if he were a being apart, as if he and his work were more worth study than the 'England' that produced them. I dare say that Wordsworth himself may be credited with finding his own technique as a versifier; but that rural sympathy of his, that strong understanding of mountains and mountain temper, that brave tender insight, that calm outlook – out of what fine social atmosphere did he as a boy (for this sort of thing develops in boyhood, I think, or hardly at all) absorb all this? Whatever it was, and wherever Wordsworth got it, it was a part of England's spontaneous living – a part of folk-life; and this is what I care to study more than literature for its own sake. I would use the famous writers chiefly as doorways into England's inner life. (SJ, II, pp. 782–3)

The 'Englishness' this seeks is resolutely local and bent on going beyond the issue of form (something that nonetheless preoccupied Sturt elsewhere). Literature, properly conceived, should not be read in a purely literary spirit. This is a long way away from T. S. Eliot's talk of 'purely literary values' (in 'Johnson as Poet and Critic')[12] but closer to Leavis than might at first appear. He takes a similar approach with at least those authors he admires most and tends to use as touchstones: Bunyan, George Eliot, the early Lawrence. In fact, Leavis's own Sturt-like interest in these writers' environment was one of the sources of his later criticisms of T. S. Eliot. His analysis of 'East Coker' in *The Living Principle*, for instance, makes it clear that he thought Eliot would have benefited from more attention to Sturt's kind of approach.

It was not, of course, simply his gift for observation that made Sturt's books unique. As the master of a wheelwright's shop himself, he enjoyed much closer daily contact with country men and women than other writers could hope for. Nor did he feel that his own roots were essentially different from theirs or speak to them as superior. He certainly felt that class and education set him at a remove from them but it was the kind of remove which sharpened rather than dulled his perception of their life. Moreover, his own language was much closer to theirs than that of the town-bred, university-educated Edward Thomas. Writing to Arnold Bennett in 1898, he recalled the 'broad Hampshire' and its 'racy Surrey variant' of his two grandfathers as a kind of speech he could still share in: 'When I was a boy, I talked a weak provincial language tinged with dialect. "Literary" English is an acquired speech with me, and it hasn't displaced the other but has merely been added to it. Many – most, of my relatives are still ignorant of aspirates ... '.[13]

The *Journals* bear this out. Many of the conversations with Bettesworth that are recorded in them show Sturt speaking dialect himself. This was an immense advantage over writers who found it hard not to think of dialect as simple or rather comic. A further advantage Sturt enjoyed was that this affinity was strengthened by his early Fabianism and his judicious but life-long interest in socialism. (As a young man, he had written for William Morris's *Commonweal*.) These things guaranteed him against sentimentalising the Bettesworths or turning a blind eye to the more grim and depressing aspects of village life. It was precisely the real and tangible qualities of that life, its unromantic earthiness, that he admired most. He had no belief in earthly paradises, either in the past or the future, nor did he need them. 'The Golden Age,' he wrote, 'is less an outward environment, than a state of inward being' (SJ, I, p. 227). Thus, his love of England did not rule out the thought that 'Englishness', far from having been realised long ago, was still waiting to be fulfilled. Among other things, his books are a perpetual *caveat* against the facile use of the word 'English'. When he writes at the end of *Change in the Village* that 'four generations have grown up and lived and died with large tracts of their English vitality neglected, unexplored' he means that the word, far from being exhausted, remains to be defined.[14]

Leavis's most important account of Sturt occurs in *Culture and Environment*, which he wrote with Denys Thompson in 1933 as a text-book for schools, to further the 'training of critical awareness'. It remains an extraordinarily lively and trenchant book, polemical where most text-books hug their neutrality. Sturt figures in a string of long quotations, mainly from *The Wheelwright's Shop* and *Change in the Village*. As John Fraser says, these are 'brilliantly selective',[15] chosen to enforce the notion of an unbridgeable divide between England present and England past:

Sturt speaks of 'the death of Old England and of the replacement of the more primitive nation by an "organised" modern state.' The Old England was the England of the organic community, and in what sense it was more primitive than the England that has replaced it needs pondering. But at the moment what we have to consider is the fact that the organic community has gone; it has so nearly disappeared from memory that to make anyone, however educated, realize what it was is commonly a difficult undertaking. Its destruction (in the West) is the most important fact of recent history – it is very recent indeed.[16]

Leavis and Thompson follow this with a passage where Sturt describes 'the slow transition from village or provincial industry to city or cosmopolitan industry'.[17] On the face of it, they are simply paraphrasing Sturt's argument; in fact, their own position is subtly different from his. For example, he has no need of an abstraction like the 'organic community' to do his work for him. Neither does he generalise about 'England' as a whole – his findings are local ones and that is their virtue. Perhaps it is especially when we feel cut off from a living sense of community that it begins in retrospect to grow abstract in the mind? Sturt, on the other hand, could afford to make it quite clear that his own village, The Bourne, from which he took his pseudonym, was not really representative of village life at all. It was only settled in around 1800 and in his day was already well on the way to becoming suburban. To Sturt, The Bourne's life was sensuous and immediate, not an idea but an experience. Yet he himself lived to see his wheelwright's shop become a garage and it is easy to understand how, by the 1930s, it had become tinged with a feeling of myth. Despite this, Leavis and Thompson never tried to idealise *contemporary* village life. They deduced from Sturt himself that, whereas Bettesworth's culture had been oral, the present-day villager was likely to be an avid reader of Northcliffe's newspapers and the novels of Warwick Deeping that Mrs Leavis had analysed in *Fiction and the Reading Public*.[18] It was this decline, as they saw it, which made them need to believe in Sturt's England in that literal way that often shades into myth. They could hardly have afforded to share his doubt as to whether an ideal village life had *ever* existed:

Some of these days I shall go in search of a village. I mean the sort of village one imagines after reading Gray's 'Elegy', or Goldsmith's 'Deserted Village', or Herbert's 'Priest to the Altar' [*sic*]. A village inhabited by Peasantry: rounded in by its own self-supporting toil, and governed by its own old-world customs. It would not at all surprise me to discover that this sort of community – if it ever existed – is extinct. (SJ, I, pp. 302–3)

This adds up to a good description of the country as most of Sturt's contemporaries would have liked to see it. Leavis and Thompson may not have believed in it but, with no later social model to believe in, it is clear that they would like to have done. Sturt's scepticism would have been difficult for them to afford and, perhaps, in their situation, beside the point.

It is not too extreme to describe this modern sense of loss as a fear that, in a deep sense, England had ceased to exist, ceased to be English any more. This is why it became necessary to reinvent it as a myth. Such, at least, was Raymond Williams's view of the belief in an 'organic community'. It may begin, he says, from a 'detailed record' of the past but it always develops into a 'conventionally foreshortened version of history'. Even *Change in the Village* moves 'from record to convention and back again'.[19] The 'organic community' always lies just in the immediate past, over the last hill we have climbed; for Leavis, in the late nineteenth century; for Sturt, before the enclosures of the 1860s; for Thomas Hardy, back in the 1840s before 'machinery' came in. There is a good deal of psychological truth in this view and Williams brings to it the authority of being country-bred himself. He too, sitting in Cambridge, must have found such images seductive. They are not, however, where an account of Sturt should rest. Certainly, he felt the pull of nostalgia, as others did, but the real point is that he never gave in to it. We find him confiding in his *Journal* that his thoughts often took a quite different direction. For example: 'the old village life was not so nice in reality as I have made out in *Change in the Village*' (SJ, II, p. 689). Elsewhere he admits to having deliberately played down the positive side of the rural labourer's lot, 'for fear of providing "gentlemen" with an excuse for preserving the present economic system' (sj, ii, pp. 261–2) When England can provoke such changing responses one knows that it is alive. It is only when responses to it harden and set that to speak of 'Englishness' seems like holding a post-mortem.

Leavis and Thompson, like Sturt himself, would have answered Williams by insisting that what they called the 'organic community' *did really exist*. It was not a literary invention of Gray's or Goldsmith's or anyone else's. They could not, however, offer the same evidence for it that Sturt could. *Faute de mieux*, they had to rely on English literature – on Shakespeare and Bunyan and, most recently, Sturt himself – to confirm its existence. They adopt the method implied by the remarks on Wordsworth in the *Journals*, though from the more estranged and painful perspective of the modern 'culture' from which Sturt himself did *not* have to begin. But things had gone too far for any indulgence in looking back to the 'good old days' and Leavis and Thompson had no time for attempts to revive their 'folk' spirit:

And we must beware of simple solutions. We must, for instance, realize that there can be no mere going back: it is useless to think of imitating the Erewhonians and scrapping the machine in the hope of restoring the old order. Even if agriculture were revived, that would not bring back the organic community. It is important to insist on what has been lost lest it should be forgotten; for the memory of the old order must be the chief incitement towards a new, if ever we are to have one. If we forget the old order we shall not know what kind of thing to strive towards, and in the end there will be no striving, but a surrender to the 'progress' of the machine.[20]

William Morris was a great man but neither he nor his disciples had any solution to offer the Machine Age. In this respect, *Culture and Environment* was at one with Sturt, whose *Journals* are peppered with sceptical references to Morris. Reading *Sigurd of the Volsungs*, for instance, he had complained of Morris's 'longing for heroes and heroic times': 'A sort of backward looking, with a sense of meanness in our own lives. 'Tis a secondhand nobility that we get, and the heroism that delights us is not our own, but our ancestor's. Ignoble pensioners we seem, doomed to a seat in the House of Poetry' (sj, i, p. 139). It is in the same spirit that Leavis and Thompson dismiss the Arts and Crafts Movement, which many of the teachers of 'English' found common cause with.

Where *Culture and Environment* did simplify Sturt, and open him up to Williams's charge of being ahistorical, was through those elements in his work it chose to omit. Its version of rural England is undoubtedly more reassuring and less problematic than his was. It too remarks on the satisfyingly varied work of the traditional labourer in comparison with that of his modern counterpart, but it remains silent on the economic system within which that work was done. Where, for instance, did the real economic power lie? Sturt, on the other hand, as the *Journals* show time and again, was deeply troubled by his own position as a (highly benevolent) employer of this labour. He felt keenly 'the misery of being a Socialist employer of Labour' (SJ, I, p. 127). That is, one part of him wanted the social change that another part regretted. We constantly see him anxiously computing how little some poor family has to live on and how brutalisingly hand-to-mouth its life must be. At moments, one imagines him going round The Bourne like Mr Snagsby in *Bleak House*, reaching into his pocket for half-crowns. Some of the most vivid and moving passages in his books are accounts of sheer grinding poverty, such as the harrowing narrative (more harrowing, I think, than the end of *Jude the Obscure*) of the last days of Bettesworth in *Memoirs of a Surrey Labourer*. Sturt's England is unusually full of poor old men, unable to work, and old women like Lucy Bettesworth, struggling against illness in unsanitary conditions without adequate food or heating.[21] It is no wonder that he felt such people were unable to 'develop *from within*' (SJ, I, p. 273) or that the only thing which kept them seemingly civilised was the middle classes with their twin curbs of 'Parson and Policeman' (SJ, I, p. 273). Sturt's 'steely and everlasting hatred of sentimentality', as Bennett called it, counted for more than just his unflinching response to poverty.[22] It also acts as a kind of guarantee that when he writes about the positive aspects of village life we can still believe what he says. For he is not, save perhaps at times in the late *A Farmer's Life* and *William Smith: Potter and Farmer*, a pastoral writer. The nearest he gets to that is in his eye for the interrupted or ruined pastoral. On the other hand, the notion of an 'organic community', even though based on history, is itself much closer to pastoral feeling. Sturt is not interested in moulding his 'Bourners' into reflections of his own ideas and feelings but in letting their own voices speak. He did not claim to understand them well enough to make a myth of them. (Once, at Farnham fair, he found himself looking at the people 'as in a Zoo one looks at animals' (SJ, I, p. 270) – he could hardly pretend to have summed them up).

   It is not my point that Leavis and Thompson failed to see this bleaker side of Sturt – they could hardly have missed it – but that their own rather different idea of rural England made it expedient for them not to draw attention to it. Rural crafts appeared more attractive without the often attendant squalor. Thus *Culture and Environment* now seems like a book about the state of the culture *without* reference to the politics which informed it, a curious blend of political implications and undrawn political inferences. Its mythology, perhaps its too specific purpose as a book for schools, prevents it from having the scope of Leavis's later social criticism. Trenchant as it still is, there are ways in which Sturt's sense of England seems deeper *and* nearer. One can say this whilst recognising that, at least in the unpublished work, Sturt shares the assumption that the culture of everyday living is more primary than the political culture that grows out of it. That view, harder to sustain in the media age, goes back to George Eliot and, indeed, to the Johnson who said, on his Scottish journey, that 'The true state of a nation is the state of common life.'[23] To the extent that this view shifts the emphasis away from the class-system and the cash-nexus it may, as Williams claimed, be called ahistorical. Sturt's notion of the 'folk' and of 'race' raised the question of England in a quite different way from the politicians of his time. It is a tricky business trying to assign political labels to him, as he realised himself, in his wryly bemused way: 'if my theories are "liberal" my tastes are often conservative' (sj, II p. 483). He could say this notwithstanding a fierce hatred of privilege and a belief that the British Empire was an 'overgrown absurdity' (sj, II, p. 503). In one pregnant passage in his *Journals* he records a visionary moment when he had the sense of 'England spreading out before and all around me.' It is characteristic that he should follow this with an account of a local Liberal Party meeting he had just attended. The meeting completely dissipated his fleeting sense of 'England'. Similar paradoxes are, of course, frequent in Leavis too. In 'Under Which King, Bezonian?', in an early number of *Scrutiny*, he argues as someone so radically at odds with the *status quo* that even Marxism seems to him to be a product of it. It is easy to present such positions as reflections of a kind of conservatism that neither Sturt nor Leavis really shared. More crucial is the fact that neither of them were really thinking of the English as a people in the modern, political sense in the first place. They did not, for instance, have very much time for Winston Churchill. In his valuable essay on Sturt in *The Rural Muse*, W. J. Keith argues that, 'had he lived,' he 'would have attempted not only a definition of 'the folk' but an extended examination of folk art and folk culture'.[24] Keith sees his concern with England as being 'not national but tribal'; the 'true antithesis to *Folk* is *Individual*' (sJ, II, p. 551). It was the individualistic middle-class who waved the flag and sang 'Rule Britannia' or agitated for the franchise, whereas a village wheelwright learnt his craft from the anonymous traditions of 'the folk'. This opposition between rural culture and individual self-culture is precisely what Leavis found in a novel like *The Rainbow* (between the Brangwens who are farmers and craftsmen and the younger Tom Brangwen who runs a colliery). Lawrence's critique of nineteenth-century individualism was, in fact, crucial for Leavis (see his discussion of 'Breadalby' in *Women in Love*) and, though he had little time for such things as the cult of morris-dancing – often associated with new approaches to 'English' in the schools – he found it necessary to posit the presence of a kind of informing 'folk' mind out of which the masterpieces of 'English Literature' could be felt to have come. This idea can be as easily illustrated from his late work as from *Culture and Environment*:

The same people that created the English language for Shakespeare's use speaks in Bunyan, though it is now a people that knows its Authorized Version. Bunyan, that is, had behind him – or rather, had around him and in him – that pervasive and potent continuity, a living culture; it was the air he breathed, the spiritual food (doctrinal Puritanism being only an element in it) that nourished him, the more-than-personal sensibility that as a writer he was. 'One writes,' D. H. Lawrence late in his life replied to a questioner, 'out of one's moral sense,' going on immediately to give 'moral' an intense special force by adding, 'for the race, as it were.' Bunyan the creative writer wrote out of a 'moral sense' that represented what was finest in that traditional culture. He used with a free idiomatic range and vividness in preaching (the tradition he preached in ensured that) the language he spoke with jailers and fellow prisoners, with wife and children and friends at home. A language is more than such phrases as 'means of expression' or 'instrument of communication' suggest; it is a vehicle of collective wisdom and basic assumptions, a currency of criteria and valuations collaboratively determined; itself it entails on the user a large measure of accepting participation in the culture of which it is the active living presence.[25]

That Bunyan is so little read now, even in universities, is no doubt a sign that we can no longer hear this language as we once did. That Leavis came to have so little faith in any modern English writing is not a coincidence. He did not believe that the greatest kind of art was still possible without some supra-individual basis. He saw this 'basis' as essentially 'popular', not as the idiom of any élite. At a key point in the first chapter of *The Living Principle*, for instance, he finds it behind Dickens's comedy:

the creative conditions that produced the English language that made Shakespeare possible have vanished on that final triumph of industrialism – even more completely in America than here. Something of those conditions were behind Dickens's work. They have gone utterly – gone for good; and with them the day-to-day creativity of the English-speaking peoples (a creativity that Eliot, in this, at least, distinctively an American, seemed unaware of). It is plain that the quasi-living language represented by the talk of the vast majority of the population couldn't have given the assured take-off and the continuous prompting that Dickens enjoyed in his time, when speech was still a popular art, belonging to a living culture. And Dickens had Shakespeare behind him, and, of great creative writers, not only Shakespeare.[26]

That is, the reduced possibilities of contemporary English cut it off from its origins, just as modern industrial England is cut off from the 'organic community' of the past. Language too has ceased to be 'organic'. To a culture divorced from its own history, this former continuity of thought and feeling is now most readily accessible in its literature.

It is, then, very plausible that, as Williams said, Leavis had a vested interest in mythologising the past and its language when he wrote about *The Wheelwright's Shop*. He was not immune from nostalgia himself. Nevertheless, he and Thompson sought to rest their case on factual reminiscences of that past and distrusted suburban myths of the village world as much as Williams did. Moreover, before we dismiss their case as purely ideological, we need to remind ourselves of our own interest in *dis*believing it. If we are really so far from that lost world, how can we any longer even recognise it for what it was? We might prefer to think of it as a myth, as a means of self-protection. If Sturt *was* only just in time to chronicle its disappearance, how are we, seventy years on, to determine whether Leavis and Thompson were right or wrong? Especially since more than the verification of external facts is at stake, as Sturt acknowledged by putting human subjectivity and not economic forces at the centre of his books. Williams *ought* to be right about the way he distorted history but it is *The Country and the City* and not Sturt which seems to have history a little bit too taped. Sturt was more careful when he presumed to generalise from 'ordinary life'. How indeed can anyone disentangle what is mythical in history from what is fact? To think of something like the Jacobite rebellions without their mythology is to think of a history that has been amputated. This may explain why Williams never fully refutes the broad thesis of both Sturt and Leavis that there was a watershed in English culture at the end of the nineteenth century. There is much in his own work which might have pointed him to a similar conclusion. He too knew that painful sense of loss that goes far deeper than mere nostalgia and that has been such a formative factor in the modern English experience (see his work on Hardy).

In making this point I bear in mind Leavis's own strictures on nostalgia, as in his backhanded compliment to Rupert Brooke ('He energized the Garden-Suburb ethos with a certain original talent …').[27] A telling example of his impatience with writers who spent their time hankering after the past occurs in his essay on E. M. Forster. Though Leavis admired the 'liberal humanist' tradition that counted so deeply for Forster he had no truck with the liberal pieties invested in 'Englishness' in *Howards End*. To him, that sort of 'Englishness' was self-consciously middle-class. Forster was claiming as a conscious feeling something which, in its instinctive form, had been lost with Hardy. As *New Bearings in English Poetry* has it:

Hardy was a countryman, and his brooding mind stayed itself habitually upon the simple pieties, the quiet rhythms and the immemorial ritual of rustic life.

It is very largely in terms of the absence of these, or of any equivalent, that the environment of the modern poet must be described. Urban conditions, a sophisticated civilization, rapid change and the mingling of the cultures have destroyed the old rhythms and habits, and nothing adequate has taken their place. The result is a sense, apparent in the serious literature of the day, that meaning and direction have vanished.[28]

Knowing this, Leavis does not pretend to feel in the way that Forster does. The thought of the past did not make him moderate his habitual stringency and toughness. There is, indeed, some reason to suppose that he himself became less certain about the 'good old days'. He never again wrote about them as he did with Denys Thompson.[29] If the loss of their 'community' remained a *donnée* in his work after the 1930s, its actual nature was something he preferred not to speculate about too much. He does not want to pretend that he is nearer to it than he really is.

This refusal to put the clock back was something Sturt whole-heartedly shared. The last page of *Change in the Village* is its classic expression:

At any rate, the hope is great enough to forbid the indulgence of any deep regret for what has gone by. The old system had gone on long enough. For generations the villagers had grown up and lived and died with large tracts of their English vitality neglected, unexplored; and I do not think the end of that wasteful system can be lamented by anyone who believes in the English. Rather it should reconcile us to the disillusionments of this present time of transition. They are devastating, I admit; for me, they have spoilt a great deal of that pleasure which the English country used to give me, when I still fancied it to be the scene of a joyful and comely art of living. I know now that the landscape is not peopled by a comfortable folk, whose dear and intimate love of it gave a human interest to every feature of its beauty; I know that those who live there have in fact lost touch with its venerable meanings, while all their existence has turned sordid and anxious and worried; and knowing this, I feel a forlornness in country places, as if all their best significance were gone. But, notwithstanding this, I would not go back. I would not lift a finger, or say a word, to restore the past time, for fear lest in doing so I might be retarding a movement which, when I can put these sentiments aside, looks like the prelude to a renaissance of the English country-folk.[30]

Such 'forlornness' was clearly a consequence of the 'neglected vitality' Sturt regrets, not just of spoliation. He understood completely that to turn the past into a dream world and a haven from the present was tantamount to betraying its human meaning. The village where he found his meanings had nothing in it that would have been obviously congenial to the Schlegels. In an essay he wrote on 'Antiquarian Sentiment' (in *Lucy Bettesworth*) he made it plain that he regarded Helen's kind of sentimental 'Englishness' as basically suburban, bearing little relation to England as he knew it:

the habit of retrospective dreaming may be indulged until it becomes a fault. You can have too much of most good things, including affection for what has departed. When this is pushed so far as to be obstructive to improvement, and the antiquary hardens into a hide-bound conservative, loving old life so well that he would cramp the new for its sake, he must not complain if sensible folk regard him as a nuisance. Besides, the future demands some consideration. In the future our own present time will have become a past to which men will look back wistfully; it is for us, therefore, to prepare for them a real and moving life to look back to.[31]

Sturt did not think of this stream of life as something which ever stopped. He speaks movingly of the antiquarian deriving 'from the monuments of death a fuller sense of those vast spaces of life, out of which for a moment or two, like a wave out of the sea, his own existence has emerged'.[32] For this reason, he cannot become a 'hide-bound conservative'. England is not some immutable Platonic entity but a culture in the process of development. Sturt has no static point outside this process from which to sum it up. Not for him that apocalyptic, moralised view of history that was dear to Victorians like Carlyle and Ruskin. Though he chronicled a broken continuity, he did not believe in hard-and-fast historical watersheds. The past and the present seemed to him neither antithetical nor separable. That is why he distrusted William Morris's Utopia's and why, it may be, he would not have been wholly convinced by *Culture and Environment*.

There have always been two ways of reading Sturt, one which dwells on his mastery of fact and one which finds in him a prophet who goes beyond simple observation to challenge our received view of ourselves. His distinction, in fact, was to be both of these writers at the same time, the most modest of the critics of 'culture'. Neither Sturt was ever allowed to undercut the other. Writing to his friend Arnold Bennett at the time he was working on *The Bettesworth Book* he insisted that he began it because 'it seemed to me a duty' but that ''tisn't literature.'[33] The implication is that his own role is artless, his only art, as a recorder of Bettesworth's talk, being to avoid arranging it artistically, yet we know from the *Journals* and from *The Ascending Effort* how deeply questions of aesthetics engaged him. Bennett himself thought of him as a *particularly* intellectual writer rather than as an artless one:

I had not been with him an hour before I was compelled to readjust my estimate of the depth of his immersion in literature. Writing occupies all his thoughts in a way I had never suspected. With the most perfect naturalness, he regards everything as 'material', and he assumed that I should do so too. A more literary temperament than his it would be difficult to conceive. He doesn't 'search' for stuff; his task probably is to cope with the masses of material which thrust themselves upon his attention. He sits down in his writing chair and handles note-books and papers with an air of custom and familiarity which I have never seen in a writer before.[34]

This Sturt consumed by his 'literary temperament' was, para-doxically, so good at getting himself out of the way precisely because he was so self-conscious. 'Hang it, I envy them their unconsciousness' he writes of his workmen as they set off to the Farnham carnival. In his position, the inner life had to be very inner indeed and masked by the practical exigencies of his day to day life as a master wheelwright. This ought not to make us forget that his own writing, so devoted to understanding the kind of men he felt himself to be excluded from, had begun, under very different auspices, in a deep admiration for the prose of Walter Pater.[35] His scope was wider than it seemed. His gift for rooting general thoughts in tangible facts was something he learnt as much from Pater's attacks on 'abstraction' as from listening to Bettesworth. Like Pater too, he knew how to evoke the colourless feeling of everyday life as well as its epiphanies. Most of his books begin by seeming oddly dull and easy to put down until they quietly start to grip us.

Sturt's avoidance of the abstract is particularly impressive in the way he uses the word 'English', where abstraction might have been expected. For few writers of the period does 'Englishness' denote more of a real thing and less a mere idea. One way of making this point, if roughly, is to compare his attitude to Bettesworth with Edward Thomas's attitude to Lob. Thomas wrote finely on Sturt in *In Pursuit of Spring* but he could not give Lob Bettesworth's flesh and blood solidity. This was not simply because he was writing poetry rather than cultural history. Thomas had to make Lob's poetry out of the way he constantly escaped from time and place. He was not so much England as an idea of England, elusive and unpredictable, evoking a throng of allusions and associations none of which could quite account for him. He is the spirit of an England which Thomas is always in search of but one does not know what it is like to *be* Lob as one does with Bettesworth. Sturt brings us firmly down from such Englands of the mind to real existing things. It follows that Sturt was most successful in making his feeling for England palpable in the kind of patient notation of rural customs that does not call for large cultural generalisations in the first place. This feeling could be said to have been deepest when there was no need for the word 'English' at all. Sturt understood that the thing most incompatible with that feeling is a self-conscious sense of one's own 'Englishness'. It did not depend on being poetical, any more than Bettesworth himself needed to be a poet in order for his speech to be an 'art'. When Sturt did try to articulate the feeling, he did so partly as a way of hanging on to it and partly in order to enact its tentativeness. It was not an obvious feeling nor one to be had for the asking and even when he felt nearest to it he was often divided from it by memory. Such revelations as he

had were slow and fitful, as if England were to him peculiarly difficult
to pin down.

Change in the Village and *The Wheelwright's Shop* are usually read as
sad celebrations of the passing of the old order of rural life. This is
only partly true. Sturt chose his subject matter out of love, not
sociological interest, a genuine love that did not romanticise its
object. His England was not an ideal one. If *Change in the Village*
begins on a note of regret it soon moves into a very different key:

> Yet there was another side to the picture. The charm of it was a generalised
> one – I think an impersonal one; for with the thought of individual persons
> who might illustrate it there comes too often into my memory a touch of
> sordidness, if not in one connection then in another; so that I suspect myself,
> not for the first time, of sentimentality. Was the social atmosphere after all
> anything but a creation of my own dreams? Was the village life really
> idyllic?
>
> Not for a moment can I pretend that it was. Patience and industry
> dignified it; a certain rough jollity, a large amount of good temper and
> natural kindness, kept it from being foul; but of the namby-pamby or soft-
> headed sentiment which many writers have persuaded us to attribute to old-
> English cottage life I think I have not in twenty years met with a single trace.
> In fact, there are no people so likely to make ridicule of that sort of thing as
> my labouring-class neighbours have always been. They do not, like the
> middle classes, enjoy it.[36]

This setting himself on guard against making a literary version of
England was typical of Sturt. He understood how partial and
transitory nostalgia was, not a product of the village world itself but
simply a way of coping with its loss. He did not think of his villagers
as leading fulfilled lives. In the *Journals* there is a revealing passage
written to rebut a friend who had been praising the 'good old days'.
What characterised those days for Sturt was how little 'the people'
were able to realise their true selves:

> The more I examine it, the more I grow sceptical of the well-being of the
> people, in these 'good old times'. I suspect that disease, squalor, poverty,
> oppression, were more plentiful than they are now. Bleak, harsh, painful,
> bitter – don't you think England may have been that, more often than not,
> to the comfortless peasants? ... Yet I will take it at its best. I will concede the
> happy peasantry, their country's pride, and admit their fine skill in rural
> handicrafts, their delight in their folk lore, their pleasing genius for song,
> their merriment. Let it all be granted, in its immense contrast to the
> dreariness of our present villages, and still – I would not go back to it... I
> think English men and women have it in them to be something better than
> peasants; and indeed, we are beginning to know it. (SJ, II, p. 622)

Endless toil and the stifling effect of an oppressive class-system had left the villagers in a state of spiritual hibernation. Their life as 'peasants' was not inevitable and progress (in which Sturt sometimes believed) might improve it. Some modern readers will no doubt set such things down to his optimism, pointing out how bitterly ironic they seem now in the light of what has befallen the 'English' since he wrote. But that is to expect too much of him. Some such faith was an essential part of what he brought to the past. He needed to think of England as alive in the fullest possible sense, that is, alive and changing. Unless this is understood, even if not shared, we are likely to confuse the way he thinks of England with the commonplace kinds of nationalism for which he had so little time. In Sturt, the word 'England' always refers to a people in the thick of an historical process; it is specific and relative, not some Platonic idea set like a classical figure on a pedestal. This England could not be defined by the possession of that middle-class requisite, a 'mission'. Its culture was not primarily literate, nor were its bonds of community political in the ordinary sense of the word. Sturt also viewed the waving of the Union Jack with distaste. The popular, oral culture he treasured had no influence in those spheres where the louder voices of the age were raised. He thought of patriotism as a poor compensation for the community that had been lost. Just as travellers like to talk endlessly about the foreign places they have been to when they get home, so the patriot needed to talk more and more about England the further from it he actually felt. Sturt wanted to feel himself very slowly into the sense of England, slowly and scrupulously, never treating it as an occasion for cheap emotion.

Of course, Sturt expressed something of his age's prevalent nostalgia too. This is clear from *A Farmer's Life* and *William Smith: Potter and Farmer*, two of his last books, written, like *The Wheelwright's Shop*, when his health had completely broken down and his own helpless distance from active life encouraged a mood of retrospection. Neither book was based on personal observation as the earlier ones had been. *A Farmer's Life* is a memoir of his uncle, John Smith, who had lived and worked in the mid-Victorian period; *William Smith* reconstructs the still earlier world of John's father, Sturt's own grandfather, and takes him back in imagination nearly to the England of Nelson and Cowper. The books were only possible because of the detailed reminiscences of his conversations with the older members of his family which Sturt recorded for years in his

Journals. Both of them have moments which are bathed in a glow of nostalgia that lights up Sturt's usually sober prose. This method corresponds to the kind of poetic guess-work which here had to take the place of documentary, yet Sturt always has his feelings under control. The remarkable thing about these books is that they can entertain such emotions without forsaking their attempt to give as humanly circumstantial an impression of this lost world as possible. *William Smith*, for example, has a picture of a pig-killing that is more brutal and realistic than the famous one in *Jude the Obscure*, and also more informative. Sturt does not witness such scenes through civilised eyes, as Hardy does by making us see through Jude's: he sees it as his business to commemorate the hardships and crudities of the old way of life as physically as possible. It is this ability to think himself into the way his forbears felt which gave Sturt the right to a certain ring of sentimentality when he wrote about the 'Englishness' of the two Smiths. It was not an 'Englishness' of the modern kind. His feeling for the yeoman virtues did not lead him into idealising them in a way that would have seemed foreign to the Smiths themselves, as Hardy had tended to do in his elegiac picture of Giles Winterbourne in *The Woodlanders*. The Smiths have the ripeness without the poetics. What Sturt aimed for was to enjoy the flowers that grew in this rural world without failing to notice the manure that had helped them to grow.

Sturt may see John Smith as 'a mirror to England's life', 'the sort of man Shakespeare knew',[37] and find in him a reflection of a 'certain dignity in the collective life of the English' and a 'serene English poise';[38] he may grow lyrical over his 'mellow country wisdom and an Old English faith',[39] but all this does not turn the plain farmer into a paragon of pastoral romance. Smith also has his faults. One aspect of his 'Englishness' is seen in his narrow mental horizons – he certainly never finds any poetic or metaphysical significance in himself. Rather, he brings home the force of Sturt's characteristic saying that 'the ordinary suffices me'. The England he embodies is quite unliterary and prosaic, an England of common sense, endurance and good temper that is too dull for poetry any less plain that Sturt's own: he 'belonged to that element of quiet strength in England which furnished no subjects for novels, no excitements for lawyer or judge or politician, no romance for poets, but kept the country orderly and industrious.'[40] Getting at this England is, in fact, a matter of seeing underneath the one the novelists and poets have created. Their 'culture' has to be peeled away to get at its culture.

The process was, of course, more intrinsically literary itself than this suggests. Literature may not have studied John Smith before but Sturt nonetheless thought of him as a true literary subject. He is like a prose version of Wordsworth's Michael.

Every character in Sturt is like the tip of an unseen iceberg. Not psychologically – their psychology is something they share with many others like themselves – but because conventional history has left half the story untold. The Smiths *are* strong individuals too but they are also vehicles for more than just self, especially in their speech. That comes from the 'race', instinctively, a measure of their belonging to 'the folk' and not to their belief in any idea of self-development. Sturt's own relation to this speech was partly conjectural: he could not define the 'Englishness' it embodied. As an exponent (and victim?) of 'culture' he had to proceed by guess-work, never quite sure of the colours of the banner he wanted to unfurl. But this was not simply a handicap to him. It had the benefit of preventing him from writing about his people as an authority or prophet engaged in spreading his word. If his England was hidden and unobtrusive he still knew that it was vital to seek for it: not just for his own private spiritual journey but for more down-to-earth reasons too:

One may infer that Bettesworth does not consider himself a particularly strong man. And of course he is right, in a sense, although one is prone to think otherwise. But the truth is, he belongs to a strong breed. There are thousands his equals in serviceable doing. All that he has ever done well, is being done no less well today by his successors in every village and town throughout the country. It is so common, a matter of such every-day occurrence, that we take it for granted, and do not notice the tough breed of men at their obscure work. Yet if their work were to cease, England would become uninhabitable before a week was out.[41]

It is as if their work and 'England', though inseparable, were not the same thing. These myriad Bettesworths do not quite belong to the only entity one would expect them to belong to. This chink in a seemingly assured sentence is a small sign of something one often feels when reading Sturt: that England, far from being indivisible, is really made up of various different Englands which never quite intersect. Sturt himself does not speak as an inhabitant of the same spiritual England as Bettesworth's, though he lives in the same place. What the *Journals* several times describe as a 'gulf' had opened up between their Englands, condemning Bettesworth to the contempt of the new middle-class villa-dwellers of the Bourne and Sturt to writing as a sort of sympathetic *déraciné*. In *A Farmer's Life* he thinks of his own knowledge and power of observation as something he is condemned to, second-best to real living:

> would he not have enjoyed consciously delights that I too have since enjoyed? More vividly perhaps. The memories called up were, for me, of things only seen; but, for him, of things actually done. I had but looked on at the hay-makings, the timber cartings; but he had taken his share in them. He was a partaker in that English life of which it had to suffice me to be a spectator.[42]

There was no glamour in such a role but the dry, honest rigour of Sturt's spectatorship at least preserved him from imagining that the Smiths' experience could be possessed – captured – by anyone who had not suffered its hardships.

  Some of the most moving things in Sturt's books occur when, though a looker-on, he is privileged with a sense of whole generations of English people, emerging through the presence of some humble peasant descendant. As he thinks of the suffering Lucy Bettesworth has had to bear, for instance, she ceases to be one, rather dirty, old woman and becomes the representative of a vast but disregarded historical force:

> The labours that have claimed so ruthlessly and have so cruelly marred this old woman are of another order. They rank among the great things for which our race has lived. Unrecognized, unrecorded, their place is beside our Armada conflict, our occupation of India, our mastery of the seas; viewed in the large, they are not less splendid, and they are more venerable than these; nor could there have been any Agincourt or Waterloo had there been no forgotten folk left at home to enforce the harvests from our English valleys.[43]

Lucy's 'swarthy wrinkled face' seems 'out of touch with our times' but it takes Sturt back to a time when it did belong, 'perhaps the fifteenth century'.[44] It is a noble vision, touched with suppressed anger but not polemical. Its human tone explains why Sturt could not regard the poor as simply deprived – objects of charity – hard as their lives are. For their deprivation is also a sign of their strength. No 'official' version of history could have provided this dramatic view of Lucy which, in itself, is like an early plea for what would now be called an 'alternative' history. This was, of course, more than Sturt himself could give but he did not understand that, without it, there could be no true account of 'Englishness'. Commenting on the 'Khaki' election of 1900 he wrote:

Consider the recent general election: how sordid and base in all its details, without one exception so far as I saw it. Only in the large does it assume august proportions: but the large does not dignify the little, which is a part of it. The English people choosing its Parliament is a great spectacle and inspiring: not so the lying candidate and his dull-witted constituents. It is because the Religion of England is not present to us: from the belief in our national greatness there does not run down through all the fabric that steadying strength which such a keystone should provide. Perhaps the belief is faulty: perhaps the greatness which is its centre is only the supremacy of bullies and knaves (indeed our leading public men are not all that we could wish): but whatever be the cause, the fact remains that as a people we are without religion. (sj, I, p. 321)

This is unusually Ruskinian and denunciatory for Sturt but it is also quite precise. The word 'religion' (which he seldom uses in so large a way) is actually used to refer us to the problem that all the Bettesworth books centre on: how are the different Englands, the 'large' and the 'little', to be joined together in one whole? Sturt's own substitute for a 'religion' was the countryside itself – but only just. His work is full of sad accounts, almost Lawrentian in feeling, of how his beloved Hindhead was being blotted out by middle-class civilisation:

villas seen from a distance seem to have broken out upon the once majestic hill like a red skin eruption, and in certain slants of the sunshine make it an uplifted horror visible for miles. There was a time when I could not see Hindhead without gladness; there are times now when I rather look away from it than endure to think what has gone from it for ever. For the continuity has gone.[45]

It is this refusal to assume more of England than he could that earns Sturt our respect today. Even in nostalgic mood he remains the tough, judicious observer, the enemy of glib generalisations and easy panaceas. In the end, he could only try to leave his subject matter where he found it. 'Englishness' was too complex and unresolved a theme to tabulate. No doubt he would have regarded what later writers made of his books with his customary wry scepticism. He himself did not want to feel that he had reduced their material to literature or the level-headed pathos of men like Bettesworth to fiction.

It is, however, misleading to think of Sturt solely in terms of the way he addressed an abstract idea like that of England, even if his aim was to make it more concrete. He made his points as a writer most strongly when he made them tacitly. He was a master of the art of letting a fact grow in suggestiveness without squeezing it for meanings. This is why his eloquently sober prose needs time for it to begin to sound. His words draw no attention to themselves but they do slowly impress on us a sense of real texture and substance, as of some sturdy hand-woven cloth. At first, though, his voice scarcely penetrates the silence in which things are held by its clear medium. But if the prose is like a windowpane there is no mistaking its deeply personal accent. Sturt did not seek to scrutinise rural life with unemotional objectivity and his finest images of it, like Wordsworth's, are all suffused with emotion. It is the thought of human distress or dignity or mere endurance that prompts him to generalise, as in this picture of the farm from *William Smith*:

It was a background: or, say, the whole background was enriched by it, whatever the subject of talk. Amidst incongruous matter – squires and rectors, village conditions, pigs, pottery, Christmas customs, the collecting of urine for steeping the seed wheat, the making of tinder and matches; and in chatter about the turnpike roads, and dog traction, and the to and fro of traffic between London and the far-off coast – from amidst and in and out of all this in its endless variety, farm words – single words such as glebe, harvest, thatching – sometimes glowed with a colour all their own, like ruddy sails on a summer evening sea. But the sea was the ancient country life and memory of an earlier era. The talk, indeed, took me back into George Borrow's time. And it seemed no mean or ugly country that I heard of. The farm – I think it must have been the farm – suggested dreams of quiet pastoral scenes, stately trees, great skies. In a word, the background was England – England in epitome.[46]

That frankly admits its own nostalgia but it is not really a 'pastoral' pastoral. In pastorals, seed wheat is not steeped in urine. Sturt imagines what William Smith was like, not what he would have liked him to be like. Though he deprecates his own description of early nineteenth-century Farnborough as a 'fancy picture' he immediately picks himself up for it: 'Sentiment has a way of picking out the otherwise unnoticed values and thus finding the deepest truths; and in this case I am persuaded that the values of a vanished rural England are precisely those which, above all others, ought to be in any imaginary view of Farnborough.'[47] What is 'imaginary' need not be 'fancy'. 'Sentiment', so often the place where thinking stops, can also be a technique of discovery.

As a young man, before taking over his father's wheelwright's business, Sturt was a great reader of Ruskin and Arnold. Later, he tried to marry Arnoldian 'culture' to his Ruskinian concern for the labouring classes who were excluded from it. When he speaks of John Smith's 'serene English poise' he does not, of course, refer to the educated urbanity Arnold valued but he did see that 'poise' as the creation of real intelligence and imagination. Far more than Hardy did, Sturt believed passionately in the intelligence of ordinary men and women. His Bettesworth is never a country bumpkin. On the contrary, Sturt likens listening to him to the pleasures of listening to an artist talking about his art: 'The man's brain is a miracle. Nothing is without interest for him. His mind is crowded with facts – local knowledge mostly – all loose and disconnected, yet all ready, so that he can refer to them whenever he wants. What a storehouse for a novelist!' (sj, i, p. 245). The rarity of these simple statements is a good index of just how divided Sturt's England was. Intelligence was the last quality that most writers – even on the country – found in the peasantry. It is, however, the quality most necessary if the 'folk mind' is to be seen as genuinely creative – a real counterpart to the creativeness of the 'higher' culture. Rural customs, when informed by it, were not just customary in the inert sense. In *Lucy Bettesworth* there is a fine essay called 'Our Primitive Knowledge' which celebrates what Sturt calls a 'knowledge not to be picked up in schools' and it was the intelligence which could use such knowledge that was the impetus of the 'folk mind'.[48] Another way of saying this is to note that that mind, as Sturt conceived of it, was the outcome of innumerable sharp individual minds like Bettesworth's.

The *donnée* of *A Farmer's Life* and *William Smith* is that these men are not ciphers, like 'Hodge', and one corollary of this is that Sturt owes it to their intelligence not to fudge what was squalid and narrow in their lives. He makes no bones about the fact that their England was 'grossly materialistic' and lacking in culture – 'books they had none, art none'.[49] Despite this, he finds in them a real inner life where, in most country writing, there is usually a sort of picturesque blank. (The early prose of Edward Thomas comes to mind). But Sturt had a gift for invoking ghosts and giving a tongue to hidden and anonymous lives. He could also use that difficult word 'race' without falling into nationalistic or imperialist aggrandisement. One such context is the last days of Bettesworth, as he goes 'weakening down, towards the workhouse horror':

I hope yet to hear many more of his tales; but it seems well to let the record of them end here on this note of endurance in himself, and of considerate helpfulness in his 'mate'; because when Bettesworth is done for and his old wagging tongue at length still, the same brave qualities, spontaneous as in him and his neighbours, will be moulding other men after his pattern, controlling their actions, shaping their thoughts, putting into their mouths conversations like these, and in them all carrying on invisibly those unconscious traditions, habits, instincts, that are surely a valuable part of what we think of as the English Race.[50]

'Race' has this large sense here because Sturt delicately sidesteps the pastoralist's fallacy of thinking of the country as the *only* true source of ancient traditions. There are and always have been as many Bettesworths at work in England's towns. Nor does Sturt doubt that their race has a future ahead of it as well as its past. But, like Leavis, he does not believe that that future will be 'English' in the old sense. The English get farther from England, not nearer to it: 'If we are winning the Cosmos we are losing touch with England.'[51] Sturt does not weep or wail over this change – 'Ours is the larger hope' despite it – because for him change was inherent in any continuity. England is not above history. There is a kind of Proustian element in his work, a need to relive what is past, and a consequent sense that its world needs to be past or passing for it to touch us imaginatively. The remembrance of things past is a means of cementing our bonds with our lost worlds, not simply a valediction to them. The sense of where one had come *from* mattered almost as much as the place itself. The personal parts of *A Farmer's Life* and the autobiographical *A Small Boy in the Sixties*, his last book, testify that for Sturt there was a *temps retrouvé* as well as a *temps perdu*.

Yet his own school was Farnham Grammar, not the fields and hedgerows, and, like Hardy, he had to study rural culture through the eyes of a written culture whose existence men like Bettesworth barely suspected. No doubt his original readers must have included some of those villa-dwellers whose arrival had, he feared, sounded the death knell of the old way of life. He too was astraddle two worlds and, in bleaker moments, must have wondered how much resonance the word 'English' would muster in the future. This was why the young Leavis could identify with him as he did not with other country writers of the time. One cannot prise open Sturt's prose to get at its emotional meaning as one takes a mollusc from a shell. Yet his muted self-effacement often does swell into resonance as I have tried to show, nowhere more so than in the weight of meaning he could give to the words 'English' and 'Englishness'. Has any modern English writer known his own particular England as closely as Sturt knew his?

NOTES

(Place of publication is London unless otherwise stated)

1 *The Journals of George Sturt* 1890–1927, selected and edited by E. D. Mackerness in 2 vols. (Cambridge University Press, 1967), I, p. 315 and given hereafter as SJ. (Vol. I has a perceptive account of Sturt's life and work. For another good brief account of Sturt see J. H. Grainger, *Patriotisms* (Routledge and Kegan Paul, 1986), pp. 99–103.)

2 *Anna Karenina and Other Essays* (Chatto and Windus, 1964), pp. 2–3.

3 *Culture and Environment; The Training of Critical Awareness*, by F. R. Leavis and Denys Thompson (Chatto and Windus, 1964), pp. 2–3.

4 *Nor Shall My Sword: Discourses on Pluralism, Compassion and Social Hope* (Chatto & Windus, 1972), p. 84. For Sturt on Morris see SJ, I, pp. 138–9, p. 174 and p. 219.

5 Leavis's prejudice against a certain type of public schoolboy was well known. H. A. Mason recollects (in a letter to the author) that he liked to think of himself as 'working-class'. Class disaffection from Cambridge would help to explain why Sturt attracted him.

6 *Culture and Environment*, p. 82.

7 *Ibid.*, p. 83.

8 *Nor Shall My Sword*, p. 94.

9 *Ibid.*, p. 41.

10 The *Journals* record several visits from lady admirers who were obviously using Sturt as a source of the kind of rural sentimentalism he loathed.

11 *Change in the Village* (Duckworth, 1955) p. 65.

12 *On Poetry and Poets* (Faber, 1957), p. 191.

13 *The Letters of Arnold Bennett*, ed. James Hepburn, (Oxford University Press, 1968), II, p. 110.

14 *Change in the Village*, p. 205.

15 'Reflections on the Organic Community', *The Human World*, 15–16 (1974), p. 61.

16 *Culture and Environment*, p. 87.

17 *Ibid.*, p. 87.

18 It is by no means certain that Sturt himself would have agreed. He often notes Bettesworth's pleasure in reading the papers (at the barber's) and thinks of it as a great advance on the old village world where a Bettesworth would not even have known the name of the Prime Minister. He had no wish for the peasantry to remain peasants.

19 *The Country and the City* (Chatto and Windus, 1973), p. 261.

20 *Culture and Environment*, pp. 96–7.

21 Sturt's informants are usually old, often dying. His younger villagers are already cut off from the culture of the past. See in particular the essays 'Dying Out', 'At the Infirmary' and 'Dickey Brown' in *Lucy Bettesworth* (Duckworth, 1913), pp. 85–127.

22 From Bennett's introduction to Sturt's *A Small Boy in the 60s* (Caliban Books, Horsham, 1982), p. xi.

23 *Journey to the Western Islands of Scotland* (Cambridge University Press, 1930), p. 20.

24 *The Rural Tradition: William Cobbett, Gilbert White, and Other Non-Fiction Prose Writers of the English Countryside* (Harvester, Brighton, 1975), p. 166.

25 *Anna Karenina and Other Essays*, p. 41.

26 *The Living Principle: 'English' as a Discipline of Thought* (Chatto and Windus, 1975), p. 52.

27 *New Bearings in English Poetry*, (Chatto and Windus, 1961), p. 63.

28 *Ibid.*, p. 61.

29 H. A. Mason recalls (in a letter to the author) that Thompson always subscribed more whole-heartedly than Leavis did to the idea of the 'organic community'.

30 *Change in the Village*, pp. 205–6.

31 *Lucy Bettesworth*, p. 276.

32 *Ibid.*, p. 275.

33 Bennett, *Letters*, II, p. 65.

34 *Ibid.*, p. 57.

35 For Sturt on Pater see *Walter Pater: The Critical Heritage*, ed. R. M. Seiler (Routledge and Kegan Paul, 1980), pp. 188–93.

36 *Change in the Village*, pp. 7–8.

37 *A Farmer's Life* (Jonathan Cape, 1927), p. 11.

38 *Ibid.*, p. 130.

39 *Ibid.*, p. 129.

40 *Ibid.*, p. 178.

41 *The Bettesworth Book: Talks with a Surrey Peasant* (Duckworth, 1920), pp. 118–19.

42 *A Farmer's Life*, p. 184.

43 *Lucy Bettesworth*, p. 5.

44 *Ibid.*, p. 4.

45 *Ibid.*, pp. 272–3.

46 *William Smith: Potter and Farmer 1790–1858* (Caliban Books, Horsham, 1978), pp. 96–7.

47 *Ibid.*, p. 103.

48 *Lucy Bettesworth*, p. 218.

49 *William Smith*, p. 208.

50 *The Bettesworth Book*, pp. 324–5.

51 *William Smith*, p. viii.

CHAPTER 5

Contending Englands: F. R. Leavis and T. S. Eliot

The present is not a salutary time for assessing how the English have studied 'English' in this century. The missionary mood of the early days of 'Cambridge English' is now difficult even to imagine, let alone share, when the subject is under threat from both without and within as never before. The only thing that everyone agrees on is that there is a 'crisis' in English studies.

This said, one needs to remember that crises are the stock-in-trade of journalists and polemicists: if enough bystanders tell you your house is on fire you will probably ring for the fire brigade. Moreover, in this context a crisis is nothing new. Arguably, 'English' was born in response to a cultural crisis, as a rearguard action against 'mass civilisation'. If it aspired to save souls, as I. A. Richards thought, that was because so many souls seemed all but lost.[1] Not that Leavis himself had much time for such hopes; every page he wrote derives energy from his insistent need to communicate what he has to say before it is too late. In other words, he located the crisis not in the discipline itself, as we do, flawed though he thought it, but in England itself. *Scrutiny* saw it as the subject's function to maintain contact with the English life and culture of the past. It did not settle, as most modern departments of 'English' do, simply for the *preserving* of 'English Literature'. It is not then surprising if 'English', for all its expansion as a subject, should seem more tangential to England than it once did.

Leavis has often been accused of being a Little Englander but no English writer in this century has been less complacent about England than he has. It is significant that his writings about 'English' rarely mention the 1924 *Newbolt Report* on the subject. They might have been expected to, if only because one of its authors was 'Q', Leavis's first professor, and Caldwell Cook, his old English master at the Perse, was a key witness to it. Perhaps the report's tone was too

confident, even nationalistic, for his taste? Yet he must have approved
of much of what it had to say. No doubt he questioned its self-
assurance, its claim to be able to renew the bonds between English
people and their 'Englishness'. In this respect, there is a revealing
contrast to be made between Leavis and Eliot's friend Herbert Read.
In 1933, Read brought out an anthology entitled *The English Vision*.
His aim was 'to present the English ideal in its various aspects as
expressed by representative Englishmen'.[2] The book is still worth
reading and it does have some common ground with Leavis ('without
a consciousness of a national language there can be no consciousness
of a nation'[3]) but, although Read cautions his reader against 'the
excessive nationalism of some of the extracts',[4] this doesn't prevent
him elsewhere from sounding like an imperialist himself: 'What I
wish to emphasise now is the universal validity of this our vision.
Alone of national ideals, the English ideal transcends nationality.'[5]
Leavis would have thought the ultra-progressive Read's transcendence self-defeating. Yet Read was quite capable of following his
remark with an endorsement of D. H. Lawrence's 'Englishness', a
quality which it would be hard to translate into any 'national ideals'.
It is therefore relevant to point out that in 1933 Leavis himself was
drawing on Lawrence for the much less euphoric thesis of *Culture and
Environment* and *For Continuity*. In comparison with those books, Read
takes his 'Englishness' for granted, as if he had some hot-line to the
past. Margaret Mathieson may be right to say, in her useful *The
Preachers of Culture*, that the 'Leavisite English teacher' in the schools
was usually 'supportive of traditional values'[6] but Leavis himself
never imagined that it was sufficient to support those values in order
to bring them back.

One thinks of Herbert Read, despite *The English Vision*, as
metropolitan and cosmopolitan, a modernist and a European from
Eliot's camp, whereas Leavis from the start proclaimed his allegiance
to English provincial life. One of the advantages of Cambridge to him
was that it was not London. Thus, his criticism laid unusual emphasis
on the relation between literature and common life – for example, in
Shakespeare and Dickens and Lawrence. When, in *Education and the
University*, he recommended the seventeenth century for special study,
he was thinking of the period as one that immediately preceded a
'new separation between polite and popular culture'.[7] In other
words, he drew an analogy between the period and the so-called
'organic community' that would later be destroyed by industrialism.

Such ideas were enough to put Leavis on his guard against Eliot's use of his Tudor ancestor's *Book of the Governour* (1531) in his evocation of traditional village England in *East Coker*. By what right did a modern American poet draw on Sir Thomas Elyot's 'Englishness'? Could his commitment to a central 'European mind' allow him to understand a culture that was provincial and regional? Leavis is on record as thinking that Eliot's genius did not function in terms of 'the social world' and he had no doubt that it was 'social' insight which *East Coker* lacked.[8]

The reader of *Notes Towards the Definition of Culture* will know that, though a conservative, Eliot was not inclined to dwell on the 'organic community'. For him, it was too secular an ideal. He saw 'the regions' mainly as servants of a classically centered, metropolitan culture. Their role was not unlike that he assigned to the 'masses': they are permitted unconsciously to possess a culture 'from which the more conscious part of culture draws vitality'.[9] The 'regions' ought never to prevail over the national culture they serve. To defend them too hotly is to become provincial and rather ridiculous:

We expect to find 'regionalists' attempting to revive some language which is disappearing and ought to disappear; or to revive customs of a bygone age which have lost all significance; or to obstruct the inevitable and accepted progress of mechanisation and large-scale industry. The champions of local tradition, indeed, often fail to make the best of their case; and when, as sometimes happens, they are most vigorously opposed and derided by others among their own people, the outsider feels that he has no reason to take them seriously.[10]

This is both lofty and blank. Eliot seems to have very little feeling for 'tradition' when it works at this level. The 'significance' of his 'regions' seems to be imposed from above, as if the representatives of metropolitan culture (or 'large-scale industry') were more entitled to determine it than those called on to embody it in their actual lives. What is more, Eliot implies that anyone who inhabits this higher sphere need feel no qualms at being an 'outsider'. Not all of Eliot's argument is as blatant as this, however, and he does go on to make more constructive suggestions with which both Leavis and Sturt might have found common ground. For instance: 'what is wanted is not to restore a vanished, or to revive a vanishing culture under modern conditions which make it impossible, but to grow a contemporary culture from the old roots'.[11] Yet this hardly reassures us that Eliot's metropolitan viewpoint would enable him to recognise the 'old roots' if he encountered them. They may be a starting point for 'culture' but they are prior to it rather than part of it.

My reason for referring to *Notes Towards the Definition of Culture* is not so much to raise the thorny issue of Eliot's politics as to suggest the spirit in which he approaches his subject-matter in the first section of *East Coker*. There too we find him contemplating a folk culture through the eyes of a culture that is more sophisticated:

> In that open field
> If you do not come too close, if you do not come too close,
> On a summer midnight, you can hear the music
> Of the weak pipe and the little drum
> And see them dancing around the bonfire
> The association of man and woman
> In daunsinge, signifying matrimonie –
> A dignified and commodious sacrament.
> Two and two, necessarye coniunction,
> Holding eche other by the hand or the arm
> Whiche betokeneth concorde. Round and round the fire
> Leaping through the flames, or joined in circles,
> Rustically solemn or in rustic laughter
> Lifting heavy feet in clumsy shoes,
> Earth feet, loam feet, lifted in country mirth
> Mirth of those long since under earth
> Nourishing the corn. Keeping time,
> Keeping the rhythm in their dancing
> As in their living in the living seasons
> The time of the seasons and the constellations
> The time of milking and the time of harvest
> The time of the coupling of man and woman
> And that of beasts. Feet rising and falling.
> Eating and drinking. Dung and death.[12]

Why does Eliot choose to summon these anonymous dancers through the rhythms of Sir Thomas Elyot? When a mind like his ventures into pastoral – even though the result for a moment recalls George Eliot in deepest Loamshire – that pastoral is likely to have a patrician cadence. It is not what Spenserian pastoral sometimes is, a means of going beyond the thought of class. It is the controlling pressure of Sir Thomas's stately English which bestows meaning on the rustic dancers, distancing them from any thought of the routine of labour. Eliot seizes on a ritual aesthetic moment in their lives, a moment through which the part can be represented as the whole. Normally, they would have been abed long before midnight to prepare to begin their toil again at dawn. Here, the rhythms of 'The time of milking and the time of harvest' are assimilated into those of the ritual dance and do not imply any mundane drudgery. The only voice we hear in the passage is Sir Thomas's and this indicates that the peasants are not there for themselves (as Bettesworth is) but for what they can symbolise. Their local customs are universalised into a timeless dance of life and death. Their mortality interests Eliot more than their culture does. In the final section of *East Coker* he makes it clear that part of the attraction which the past has for him is precisely its inscrutable pastness, the fact that it remains obscure enough to be malleable to present emotion. The past has to feel strange but not estranging, not inaccessibly other:

> not the lifetime of one man only
> But of old stones that cannot be deciphered
> There is a time for the evening under starlight,
> A time for the evening under lamplight
> (The evening with the photograph album).
> Love is most nearly itself
> When here and now cease to matter.[13]

The effect of approaching history as a theme for religious meditation is to conflate one period with another and counteract the sense of historical change. *Four Quartets* does not think of the sixteenth and seventeenth centuries as a dynamic force behind modern culture (as Leavis does) but rather as a past which he can adapt to his mood. Just as the past seems most moving when it is malleable, so one suspects Eliot of not really *wanting* his 'old stones' to be 'deciphered' or to have daylight rather than 'lamplight' falling on 'the photograph album'. It is part of the attraction of history that it prevents us from coming too close to actual living. Thus, when we read, in *Little Gidding*, that 'History is now and England'[14] England seems not so much a place or a tradition as a state of mind, a kind of poignant Platonic essence that has been distilled from the raw stuff of historical change.

It is not difficult to see why Leavis should have demurred at the opening of *East Coker*. In *The Living Principle* he uses it to illustrate where his own sense of England diverges most sharply from Eliot's. Quoting the passage about the midnight dance he observes how Eliot

shifts from 'the "now" of present actuality to a "now" of the past –
that is, to one imagined and essentially non-tangible and un-
approachable.'[15] Though he finds Eliot sincere he nonetheless sees 'a
most gravely disabling ignorance' in his consequent presentation of
'the country-folk of pre-industrial England'.[16] What triggers his
dissent is the bluntness of the words 'Dung and death':

I don't see how that can be explained away. In its reductivism it is so
patently innocent, and it is the innocence that is so revealing. One might
have thought, how surprisingly close to the Lawrence of *The Rainbow*! –
until the final touch. That leads one to reflect that the intuition Lawrence
expresses in the places one would point to may be called religious, while
Eliot is hardly thinking of such an adjective as applying here in his poem; he
appropriates it (one divines) to a kind of context that is very different. Why
then, one is impelled to ask, did he earlier in the same paragraph work into
his verse that passage from Sir Thomas Elyot's *The Governour*? –

> The association of man and woman
> In daunsinge, signifying matrimonie –
> A dignified and commodious sacrament.

It could hardly have been with a profane intention – whether or not
directed at Sir Thomas. The explanation surely is an intention of a different
kind that possessed him – possessed him with monopolizing completeness.
The name, as both that of a well-known Tudor writer and his own, having
attracted him, he found, disposable as Eliotic verse, a passage to quote that
suited his strongly emotional purpose, which was to present the sixteenth-
century 'now', and to present it in a way that would give a grim resuming
force to the concluding 'Dung and death' (for that was certainly in view,
and working decisively in his mind). The close itself, if one likes, is an irony
– an Eliotic one. The poet's unconsciousness of the effect in relation to Sir
Thomas's 'sacrament of matrimonie' emphasizes the reductive force of 'the
coupling' in that culminating sentence, and can't but be judged to exemplify
another of Eliot's traits – the distaste he tends to assume as proper and (in
a higher sense) normal at the thought of sex.

The given reductivism is in keeping with Eliot's conception of the rural
English populace contemporary with his Tudor namesake. He clearly thinks
of them as yokels, clumsy, crude, gross and incapable of the spiritual or
cultural graces.

> Rustically solemn or in rustic laughter
> Lifting heavy feet in clumsy shoes,
> Earth feet, loam feet ...
>   ... Feet rising and falling.
> Eating and drinking. Dung and death.

Yet it was they who created the English language – robust, supple, humanly sensitive and illimitably responsive and receptive – and made possible in due course Shakespeare, Dickens and the poet of *Four Quartets*. A language is a cultural life, a living creative continuity, and English, remaining English, took into its life the values, perceptions, refinements and possibilities of a complex civilization. The culture inherent in it was more than a matter of agriculture, craft-skills and bumpkin socialities.[17]

Although Leavis detects the way the brutal words 'Dung and death' are part of a vain effort Eliot is making to present the past as more substantial than it really is to him, I would argue that in objecting to them Leavis is appealing to a world that is not wholly real to himself either. In invoking a 'human world that has vanished' they are both prone to mould it to their own purposes. For what has vanished is ripe for mythologising. It is arguable that both writers shared a familiar sense of enforced distance from the past, that each rationalised it in his particular way. Just as Eliot dwells on the thought of 'Dung and death' so Leavis cites *The Rainbow* as an instance of what Eliot omits. Just as Eliot recoils from rural mortality, recoiling really from rural vitality, so Leavis seems over-anxious to think of rural life as intrinsically life-enhancing. Both seek to impose a pattern on the past. This comes out in what I would describe as a certain squeamishness which – for all their differences – I think they both share. For instance, if Eliot's word 'coupling' suggests prim distaste, despite its attempted frankness, Leavis seems reductive in an opposite direction. He is so bent on pointing to the vitality of sixteenth-century English that he virtually forgets about the desperately brief lives of those who embodied it. His past seems hygienically limited to the degree that, unlike Eliot, he imagines no place in it for death.

In suggesting that Leavis gave a doctored version of pre-industrial England, I do not mean to imply that he also gave an unhistorical one. I would prefer to say that he chose to dwell on particular aspects of English history which for him summed up what was essentially English, and then let them stand for the whole. It is on behalf of one such England that he objects to the 'bumpkin socialities' of Eliot's dancers. Yet one suspects that Leavis would have preferred something more like the mellow 'realism' of *Adam Bede* to a realistic picture of the disease and distress of sixteenth-century peasant life. It is not, after all, the aesthetic colouring of Eliot's dancers that he criticises but the way Eliot handles the non-pastoral sides of his picture. In looking to the past for an authentic 'Englishness', such as he finds in the language of Shakespeare, Leavis is as liable as Eliot to move from the domain of history to that of metaphysics, to posit a creativeness that is as timeless in its way as Eliot's 'timeless moments'. Leavis feels no hesitation or embarrassment in speaking on behalf of this 'Englishness' against Americans like Eliot and Pound who, presumably, cannot participate in it as he does himself. It is not his view, as one might expect it to be, that the pre-industrial sensibility has become irrecoverable to a modern English writer who is the heir to everything the last two centuries have done to obliterate it. Like Lawrence, he believes in an essential England which still exists in spite of what England has become.

One reason that the notion of 'the organic community' sometimes seems too abstract is that, though its apologists stress its 'organic' character, they do little to explain how change occurs *within* it. Their emphasis falls instead on the pressures exerted on it from without, by the modern world. In consequence, one easily receives a paradoxical image of a society in which change does not entail disruption and loss. What is supposed to be organic and growing can turn out to seem historically static. This is to some extent the case with *Silas Marner*, a novel admired by both the Leavises for its historical fidelity. The note of pastoral idealism that tinges George Eliot's picture of the rural English past clearly found an echo in Leavis. It corroborated his own (rather Victorian) tendency to make loaded contrasts between past and present. There is usually an element of retrospection in his most positive images of culture. To compare his accounts of Augustan or Elizabethan England with what he says about the 1930s, is to feel that for him the past, being concluded, is more solid, its imperfections less galling. One cannot imagine the chronicler of the grim, lingering deaths of the Bettesworths baulking at the 'Dung and death' of *East Coker* as fiercely as Leavis did. The note of disgust in Eliot's lines (and also in Leavis's reaction to them) perhaps came from a lack of the countryman's first-hand knowledge of such things.

It is significant that, despite his admiration for novels like *Adam Bede* and *Silas Marner*, Leavis was not more drawn to the novels of Hardy. No doubt Hardy's obsession with the bleaker aspects of Wessex life counted for something in this. Leavis found a more congenial illustration of rural England in the Wordsworth of *Michael*,the Wordsworth who lies behind *Silas Marner*. There is, of course, acute suffering in poems like *Michael* and *The Ruined Cottage* but it is never demoralising in the way Jude Fawley's is. In

Wordsworth, far from belittling humanity, suffering sets a seal on human dignity. His most characteristic tragedies are uplifting and salvage an ideal endurance from the contemplation of grief. In *Jude the Obscure*, pain simply becomes more excruciatingly painful as the story goes on. It is therefore impossible to think of Hardy's characters as embodiments of the creativeness of the English folk in the way George Eliot and Sturt think of some of their people. Of course, Leavis had more specific literary objections to Hardy's novels, but that does not alter the fact that Hardy was always unlikely to assuage his own need for good images of the rural past. His anxiety to recover an untarnished, life-enhancing England could never have been fostered by such scenes as that of Tess working in the fields at Flintcombe Ash. To say this is not to argue that Leavis was not interested in trying to understand the English past as it actually was – in pointing to it he plainly hoped to remind his readers of realities he felt *they* had forgotten – but to suggest that he sometimes wanted that past to be hygienically packaged. Would he, for example, have detected the germs of decay *within* the old, 'organic' order as Hardy did in *The Woodlanders*? Present cultural needs sometimes led him to play down the less fulfilled aspects of the Englands of writers like Bunyan and George Eliot, Englands he deeply needed to believe exemplary.

Despite Leavis's obvious wish to place and refute the Eliot of *East Coker*, the mixture of attraction and repulsion he came to feel for the poem suggests that he found it harder to dissociate himself from it in practice than he did in principle. Raymond Williams has noticed how even in his late books he was still 'trying to drive the Eliot and Lawrence horses together'.[18] The risk he ran in doing this comes out in the way he enforces the criticism that Eliot's reference to 'Dung and death' portends something reductive in his response to life. He begins from a consideration of the 'Lady, three white leopards' poem in *Ash Wednesday* in which, he says, Eliot 'accepts extinction as an escape':

There is the vocation of emptiness, but the emptiness is charged with an enchantment of spiritual suggestion, and there is no hint of any obsession with age and decay that had to be exorcised: the bones are sterile, and consort with the heraldic white leopards. But 'Dung and death' is unequivocal recoil: this is death as it is brooded on by Hamlet in the grave-diggers' scene. Eliot contemplates the fact in its unacceptableness. What we also note is that the frankness of the contemplating relates in an obvious way to the insistent positive preoccupation of *Four Quartets*, the concern to establish the apprehension of a state that is neither death nor the life that is 'only living' and so 'can only die'. It seems certain that he will end satisfied – to say which is to anticipate the severest judgment exacted by the complete poem.[19]

Certainly there is something a little prim and grudging in the matter-of-fact tone of 'that which is only living can only die' and the mention of *Hamlet* is enough to make Eliot's hunger for solutions seem evasive. However, it is easier to see this than to see how Leavis would himself integrate the thought of death or loss into his belief that, 'A language is a cultural life, a living creative continuity, and English, remaining English, took into its life the values, perceptions, refinements and possibilities of a complex civilization.' How can so positive a view of tradition cope with Eliot's realisation that, however nourishing, the past *is* past, the dancers *are* 'all gone under the hill'? When Leavis complains that 'it seems certain that [Eliot] will be satisfied' his words tend to boomerang back on himself. Sometimes one wants to say the same thing about the way he uses words like 'life' and 'living', not just with unusual positive force but also with a more exclusive, selective meaning than most people – Eliot included – give to them. In this connection, his description of Shakespeare's and Eliot's theme as the 'unacceptableness' of dying is revealing: surely their point is that dying is something we have to learn to accept? Eliot's acceptance may be facilitated by his fear of 'life' but, in this context, 'unacceptable' also suggests a degree of evasiveness and resistance to experience. In using the word 'squeamish' to describe such reactions I had it in mind that squeamishness is not just a characteristic of such things as Eliot's reference to the 'coupling of man and woman / And that of beasts'. Even the potent word 'life' can be used to insulate ourselves against some of the more disturbing things which life is usually felt to comprise.

It is very difficult to discuss Leavis's reading of *Four Quartets* without seeming to be splitting hairs but there is a good excuse for this. Reading *The Living Principle*, one finds it increasingly hard to draw a line between where Leavis is making genuinely objective criticisms of the poetry and where his own preoccupations sway and colour his sense of Eliot's. The fact that he brings his own creative reading of the English past to bear so powerfully on the poem's makes the reader's quandary even sharper. Yet what is at issue is by no means a simple opposition or antagonism between two minds which have parted company. Leavis and Eliot share certain kinds of experience even in their different ways of responding to it. That is why they provide an instance of the way the thought of England and the English past is always, in practice, a subjective thought. The past that matters most to us is the past we need to invent. Even when Leavis's concern is to express Eliot's 'disabling ignorance'[20] of vital aspects of English culture his appeal is never confined to straightforward historical scholarship. The past for him is not a vast collection of data but a moral force; it is therefore only morally that it can be apprehended for what it is. Where Eliot fails it is not in knowledge but in sensibility: that is where the real 'ignorance' lies. The study of 'English' as a 'discipline of thought' seeks to diagnose and make good such ignorance. This is why, for Leavis, it is committed to value-judgements and, as their basis, to a version of the history of English literature that is uncompromisingly opposed to the commonplaces of traditional literary history. 'England' and 'Englishness', that is, are not things that are given, but changing, malleable concepts which the critic must strive to create afresh. Leavis had little time for the notion of a literary canon in the inert sense of a received orthodoxy – witness his treatment of Milton – nor for any kind of 'Englishness' that presumed to pin down and immortalise the past. Not for him an England that is 'never and always', exemplary and yet a possible release from time and struggle.

This is where Eliot's purpose in *Four Quartets* is most radically different from Leavis's in *The Living Principle*. For the idea of England to satisfy Eliot's imagination he needs to imagine it as timeless:

> the intersection of the timeless moment
> Is England and nowhere.[21]

Continuity is assured by cancelling out change. This process is only completed in the third part of *Little Gidding*, towards which the opening of *East Coker* can be seen to have been moving. Death ('the moment of the yew tree') transfigures the chaos of history into a significant 'pattern':

> If I think, again, of this place,
> And of people, not wholly commendable,
> Of no immediate kin or kindness,
> But some of peculiar genius,
> United in the strife which divided them;
> If I think of a king at nightfall,

Of three men, and more, on the scaffold
And a few who died forgotten
In other places, here and abroad,
And of one who died blind and quiet,
Why should we celebrate
These dead men more than the dying?
It is not to ring the bell backward
Nor is it an incantation
To summon the spectre of a Rose.
We cannot revive old factions
We cannot restore old policies
Or follow an antique drum.
These men, and those who opposed them
And those whom they opposed
Accept the constitution of silence
And are folded in a single party.
Whatever we inherit from the fortunate
We have taken from the defeated
What they had to leave us – a symbol:
A symbol perfected in death.[22]

The fact that the poet who 'died blind and quiet' had signed the
death-warrant of the 'King at nightfall' does not render their union
in Eliot's pattern at all problematic: history is transformed into a
'symbol perfected in death'. Its battles have all been fought and are
all long over. The past is both sublimated and cancelled. It heals but
cannot haunt us. As John Lucas has argued, the result is as much
sectarian as mystical: ' "England" is offered as an ideal, a wished-for
cultural unity, very different from the bitterness of faction and class-
interests that make its actual history ...' Eliot's 'single party', Lucas
says, is in reality 'Anglo-Catholic, monarchist, authoritarian'.[23] It is
certainly hard to imagine the 'blind and quiet' Milton having any
truck with it. Like Leavis, Lucas puts Eliot's ideal England down to
his being an American who is unable to 'understand or to be aware
of the tensions created by the complexities of the past'.[24] Whether this
should be set down as especially American seems to me to be
doubtful. 'England', as Eliot thinks of it in *Four Quartets*, is essentially
a symbol for the life-process itself (something he needed to sublimate);
as such, being in touch with it can hardly depend simply on
nationality. Moreover, the project of transforming the life-process
into a symbol that is *only* 'perfected in death' can hardly be summed
up in merely political terms, even if politics is clearly at issue in it.
Presumably the factionalism of either side in the Civil War is felt to

be transcended. Sometimes a poet will use history and nationality not as ends or objects in themselves but as the means of exploring something beyond either of them. That, at least, would be a possible way of defending Eliot against Leavis's critique in *The Living Principle*: it would also be a way of arguing that, in his account of *East Coker*, Leavis allowed his own commitment to the continuity of English culture to come between himself and the poetry.

What Leavis's reading of *Four Quartets* comes down to is fundamentally a confrontation of two incompatible conceptions of what it means to be *religious*. This is why Leavis's argument can seem both to expose its object and yet somehow fail to meet it head on, on its own terms. If literary criticism *can* come to rest in spiritual diagnosis then Leavis's conclusions are hard to resist. But such a diagnosis easily cuts a critic off from a poem if it becomes confused with the process of reading itself. It too needs to be diagnosed and, perhaps, 'suspended' as Coleridge said. H. A. Mason has written penetratingly of the way Leavis's value-judgements could sometimes be enlisted to protect himself against certain kinds of emotion which he was reluctant to give himself up to.[25] One of his examples of this is the way Leavis needs to insist on the value of 'concreteness' as a defence against the unbridled emotionality of a poet like Shelley. In this connection, the lacunae in Leavis's account of *Little Gidding* (which he treats more briefly than *East Coker*) seem particularly revealing. Remarkably little is said about its final vision of 'love' when 'all manner of thing shall be well'. To the more stoical Leavis, it clearly represents another capitulation to the wrong sort of emotion. In fact, his account of *Little Gidding* is nearly all concerned with the quartet's second section, the poet's chastening meeting with his admonitory 'familiar compound ghost', and has nothing to say about the lyrical release from doubt of its conclusion:

> At the source of the longest river
> The voice of the hidden waterfall
> And the children in the apple-tree
> Not known, because not looked for
> But heard, half-heard, in the stillness
> Between two waves of the sea.
> Quick now, here, now, always –
> A condition of complete simplicity.[26]

To pass over the music of this in silence, neglecting to set its rhythms against the very different movement of the second part of *Little*

Gidding, is to risk appearing to want the part at the expense of the whole. It is as if Leavis were unwilling to give himself to one element in what he nonetheless praises as the poem's complexity. Perhaps, in the end, we are talking about a place which his mind did not want to go to.

Today, Leavis's 'humanism' (as current orthodoxy terms it) is as out of fashion as Eliot's Anglo-Catholicism was in the 1930s. He is not, of course, linked to any specific kind of humanism – Russell's, say, or that evoked by The Conway Hall – but there is a widespread assumption that his criticism was founded on a naively universalising belief in 'human nature'. This use of the word 'humanist', to indicate no more than a vague frame of mind, operates in a conveniently catch-all way. It is this that makes it such a convenient polemical weapon: one is under no obligation to define what it means. (Hence the kind of modern Shakespeare critic who cheerfully writes off his predecessors, Wilson Knight as much as Bradley, as 'humanists'.) For critics like Terry Eagleton and Catherine Belsey Leavis, despite his proclaimed empiricism, sought to set literature on a metaphysical plane. Belsey's interest in *The Great Tradition*, for instance, is confined to its value-judgements; she disregards the process of reading by which he arrives at them.[27] In this way, she can give the impression that he seeks to impose an ideology on to the writers he discusses. He doesn't, of course, admit that this is what he is doing because his 'humanist' ideology is too ingrained for him to realise its presence in his thought. It is axiomatic for her that the 'humanist' critic never realises that he is *being* a 'humanist'. This makes it all the easier for her to put his own unspoken position into words for him. She manages, for example, to pass over his own view, in his famous reply to René Wellek's objection that he never stated his own position, that to avoid ideology was not an evasion or retreat but a precise and demanding intellectual engagement. For Leavis was hardly a writer unwilling to come down from his ivory tower. One thinks of his life-long instinct for the pertinent critical occasion, the way his writing so often intercepts his culture at a particular juncture in time. (His work on both Lawrence and Eliot has to be seen in the light of their respective reputations at the time of his writing about them.) Criticism to him is an intervention, not a lofty meditation *in vacuo*. Its commitment to disinterestedness never entailed any refusal to expose himself to the resentment of current orthodoxies. 'Humanist' or not, he never expected all his readers to agree with him. If there is one underlying ideological position behind his work it is far from being a vague, abstract belief in 'human nature', though he certainly thought of himself as writing for human beings. He may lean heavily on the word 'life' but not in the way a philosopher would. It is axiomatic for him that such 'necessary' words should be indefinable. What gives them meaning is their context in some specifically *English* 'human nature', apprehended at some particular moment of English history. One can't get far towards defining his critical position without proper recognition of the strong element of the social in it. Hence, his emphasis on 'Englishness', that being the most tangible and specific form in which he encountered 'human nature'.

Leavis's conception of English society takes us back to his account of *East Coker*. This reminds us not only of his debt to Sturt but of the deepening sense in his work of the essentially social nature of the English novel. The 'reality' evoked by Eliot's poem is implicitly set against the sort of social reality evoked by Dickens and George Eliot. Their novels demonstrate in incomparable detail what he had already learnt from Bunyan and Sturt, that an art that is truly humane can never be abstract or generalised. (Eliot's Tudor peasants represent *all* peasants in general and none in particular.) For Leavis, a rich sense of social difference was an intrinsic component of an authentic spiritual life. Without the nineteenth-century novel and the England it could still remind him of, even in a period of broken continuity, he would have felt stranded. It was this commitment to history over metaphysics, literature over philosophy, that made a Marxist critic like Raymond Williams acknowledge that *For Continuity* had won its argument with 1930s Marxism hands down. For Williams, *Scrutiny* represented a partial legacy that needed to be developed, not simply a conservative false direction to be repudiated, but later left-wing critics have tended to accuse Leavis either of obstinately confining his insights to the field of criticism or of allowing that criticism to turn into something else, usually 'morality'.[28] Two influential exponents of these views are Chris Baldick and Francis Mulhern and, between them, they are sometimes felt to have laid Leavis's ghost for good as far as the left is concerned. For Baldick, the upshot of the critical effort of *Scrutiny* was that, 'Criticism in its most important and its most vital sense had been gutted and turned into its very opposite: an ideology.'[29] For Mulhern, the 'logically necessary effect' of *Scrutiny* was '*depreciation*, a *repression* and, at the limit, a *categorical dissolution* of *politics as such*.'[30] Since 'ideology' presumably entails 'politics as such' it isn't clear how both objections can be true at the same time, though this has not prevented some readers subscribing to both together. Polemical convenience is thicker than water. But the flaw in this two-pronged attack lies in the assumption that Leavis's position is inherently conservative. Would a simply conservative writer have counted as much to Raymond Williams as Leavis did? Were even the things that Leavis most wanted to conserve in the English experience – things like *The Pilgrim's Progress* and the novels of George Eliot – themselves conservative? Leavis may not have adhered to the left, any more than to the right, but his deep disenchantment with the state of England as it was certainly shared common ground with it. There is, for example, nothing surprising in the fact that he was as opposed to the hierarchical, Anglican England of *Four Quartets* as a modern, left-wing critic like John Lucas is.

At this point I need to introduce the notion of class. Its relevance to my argument will already be plain. Leavis's championing of D. H. Lawrence, for example, is inseparable from his plea for the recognition of the culture of another England than that celebrated in *Four Quartets*. This England, most fully evinced by the English novel, is Protestant in religion and non-middle-class in its roots. The subtlety of its awareness of the gradations and fluctuations of class makes *East Coker* look like a mere mystical refinement of the social hierarchy. Maggie Tulliver, Arthur Clennam and Ursula Brangwen are all specific instances of a social mobility which threatens to transform the England of the *bourgeoisie*, the England of Bloomsbury as much as the England of Podsnappery. Where Eliot looks back to Hooker, Leavis starts from John Stuart Mill.[31] Thus, his critique of *East Coker* hinges on class, on the need to see those dancing peasants more clearly than Eliot can afford to. This is an implicit question throughout *The Living Principle*: which class really made Shakespeare possible? Leavis's answer is unambiguous: Shakespeare, like Dickens, would be inconceivable without the popular culture, the wider English language, from which he came. This is why there is no excuse for those who say that Leavis drew up at actual politics. Politics and literature were inseparable (one reason why an avowedly 'political' approach to literature would not have made sense to him). No doubt he writes about class as someone who was born at the end of the

Victorian age. Class is a vaguer thing now than it was then and it may be possible for us to disregard its presence in his criticism in a way that he himself could never have imagined.

At this point one is hampered by the lack of a full biography of Leavis.[32] (We may not get one before it is too late to draw on all the first-hand knowledge it needs.) Yet it is plain that Leavis's own class background ensured that any 'élite' he spoke for would have little in common with an existing 'élite' like 'Bloomsbury'. Whereas that was conscripted from the public school establishment, the early Scrutineers were looked down on in Cambridge as products of the grammar schools, cultural *arrivistes*. The Perse, where Leavis went himself, was not a public school in his day. His grandfather, a strong influence on him, had been a horse-dealer (as Bettesworth had been at one stage of his life) and his father made and sold pianos in Regent Street, Cambridge. He himself (unlike Richards and Empson) was first-generation university and his urban, lower middle-class origins had their roots in a more rural world that was disappearing at the start of the century with the advent of the motor car. In other words, he had to construct his own sense of class for himself. That is precisely what his criticism of the novel shows him to be engaged upon. In two generations, his family had moved from the land to commerce to the intelligentsia. The process cannot have been without its disorientating side and it is quite understandable that the Coleridgean notion of 'the clerisy', a social grouping which cut across class lines, should have had a strong appeal to him. Leavis's actual social trajectory was subtler than this suggests (it included the decisive experience of the war years, for example) but some notion of a transitional class-consciousness is needed to explain many of his later positions. Both his sympathy for the young (Eastwood) Lawrence and his distrust of 'Bloomsbury' no doubt went back to early feelings of displacement. It is surely no accident that the books which most clearly represented 'Englishness' for him – *The Pilgrim's Progress, Adam Bede, The Rainbow* – should all celebrate an artisanal and yeoman culture existing below the level of Culture with a capital C. *Scrutiny* was therefore a very different sort of 'élite' from a more traditional one like 'The Apostles'. If it sought to transcend the traditional class hierarchy it also had its roots in another England altogether. Its *points de repère – For Continuity, Culture and Environment* and *Fiction and the Reading Public* – all deplore the desecration and disappearance of that England, rather as Sturt deplored the effect of the new villa-dwellers on his

Hindhead. The world of journalism and the mass media was bent on nothing less than the obliteration of that England. In the name of democracy it was not only levelling the old class barriers but undermining the popular culture itself.

Leavis would not have thought it reductive to see his reading of *East Coker* as an expression of his solidarity with a kind of English experience which Eliot had slighted. (Eliot had always looked down on Lawrence's Eastwood). As usual, one finds Leavis standing for provincial and regional values where Eliot stood for metropolitan ones. Eliot's late essay on Virgil, praising the urbanity of a truly 'European' mind, spoke for values which meant relatively little to him. Not only did the 'history' of *Four Quartets* exclude large areas of 'Englishness' as Leavis understood it, it singled out a patrician England to which he neither could nor would have wanted to belong. His sort receive no invitation to the national gathering that crowns *Little Gidding*. Some Englands are incompatible with others.

It is one step from this opposition of two Englands, neither of which can accommodate the other, to the belief that one of them is the more authentic. This is where Leavis's work on the English novel took him; even though he believed in the existence of an England which Americans like Eliot would never be able to understand, he was too scrupulous to exaggerate his own connection with it. Class, as Jane Austen or George Eliot understood it, no longer existed (only class-conflict remained) and he never tired of reminding his readers that, in this respect, we are all Americans now. Nonetheless, his work on the novel still takes class as an intrinsic element in the English spiritual heritage. If we fail to understand its workings we fail to understand the novels themselves. It is, for instance, crucial for Leavis that we should understand why Dickens is a more deeply 'English' novelist than Thackeray, with his clubman's wit, could ever be. No value-judgement could be purely aesthetic. Thus, he would praise poets according to what he saw as their fidelity to the true spirit of the language. 'English must be kept up,' as Keats said, and Leavis was in no doubt that Shakespeare and Donne kept it up more than Spenser did, or Keats himself more than Milton or Tennyson. Poetry always risks becoming arcane and rarefied when it forsakes its roots in the spoken language and seeks foreign and literary models. Hence the crucial importance to Leavis of *The Pilgrim's Progress* as the voice of the English people. English Literature mattered to him not only in and for itself but because of the England that made it possible in the first place. It seems remote from anything that English departments stand for today. We tend now to study English writers not for the sense they give us of England but in lieu of it. We feel on safer ground with 'theory' than 'tradition'. This is surely something which Leavis, with his hatred of our 'technologico-Benthamite' civilisation, might himself have foretold.

If Leavis is oddly silent about Eliot's reassuring 'world elsewhere' at the end of *Little Gidding* that is because he brought to Eliot's religious feeling an opposing sense of social reality that was itself on the brink of religious feeling. But though he saw this as an either/or confrontation it would be crude to think of him as merely antagonistic towards Eliot. Donald Davie has spoken of his 'lack of pity' for Eliot's need to 'sham dead', an impulse he himself was too courageous and intransigent to share, but more than personal feeling is at stake in his later critiques of Eliot.[33] And Leavis needed to distinguish his own position from Eliot's precisely because he had been so deeply influenced by him. If it is true that, without Eliot, Leavis would not have been completely Leavis that is, paradoxically, because of Eliot the social critic as well as Eliot the poet. Because in Eliot those two roles seemed to him to divide, Leavis was able to understand how important it was to bring them together. The unusual weight he puts on the word 'life', meaning life as it is lived in specific social contexts, is an indication of this. Hence the importance of Lawrence as a sort of antidote to Eliot. It would, however, be wrong to give the impression that he simply saw himself as trying to refute what Eliot stood for. One of the most remarkable things about *The Living Principle* is the potency of the spell which *Four Quartets* could still cast over him in his final years. Moreover, in dissenting from Eliot's notion of 'culture' he makes no bones about the partialness of his own position: 'Better, then, be provincial than cosmopolitan, for to be cosmopolitan in these matters is to be at home nowhere, and he who is at home nowhere can make little of *any* literature – the more he knows, the larger is his ignorance.'[34] And Leavis cannot resist adding, in case the point had escaped us, that 'the idea that being provincial is what we suffer from is itself American.' Yet it seems to me one thing to accept that there is a necessary provinciality in 'Englishness' and another to dismiss what is not English with a generalised slur on what is 'cosmopolitan', glancing no doubt at Eliot the student of Irving Babbitt and proponent of 'the mind of Europe'. In practice the distinction doesn't work. One only has to think of what Lawrence himself learnt from, say, Verga or Dostoievsky to see this. Of course, Leavis was not against reading foreign literature, whether in translation or in the original, but he was in no doubt that it was in reading in one's own language that literature had its full meaning. Such reading may also be a discovery but the crux of it lies in a kind of consolidation of what, as a speaker of the language, one already knows:

Individual human beings *can* meet in a meaning because language – or let us rather say *a* language, meaning the English language (for there is no such thing as language in general) – is for them in any present a living actuality that is organically one with the 'human world' they, in growing up into it, have naturally taken for granted. There is in the language a central core in which for generations individual speakers have met, so that the meeting takes place as something inevitable and immediate in relation to which it would seem gratuitous to think of 'meeting' as being involved in meaning, or of conventions at all.[35]

There is a tincture of exclusiveness in this fine – and humane – passage. The 'central core' of the language, which Leavis hoped to recover and reinstate in the Classics-dominated institution of the university, surely acquires much of its meaning from outside England itself. If there is 'no such thing as language in general' neither is there such a thing as an 'English language' that is sealed off from the other languages that have helped to shape it. The model of the language as a sort of wholly indigenous community becomes as much a means of defence against other languages and literatures as a place in which to meet. Of course, Leavis is speaking positively rather than judiciously and I am not suggesting that he was ignorant of etymology. Nevertheless, the passage does help to suggest why he could never, either as writer or teacher, give a satisfactory account of the relation of 'English' to other languages and disciplines. This is not to accuse him of insularity – he understood the importance of Arnold's and Eliot's idea of 'culture' as well as the next man – but of trying to make the words 'England' and 'English' do more than they really could. This was perhaps because he felt a need to insist on something which, in the age of Northcliffe, was in danger of being forgotten. Looking back, one can hardly say that he was simply wrong.

But for all its betrayingly Olympian perspective Eliot's European 'humanism' could not be resisted without paying a price. The Classics themselves were never really an alternative to 'English', even if the Classicists themselves perhaps were. To confuse the two was fatal. When, back in the nineteenth century, R. L. Nettleship had pleaded, 'For heaven's sake don't let us murder Shakespeare, etc., by treating them as we treat Aeschylus and Sophocles' he was implicitly asking for a new kind of Classics as well as for the study of 'English'.[36] John Churton Collins, another early advocate for the subject, had argued that the two subjects should be taught in conjunction with each other. There is a residue of this belief in *Education and the University* (Leavis assumes that the student of 'English' will have a thorough grounding in the Classics) but also an insistence that 'English' should be the 'humane centre' around which work in the humanities should turn. (If Arnold proposed a 'centre' it was Homer.) Clearly, a student would need to know more than just 'English Literature' to be able to understand *Venus and Adonis* or *Lycidas* or *The Rape of the Lock*. Leavis himself had had a particularly good classical education at the Perse and, even in old age, made a regular habit of reading his Virgil. Nonetheless, he always drew a sharp distinction between English English and Latinate English and it is difficult to read him without coming away with the impression that, say, Bunyan is a more authentically English writer than Milton. The English poets he has most reservations about – Spenser, Milton, Tennyson – were all especially receptive to foreign influences. It may be hard for us to understand this today, when as often as not the Classics are taught in translation, but perhaps, at the same time, Leavis's embattled defensiveness on behalf of 'English' was inevitable. Moreover, England had seldom been so open to European influences as it was when *Scrutiny* was founded, in the heyday of Eliot's *Criterion*. For 'English' was born as much out of a sense that England as it had been was breaking up as from any sense of it as a living presence. The language mattered so much precisely because it was under threat. Since then, things have changed and they have not changed. 'English' now implies an increasingly mechanical professionalism and a corresponding loss of its early sense of having a mission. But we still lack any clear, coherent sense of what 'English' and 'English Literature' actually are. Perhaps the name itself is to blame? At all events, the successes and failures of Leavis and *Scrutiny* can still help us to understand our predicament.[37]

NOTES

(Place of publication is London unless otherwise stated)

1 *The Principles of Literary Criticism* (Routledge and Kegan Paul, 1960), e.g. p. 184.
2 *The English Vision*, ed. Herbert Read (Eyre and Spottiswood, 1933), p. v.
3 *Ibid.*, p. ix.
4 *Ibid.*, p. ix.
5 *Ibid.*, p. vii.
6 *The Preachers of Culture: A Study of English and its Teachers* (George Allen and Unwin, 1975), p. 209. Considerable support for this thesis can be found in Peter Burke's *Popular Culture in Early Modern Europe* (Temple Smith, 1979).
7 *Education and the University: A Sketch for an 'English School'* (Cambridge University Press, 1979), p. 56.
8 *English Literature in Our Time and the University* (Chatto and Windus, 1969), p. 119.
9 *Notes Towards the Definition of Culture* (Faber, 1962), p. 50.
10 *Ibid.*, p. 52.
11 *Ibid.*, p. 53.
12 *The Complete Poems and Plays of T. S. Eliot* (Faber, 1969), pp. 177–8.
13 *Ibid.*, p. 182.
14 *Ibid.*, p. 197.
15 *The Living Principle: 'English' as a Discipline of Thought* (Chatto and Windus, 1975) p. 194.
16 *Ibid.*, p. 195.
17 *Ibid.*, pp. 195–7.
18 *Politics and Letters: Interviews with New Left Review* (New Left Books, 1979), p. 68.
19 *Living Principle*, p. 198.
20 *Ibid.*, p. 195.
21 *Complete Poems and Plays*, p. 192.
22 *Ibid.*, pp. 195–6.
23 *Modern English Poetry from Hardy to Hughes* (Batsford, 1986), pp. 148–9.
24 *Ibid.*, p. 149.
25 See his 'Wounded Surgeons', *The Cambridge Quarterly*, vol. 11, no. 1 (n.d.), 189–223. (One of the most challenging things ever written on the enterprise of 'English'.)
26 *Complete Poems and Plays*, pp. 197–8.
27 Catherine Belsey, in *Re-reading English: Essays on Literature and Criticism in Higher Education*, ed. Peter Widdowson (Methuen, 1982), p. 75.
28 *Writing in Society* (Verso, n. d.), p. 197.
29 *The Social Mission of English Criticism* (Clarendon Press, Oxford, 1985), p. 234.

30 *The Moment of 'Scrutiny'* (Verso, 1981), p. 330.

31 J. S. Mill, *On Bentham and Coleridge*, ed. with intro. by F. R. Leavis (Cambridge University Press, 1950). (A crucial book in Leavis's development.)

32 Some of the basic facts can be found in Ronald Hayman's *Leavis* (Heinemann, 1976). A good general discussion of Leavis can be found in Michael Bell's *F. R. Leavis* (Routledge, 1988).

33 'A Voice in the Desert', *Times Literary Supplement*, 1 October (1976), 1233. (A trenchant review of *Thought, Words and Creativity*.)

34 *Living Principle*, p. 55.

35 *The Common Pursuit* (Penguin, Harmondsworth, 1962), p. 71.

36 Quoted in D. J. Palmer, *The Rise of English Studies* (Oxford University Press, for the University of Hull, 1965), p. 83.

37 For a lively (if partial) account of the history of 'English' see Brian Doyle, *English and Englishness* (Routledge, 1989).

CHAPTER 6

Englands within England: Waugh and Orwell

The 'thirties' is the age not of the thatched cottage but of the Shell Guide and the Greenline bus. For the first time, writers see the country as truly contemporary rather than timeless. Orwell's *Coming Up for Air* comes to mind, though it was a close contemporary of John Cowper Powys's *A Glastonbury Romance* which mythologises England all over again, as if Drayton had never gone out of fashion.

Such juxtapositions are to the point – nothing puts one off 'the Thirties' more than the notion of them as a 'decade' in which writers merged in monolithic orthodoxy. If there was any representatively 'thirties' view of England, it was surely the upshot of coexistent but contradictory Englands. After all, people had believed no less in Edwardian England because Kipling and Elgar and Edward Thomas had each imagined it differently. One expects an imperial nation to be multifarious. In fact, what the different available versions of England had in common was probably their underlying sense of loss and fragmentation, the modern fear that 'the centre cannot hold': the very breaking down of national identity turns out to be itself a kind of cultural cement. If we substitute other names for the cliché ones evoked by such phrases as 'The Age of Auden' – Lewis Grassic Gibbon, say, or Leavis or the Powys brothers – the age will seem to undermine its own stereotypes. Can we fit Priestley and Empson and the young David Gascoyne together, save with the distortions of literary history?

This chapter will be representative enough if it is not *too* representative. How to effect this is a matter of choice. Mine is to concentrate on two quite dissimilar writers who both came to notice in the 'thirties': Waugh and Orwell. The first pinpointed a narrow and disappearing class and looked back through it to the past; the second scanned his present for clues to the future. Waugh begins from Dickens as filtered through Firbank; Orwell takes up the novel more or less where Gissing had left it and then crosses it with Swift and Bunyan. Thus, when they do seem to touch on a common sense of 'Englishness', this implies that their subject matter has been derived from the culture itself, not just from their own *parti pris*. If they did belong partly together, that was because they shared certain underlying preoccupations which went deeper than their conscious beliefs. An anxiety over what was becoming of England was one of the most important of these. This anxiety begins before the 'thirties' and extends much later. Thus, both Waugh and Orwell sought ways to build bridges: between the seemingly unbridgeable pre-war and post-war worlds. It is this that marks them off from Forster and Lawrence. For, despite numerous differences, such books as *Sword of Honour* and *Nineteen Eighty-Four* share the ambition of reflecting on the experience of the century as a whole. Even if their authors begin in an up-to-the-minute contemporary way – and *Decline and Fall* and *Down and Out in Paris and London* are nothing if not topical – they can be seen, with hindsight, to pursue their particular material to more general ends.

In Auden's most famous lyric the reader is invited to look on England from above:

> Look, stranger, on this island now
> The leaping light for your delight discovers,
> Stand stable here
> And silent be.[1]

England is strange despite our closeness to it. Whether it is also strange to the poet himself is left unclear – the words 'this island now' carry an opposite feeling of intimacy. The bird's eye view implies both detachment and the kind of overview that only familiarity can make possible. It is no wonder, then, that John Betjeman should have seized on this poem as a prologue to his famous television anthology of poems about England, reciting it over a heart-stopping aerial view of the white cliffs of Dover. But Betjeman gives the impression of carrying his England in his pocket, accessible and ready-made, whereas Auden is cooler and more circumspect about his. This distance at which his poem holds his emotion is the hallmark of a good deal of writing in the 'thirties'. Auden's detachment reminds one of the tone of the early Evelyn Waugh: exact, ironic and disabused. For both of them, England is changing too fast to be entirely familiar, less something given and Elgarian than 'a cooling star / With half its history done.'[2] In a similar way, neither Waugh nor his heroes quite belong to the world his novels describe. The retreat offered by Catholicism in the later books is a desideratum from the start. Indeed, in the earlier books, we frequently feel like zoologists being conducted around a particularly eccentric menagerie. Fellow-feeling is something Waugh appeals to only sparingly and in a two-edged way; the infectious laughter feels cold and, sometimes, cruel. It is not, as in Dickens, convivial and conducive to a feeling of solidarity. If Paul Pennyfeather and Tony Last and William Boot were not funny they would seem frighteningly lonely.

Nothing, it seems, could be farther from Waugh's laughter than George Orwell's constant appeals to our common decency. In the world of Jock Grant-Menzies and Agatha Runcible, Orwell seems incorrigibly middle-class. Yet Orwell's very ordinariness, enshrined in his reassuring pseudonym, was, of course, partly assumed. Raised in the heart of patrician England, a scholarship boy among the upper classes, he needed to detach himself from his background as a matter of conscience. A book like *The Road to Wigan Pier* is about losing a class as well as discovering another. Its solidarity had to be based on a voluntary alienation (though in Wigan Orwell always had the accent of a gentleman). Like Waugh, he preferred to study society at one remove. Though their beliefs and allegiances could hardly have been more different, their strategy as novelists had something in common, as their common popularity attests. Underlying both Waugh's sprightliness and Orwell's dourness is the same detached stance of the anthropologist and the traveller. In a famous compliment to Orwell, V. S. Pritchett described him as 'a writer who has "gone native" in his own country'.[3] Waugh too was essentially a traveller through England, as in more exotic parts; for several years, after the break-up of his first marriage and before his second, from 1930 to 1936, he was continually on the move and had no fixed address. Like Auden's island, their England seems at the same time both 'home' and a kind of 'abroad' too. The 'real' England of a book like *A Clergyman's Daughter* – hop-picking in Kent, down and out in Trafalgar Square – comes with all the force of foreignness to the middle-class heroine. Similarly, there is no great difference between the way Waugh describes Africa in *Black Mischief* and *Scoop* and the way he describes Mayfair in *Vile Bodies*; in both cases, he depends on comic sleight of hand to make the improbably exaggerated seem believable. Both writers set out to explore England in the same spirit other explorers set out to navigate the upper Amazon. They never took it for granted. Neither did they rest content with 'Englishness'. Though the later Waugh's persona of a country squire, dressed in improbably loud checks, seems the antithesis of Orwell's, both men were equally mobile socially and both invented their own final class roles. In their persons, one kind of 'Englishness' consciously overlaid another and, in their novels, the crucial index of change is the supplanting of one class by another, that of Guy Crouchback by Trimmer or, conversely, the discovery by the genteel Dorothy (and Orwell himself) of what life is like for the destitute. In both cases, the movement is away from the middle class.

Waugh's great contribution to English writing was to see that England – long the preserve of the wistful and the elegiac – could also be comic. The tautness and sparkle of his early books leaves no room for nostalgia. His idle rich inhabit a vacuum of glitteringly hollow modernity, epitomised in Mrs Beste-Chetwynde, the cynosure of *Decline and Fall* and *Vile Bodies*. She it is who embroils Paul Pennyfeather in the white slave trade after his rustication from Oxford. In later books Waugh tended to romanticise this brittle society but in *Decline and Fall* its brittleness is everywhere apparent, yet never a pretext for moralising. Mrs Beste-Chetwynde's real symbol is not her landed estate (with adjacent parish church) but a cocktail, mixed by her precocious son Peter. Her world is relentlessly modern and Waugh – who has little enough feeling himself for traditional village England – shares in it with relish. When traditional values do appear in early Waugh it is usually to be mocked. Everyone wishes good riddance to the nineteenth century. Yet the later Waugh – who could be just as funny – cultivated an increasingly backward-looking stance as protection against the modern world. In some way, there must have been some nostalgia implicit in his early novels too. Otherwise, it would be impossible to trace the continuity from them to the later ones. The problem is to explain what linked the creator of Mrs Beste-Chetwynde to the Waugh who lamented the passing of the obsolete but beautiful world of Brideshead Castle.

In *Decline and Fall* there is a long description of Mrs Beste-Chetwynde's country seat, King's Thursday. It is half-timbered, Elizabethan and hopelessly old-fashioned:

very little was known about Margot Beste-Chetwynde in Hampshire, and
the illustrated papers were always pleased to take any occasion to embellish
their pages with her latest portrait; the reporter to whom she remarked, 'I
can't think of anything more bourgeois and awful than timbered Tudor
architecture,' did not take in what she meant or include the statement in his
'story'...

'It's worse than I thought, far worse,' she said as she drove up the main
avenue which the loyal villagers had decorated with the flags of sometime
allied nations in honour of her arrival. 'Liberty's new building cannot be
compared with it,' she said, and stirred impatiently in the car, as she
remembered, how many years ago, the romantic young heiress who had
walked entranced among the cut yews, and had been wooed, how
phlegmatically, in the odour of honeysuckle.[4]

Faced with such a dinosaur she calls in Otto Silenus, a modernist
German architect whose only completed work is 'the décor for a
cinema-film of great length' (p. 119), and gets him to turn the house
into a 'surprising creation of ferro-concrete and aluminium' (p. 120).
The slick splendour of the new King's Thursday may be a travesty of
Bauhaus architecture but it is not Waugh's point to compare it
unfavourably with the torpid traditional house it replaces. That is
equally absurd itself in the twentieth century. There is no hint of the
Pugin-like 'contrast' one might have expected from John Betjeman.
The deracinated Mrs Beste-Chetwynde is no more ridiculous than
the rural gentry of the county who try to save King's Thursday but
are 'blazing away electricity' in their own homes. Between such a
past and such a present, the traditional countryside depicted by a
writer like Jefferies might never have existed. Metropolitan values
have invaded the 'heart of England'. Rural England, mere food for
comedy, hardly seems worth preserving.

Vile Bodies (1930), centered in London, tells a similar tale and *Black
Mischief* (1932) translates Mayfair, in the person of Basil Seal, to
Africa. Throughout these novels, a cold laughter at revered English
institutions sets the tone. Nothing national is sacred, least of all a
scapegrace Englishman abroad like Basil (the forbear of so many
others in Amis, Lodge and Bradbury). There is a strong vein of
anarchism in the comedy. As early as his Lancing diary Waugh had
expressed his distaste for the patriotism of the war generation. This,
for instance, was his comment on the first Armistice Day ceremony in
1919:

At 11 am today we had the King's amazing proposition of two minutes
silence to commemorate last year. It was really a disgusting idea of artificial

nonsense and sentimentality. If people have lost sons and fathers they should think of them whenever the grass is green or Shaftesbury Avenue brightly lighted, not for two minutes on the anniversary of a disgraceful day of national hysteria. No one thought of the dead last year, why should they now?[5]

This is the voice of youth with a vengeance. It is a far-cry from the old-world Guy Crouchback in *Sword of Honour*, so anxious to impute moral meaning to a later war. In the early novels England has none of the aura of mystery Waugh gave it later, nothing of the ineffable distinction of Howards End. All that could be either forgotten or debunked.

Some readers see these brilliant early books as superficial but could anything so crisply written be *merely* superficial? Perhaps they were a necessary reaction against an old and weary civilisation (not unlike the brasher reaction of the Italian Futurists)? This is not to deny that Waugh's tone is often cold – chilly and over-precise when dealing with warm feelings or sexual emotion. Instead of warmth Waugh offers a comic elation, often near to violence. No one else comes half as near the manic comedy of early Dickens. The unremitting sequence of partying and over-drinking of the *Diaries* sounds both excited and frigid. Like Betjeman, the middle-class Waugh could never have enough of the upper-class set he got into at Oxford. Nevertheless, I myself prefer a novel like *Party Going* (1939), by Waugh's friend Henry Green, to *Vile Bodies*. Green's bright young things have a subtle penumbra of poetry to them. They are human enough to be touched by mortality – from the apparition of a dead pigeon on the very first page; also Green is not seduced by the pleasures of contempt as Waugh was. To set Green's book beside early Waugh is therefore to question whether the brilliant detachment from which Waugh saw his world was not too easily won. One should add, though, that Waugh might have conceded this, being a great admirer of Green himself.[6]

The plight of Tony Last in *A Handful of Dust* (1934) is another matter. The comedy there is less elated and, as well as the familiar baleful Waugh eye, the novel has a special dry pathos. It's subject is, of course, close to Waugh's divorce from his first wife, the most painful and probably the most decisive event of his life. It is from this time that he begins to think of England in before and after, past or present terms – as Tony's comically ominous name suggests. Nicely poised between the early high spirits and the mood of *Brideshead*

Revisited (1945), *A Handful of Dust* is for many readers his finest novel. It begins with Tony's Gothic mansion Hetton – a sort of Victorian King's Thursday – which is eating up all his patrimony, and it reaches its crisis with the death of little John, his heir, in a hunting accident. Waugh has none of Betjeman's fondness for Victoriana and it is a moot point whether the picture of an England swathed and stifled in its Victorian past is funny or sad. When Tony calls Hetton 'a definite part of English life' even he realises that he sounds pompous.[7] Waugh himself prefers to have fun with the house's dilapidated bedrooms. The vapid John Beaver, for instance, who becomes Brenda Last's lover, is put in 'Galahad' because 'no one who sleeps there ever comes again' (p. 25). There is, of course, a traditional village with a home farm at Hetton but they are farcical versions of the real thing and never ring quite true. The parson, for example, is a former army chaplain who is still recycling the sermons he preached to the troops in India: at Christmas he commiserates with the villagers for 'the harsh glare of an alien sun' (p. 60). Hetton is no 'organic community' and the past it represents seems played out. Tony, 'the old boy', is a stick-in-the-mud and when Brenda leaves him for London and Beaver she knows only too well that her lover is 'second-rate and a snob ... as cold as a fish' (p. 51). Hetton bores her. Why not divert the money meant for improvements to it to renting a flat in Mayfair? When her son dies during the fox-hunt, the accident is caused by a motorbike which frightens one of the horses. Hetton has no immunity from the modern world. Jock Grant-Menzies goes off to break the news to Brenda in an aeroplane belonging to a rich, vulgar American woman he has in tow. Whether this is less appropriate to the occasion than the Master of the Hunt offering to play 'Gone to Ground' at the funeral is a moot point. In this England, nothing quite fits the image it ought to have. This is one reason why our emotions never have free sway, despite the subject-matter. Instead of the overblown regret of *Brideshead Revisited*, Waugh deliberately refuses to let the tears flow, as in the chilling scene where Brenda imagines that it is John Beaver who is dead and then realises with relief that it is only her son. Pathos hardens into comedy as Tony plays Animal Snap with Mrs Rattery on the night of John's death. Inevitably, he is forced to sell Hetton to pay for his divorce: 'A whole Gothic world had come to grief ... there was now no armour glittering through the forest glades, no embroidered feet on the green sward; the cream and dappled unicorns had fled ... ' (p. 151). Tony's lament for the lost past recalls Ryder's last visit to Brideshead, save that Waugh obviously doubts whether there had *ever* been armour or unicorns at Hetton. Even if we sympathise with his loss we remain unsure how much value to put on the England he wants to preserve. There is certainly no question of embalming it like Brideshead. Tony himself becomes an 'explorer', in search of a 'city' in the Brazilian jungle, a 'transfigured Hetton' (p. 161). Waugh switches dryly back to the mode of *Black Mischief* when pathos looms. In the end, Tony is overcome by fever and the trauma of his divorce and loss of Hetton become part of his hallucinations: 'I will tell you what I have learned in the forest, where time is different. There is no City. Mrs Beaver has covered it with chromium plating and converted it into flats. Three guineas a week, each with a separate bathroom. Very suitable for base love' (p. 207). This scene reflects the interest Waugh showed in *Ulysses*, particularly in 'Nighttown'. Derision turns out to be truth. Tony's final torture, at the hands of Mr Todd, condemns him to read and re-read Dickens aloud forever, evoking that nineteenth-century world that he knows has gone for good. The ending, funny as it is, is an instance of Waugh's violence towards his characters. There is no final illumination for Tony. Watching a native dance, 'he shut his eyes and thought of England and Hetton and fell asleep' (p. 215). The old order fades in savage farce and the novelist, alternating between self-repression and exhilarating self-release, keeps emotion at bay once more. His brilliant oscillation between bitterness and satiric joy leaves one unsure how far Waugh had opened himself to the tragedy he has no qualms in inflicting on Tony Last. Self-exposure, however, was not on the early Waugh's agenda at all.

Even after the sombre comedy of *A Handful of Dust*, Waugh could seldom resist an opportunity to cock a snook at traditional English life. Both *Scoop* (1938) and *Put Out More Flags* (1942) do so with gusto. *Scoop* is like a triptych, a sandwich with parodied Beaverbrook journalism and African politics laid between two slices of parodied English rural life. Ostensibly, it contrasts the serenity of the country with the primitive world of African politics but the two turn out to be less different than at first appears. Civilisation, whether at Boot Magna or Mayfair, actually rests on none of the roots it claims to. The Boot family has little more connection with the land than Mrs Beste-Chetwynde did. Their world is merely a distortion of the modern one, as William Boot's spectacular success for the *Daily Beast* indicates, just as, beneath the glittering surface of *Vile Bodies*, lies not so much a spurned English tradition as the pit itself. In other words, Waugh's England is the opposite of Howards End, with its special brand of conservative liberalism. In *Scoop*, there is no Margaret Schlegel to transmit the culture of the past and no old retainer like Miss Avery to tend it – just a gang of ludicrous servants and bed-ridden nannies. William himself is a parody of the rural Englishman. He pays for his country life by writing a weekly column in *The Beast*: 'LUSH PLACES, edited by William Boot, Countryman.'[8] A debased descendant of Thomas's *Roseacre Papers*. Waugh associates rural England with naiveté: outside Boot Magna, William is in 'a foreign and hostile world' (p. 24). In darkest Africa he cries out, like any Georgian poet: 'am I still to be an exile from the green places of my heart?' (p. 166). Such a man is not a representative of an older way of life, as he might be in Forster, so much as one of the damaged halves into which the English soul has been fragmented. Another is Mr Salter of Welwyn Garden City, the luckless foreign editor of *The Beast*, to whom 'the country' is 'what you saw in the train between Liverpool Street and Frinton' (p. 26). At the end of the novel, Salter goes to Boot Magna to entice Boot back to *The Beast*. His journey from the station is more traumatic than Boot's progress through Africa. Trudging over ploughed fields and through hedges in the dark he feels 'like a Roman legionary, heavily armed, weighted with the steel and cast brass of civilisation, tramping through forests beyond the Roman pale, harassed by silent, elusive savages...' (p. 210). If the metropolis gets its comeuppance here the country turns out to be equally barbarous. The only moral to draw from this divided England is that the torpid countryside will probably last the longest. *Scoop* ends where it began, with Boot composing the next LUSH PLACES: 'maternal rodents pilot their furry brood through the stubble...' (p. 222).

Waugh's last purely comic novel was *Put Out More Flags*, a slight but sprightly satire on the 'phoney war', in which the author already felt himself to be dealing with 'a race of ghosts'.[9] It marks the re-appearance of the appalling Basil Seal, of whom his brother-in-law says, 'You can't blame Ribbentrop for thinking us decadent when he saw people like Basil about' (p. 16) but whose sister sees him as a cross between T. E. Lawrence and Rupert Brooke. Basil is well calculated for the comic catharsis the early books rise to so effortlessly. The flimsy plot hinges on his lucrative exploits as war-time billeting officer in finding rural homes for evacuee children, in particular the dreadful

Connolly family from Birmingham. 'The Connollys' are an arm of that modern world which is so feared in later Waugh. Basil sets out to place them in the typically 'English' homes of the retired and artistic middle-classes, homes not unlike Howards End. Once their owners realise how awful the children are, Basil charges to take them away. Making fun of their traditional taste, he marauds across this England of modest *rentiers* where 'the tribute of Empire flowed gently into the agricultural countryside' (p. 114). The novel is an infectious spoof of 1939–40 patriotism and also an ironic epitaph on the vanishing Mayfair of Basil Seal and the vanishing rural England of the victims. It gives a foretaste of the changing England of *Brideshead Revisited*, though its mood is not upholstered with that novel's resonant feeling of *Et in Arcadia ego*. In *Put Out More Flags*, the middle classes' fear of the masses is not dressed up at all. No doubt the laughter is rather cold, even spiteful, but it is also clean and frank and it makes *Brideshead Revisited* seem a bit soggy in the middle. I think *Put Out More Flags* will be readable when *Brideshead* seems stale and decadent, although there is a much headier emotion in *Brideshead*. Waugh came too late in the day to imagine England as he would have liked it to be. It was more vivid to him in grotesques like King's Thursday, Hetton and Boot Magna than in the desecrated and echoing shell of Brideshead Castle.

In *Brideshead Revisited* an overblown nostalgia takes over. It is a feeling quite foreign to the young Waugh but, even though it is chastened in the *Sword of Honour* trilogy, it conditions the way he came to think of England after the war. This means re-writing the England of the 'thirties'. In *Brideshead* the feckless Oxford of Paul Pennyfeather becomes 'irrecoverable as Lyonesse'.[10] It is used as a foil to the bleak period of 'soya beans and basic English' (p. 7). In retrospect, a shallow world seems sumptuous, even though Waugh knows that he is writing a 'panegyric preached over an empty coffin' (p. 7). After *Scoop*, the mood of *Brideshead Revisited* feels languid, a tremulous lament for the 'august, masculine atmosphere of a better age' (p. 133). In the dreary, egalitarian world of Hooper and the pushy Rex Mottram the heedless, upper-class 'thirties' figure as a land of Cockayne; when the war ends, the Goths are at the gates. As in Lawrence, free individuals have to make room for the average man; by the end of the book, Marchmain House is converted into luxury flats for the likes of Rex, Brideshead is left desolate and 'Arcadia' has gone forever. The groundnote is regret: 'we possess

nothing certainly except the past' (pp. 215–16). Yet when Waugh
sounds this note he begs the real question. Do Ryder and Julia really
possess the past themselves? Was it worth possessing?

Brideshead Revisited is a conservative, not to say reactionary, novel
but that does not tell us what it is that Waugh would like to conserve
if he could. What is the past the book hallows? The Paterian prose
devoted to the Flytes and their houses is by no means clear about this.
In fact, Waugh might be accused of betraying the past himself, selling
it short by enshrining its spirit in characters who are too small to
represent more than bits of it. Whereas his modern characters are
indelibly actual, the Flytes shade into myth and romance. If they *are*
the past they are not the past of English history so much as an
alternative version of it, full of missals and priest-holes, a past *not*
responsible for having brought forth the present Waugh regrets so
much. The great recusant families were innocent of having a shaping
hand in the modern world. It is as if Waugh had opened up a trap-
door down which history could disappear and from which religion
could spring out. The thought of Brideshead is one Charles can
indulge in because its owners, however aristocratic, have never
clashed with the middle-class from which he comes himself. Their
distance from that world is a measure of their nearness to the next.
When the alcoholic Sebastian dies in North Africa we are asked to see
him as 'holy'. Even Lord Marchmain finally takes the last rites.
Waugh indulges in a convert's dream of an alternative England that
masquerades as England itself, an England 'the age of Hooper' is
about to blot out, a noble never-never land. *Brideshead Revisited* was a
great popular success for Waugh but, with hindsight, one wonders
whether this wasn't because its original readers had *never* known the
England it celebrates. Instead of finding continuity and change in the
England of 1945 Waugh preferred to see it as an historical watershed,
an either/or choice between civilisation and, if not barbarism,
democracy.

Fortunately, this is not the whole story. Waugh puts a saving *caveat*
into the mouth of Charles's affected, homosexual friend Anthony
Blanche, a star from their lost Oxford. Blanche visits Charles's latest
exhibition at the end of the book and pins it down in a formula which
could fit the novel as a whole: he finds his South American pictures
simply 'too English' (p. 259), too full of 'creamy English charm,
playing tigers'. 'Charm', he says, is 'the English blight' (p. 260). Just
so, 'charm' is the blight of *Brideshead Revisited* itself, from the first

entry of Sebastian clutching his teddy bear. This explains the book's success. Waugh can't resist this romantic still-born past that never was and clearly prefers it to real history. The reader's consolation is that he was too good a novelist, too aware of the real England he loathed, not to sow a doubt in our minds about everything Brideshead is meant to represent.

This knowledge is developed more subtly in *The Sword of Honour* trilogy (1952–61), mostly without the wistful hankering for bygone days. The Crouchbacks are also recusants but they have given up their ancestral home, Broome, to a convent and are diffidently trying to come to terms with the century they live in. They still see England 'divided neatly into two unequal and unmistakable parts'[11] and the last monarch they acknowledge is James II but this does not mean that they are a cue for nostalgia as the Flytes are. The trilogy is more comic in tone and if it is never uproarious like *Vile Bodies* or *Scoop* it has a frightening new interest in frankly irrational figures like Ritchie-Hook, Apthorpe and Ludovic. But Waugh now views such characters from a distance, through the sober eyes of the ageing Guy Crouchback – 'Uncle' to his comrades – who carries his sword quixotically through an unheroic war to a dubious peace, standing for precisely those values which England is discarding. Guy is 'a good loser – at any rate, an experienced one' (p. 168) but not a comic butt like the early heroes. The comedy is always giving way to a muted pathos. Guy is both of his time and *not* of it. He offers Waugh a vantage on the present and a possibility of refuge from it when, at the end of the trilogy, he inherits far more from his father than he had expected to and is able to marry the Catholic noblewoman who has cared for his child and to set up as a traditional country landowner himself. Though on its fringes, he has a bigger place in the post-war world than Waugh admits and one not unlike the novelist's own, ensconced by this time in the remote grandeur of his own country house.

Despite material success, Guy retains the futile distinction that to Waugh is the badge of the recusant. Like his unworldly Uncle Peregrine, he has an 'indefinable numbness' (p. 482) that sets him apart, a quality which, however inert, Waugh likes to equate with goodness itself. So, when Guy's father, Gervase, dies at Matchet the Brideshead nostalgia floods back and he pictures him as 'the best man, the only entirely good man, he had ever known'. Mr Crouchback possesses 'something rare in English armoury – a device that had been carried into battle' (p. 65), though it is not clear what battle he, as a retired landowner and prep school teacher, has been through. Matchet is simply a plangent counterpart to the tawdry England of Trimmer, the common soldier who, symbolically, fathers Guy's heir on his brash ex-wife Virginia. The old order yields its place to the new in more ironic ways than it does in *Brideshead Revisited* and the novel is more moving in consequence, closer to current realities. Waugh is more aware of where his comic strengths lie, in Trimmer and not in the Sebastian Flytes of this world. *Unconditional Surrender* is not an over-ripe apotheosis to the novel but a way of facing a post-war world which Waugh both fears and dislikes. Box-Bender loses his seat to a Socialist, Ludovic buys Castello Crouchback on the profits from his best-seller and Guy re-marries, to the kind of girl he should have married in the first place. There are no cloud-borne angels or holy sinners, no scent of incense. The England Waugh ends up in is funny but recognisable, inhospitable but familiar, and the transition from pre- to post-war is credible as it never is in *Brideshead Revisited*.

Whether Waugh managed to take all of himself across this divide may be questioned. He was perhaps most fully himself in his early books, before he tried to come to terms with the modern world or quite realised that it was not flowing in his direction. It may even be questioned whether his world could ever have been as comic, once there was a Labour government in England, as it was in the 'Thirties'. *Sword of Honour* is perhaps admired for qualities which are not unique to Waugh. Set beside *A Handful of Dust* it seems neither as spontaneous nor as original. Some Englands, one suspects, are 'irrecoverable'.

What strikes a later reader is how much both Waugh and Orwell, despite their differences, were still able to make England the centre of their world. They travelled widely but doing so never made them doubt this centrality. Auden, who was soon to give up England for America, doubts it all the time. In 'Dover', for instance, he imagines aeroplanes in 'the new European air':

> On the edge of a sky that makes England of minor importance;
> And tides warn bronzing bathers of a cooling star
>   With half its history done.

It is a moot point whether the Orwell who went to Spain ever breathed this air. He certainly had to leave one England but he did so in order to discover another, to confirm his own 'Englishness'.

This is probably what most people still read him for and it also explains the common ground he had with a political opposite like Waugh. Waugh, in fact, visited him several times when he was on his death-bed and each had a guarded respect for the other. Orwell described Waugh as 'about as good a novelist as one can be ... whilst holding untenable opinions.'[12] Such doubts did not stop them from sharing certain assumptions in common, for instance, a jaundiced view of the future. There is little to choose between George Bowling announcing in *Coming Up For Air* (1939) that 'the bad times are coming'[13] and Charles Ryder glumly noting the arrival of 'the age of Hooper'. Both writers assume that the twentieth century is inimicable to civilisation, even if their political premises differ. It is easy to forget that *Nineteen Eighty-Four* is in many ways simply an underlining of the gloomier predictions of *Brideshead Revisited*. Its speculations about the course of communism too easily distract us from Orwell's fears of what English democracy itself might become. Moreover, Waugh himself more than once wrote dystopian fictions of a lighter but similarly baleful sort to Orwell's (*Love Among the Ruins* and *Scott-King's Modern Europe*, for example). It is hard for us now to think of an Orwell who was not a socialist but Bernard Crick has amply shown that that name does not really apply to him before *The Road to Wigan Pier* (1937) and not fully until *Homage to Catalonia* in 1938. Before then he liked to see himself as a 'Tory Radical', like Swift, and that label would have fitted the satirical Waugh almost as well. When Gordon Comstock, in *Keep the Aspidistra Flying*, longs to escape from decency – 'down, deep down, into some world where decency no longer mattered'[14] – he comes nearer to Sebastian Flyte than meets the eye. Both writers found in practice that their love of England conflicted with their disgust for the particular middle-class England into which they had been born. Each needed to distance himself from the democratic average, even if Orwell did so only obliquely, by being an outspoken columnist in *Tribune* who had an unerring gift for rubbing his own side up the wrong way. (When he imagined an average man like Bowling he made sure to make him disillusioned with average modern life). This distance is what one would expect in an avowed conservative like Waugh but in a writer who aspires to speak for the people it is more problematic. The fact is that 'Englishness' and socialism do not make easy bed-fellows, though Orwell invested heavily in both. I think this is why, as well as wanting to get close to ordinary English life, he was always on his guard against it. In practice, he needed to make a distinction between English people and English society. He could not afford to give a free rein to the feelings that came most naturally to him as an Englishman though he certainly drew on them in everything he wrote. His England was as if refracted through his anthropologist's curiosity, a commitment that did not preclude neutrality when necessary. This was part of his strength since it enabled him to avoid the more facile and sentimental kinds of identification with the working class that many of his contemporaries went in for. In fact, it was precisely at the point where his socialism touched on his patriotism, in *The Lion and the Unicorn*, that Orwell gave most offence to his own side. Whoever first thought of him as a plain man surely underrated plainness.

Orwell has so often been seen as the epitome of English decency and common sense that it is all too easy to think of his kind of sense as simpler than it was. We have the added temptation of finding our own common sense enshrined in his. No doubt the English like to think that rugged individualism *is* their normal moral condition. The strangeness of Orwell's case only becomes apparent when one reflects that the virtues he is usually felt to embody are essentially middle-class ones – we associate them with the professed values of the class into which he was born and which he spent so much time distancing himself from. What I call 'decency and common sense' may distinguish the prose of his essays and journalism but the same qualities, in another guise, were the traditional virtues of colonial administrators like his own father or business-men like Forster's Henry Wilcox. Raymond Williams, who rightly sees the knowledge that came to Orwell through his Imperial background as a strength when it came to understanding his England, also points out that he needed to reject this 'ruling-class network' in order to discover a more 'ordinary England' for himself.[15] The problem is that 'decency and common sense' might be discovered in *both* Englands although the one England is culturally and economically opposed to the other. Are we to conclude that Orwell's magic trick was somehow to bridge this gap, rather as Kipling did from a contrary position when he managed to get his 'If' framed and displayed in so many ordinary homes? What exactly do we identify with if we think of Orwell as one of us and his kind of 'Englishness' as ours?

Orwell's early books usually set a middle-class character the task of trying to understand the lives of those lower down the social ladder: in *Burmese Days*, Flory has to come to terms with the consequences of

Imperialism; Dorothy, in *A Clergyman's Daughter*, is made to undergo life as a down-and-out; Gordon Comstock, the needy poet-hero of *Keep the Aspidistra Flying*, tries to opt out of the world of middle-class work and is forced to realise that 'in a country like England you can no more be cultured without money than you can join the Cavalry Club' (p. 8). In *The Road to Wigan Pier* these fictional journeys of discovery are re-told from real life. In other words, Orwell sets out to uncover what England actually is, underneath all the myths about it with which members of his class had grown up. When he went looking for England he did not know what he was going to find – any more than Dorothy or Comstock did. His England was, in many respects, a foreign country, less a 'home' than a *terra incognita*. After Burma, he worked from the premise that his received ideas about it were mostly a sort of camouflage. To identify with his England too easily is therefore to fall right into the trap that he managed to escape from, the notion that England is one thing and we all know what it is. As an old Etonian and former colonial civil servant, Orwell knew that any feeling of solidarity with 'ordinary' English life that he won through to was likely to come at the cost of a sense of dislocation from the class into which he had been born. To belong to one England meant exile from another. It was the kind of knowledge that he could have got from Lawrence, though Lawrence came at it from the opposite direction. It taught Orwell how relative his sense of nationality was, how conditioned by class, as well as how other people at other points in the class-system felt; he knew whose back he was standing on. As he put it, in *The Road to Wigan Pier*, with a rather shame-faced aggressiveness, 'You and I and the editor of the *Times Lit. Supp.*, and the Nancy poets and the Archbishop of Canterbury... really owe the comparative decency of our lives to poor drudges underground, blackened to the eyes, with their throats full of coal dust... '[16] All his life, Orwell disliked the sort of intellectual who preached revolution in ignorance of what this taste of coal dust was like. Notoriously, he described Auden as a 'gutless Kipling'[17] and argued that the 'amoralism' of a poem like 'Spain' was possible only 'if you are the kind of person who is always somewhere else when the trigger is pulled'.[18] This does not mean that he presumed to identify with miners and their like but that he wished to *affiliate* himself with them. If, when he spoke of 'England' in later years, it was often of their England that he spoke, he did not disguise the fact that understanding it had required much conscious effort on his part. This is one reason why one distrusts readers who lay claim to intuitive fellow-feeling with his own 'Englishness'.

Most imaginary Englands are pleasurable, more so than the real thing. Thus, Orwell himself noted that the spirit of *A Shropshire Lad* (which, as a boy, he had known by heart) was 'not tragic, merely querulous; it is hedonism disappointed'.[19] For most writers on the subject, the thought of England is a cue for self-indulgence. For Orwell, it was more likely to mean guilt and self-mortification. His own equivalent of the 'blue remembered hills' was the squalor of the tripe shop (though there was perhaps a kind of perverse pleasure to be had there too). *A Clergyman's Daughter*, for example, begins and ends with the heroine toiling late at night over a smelly gluepot, making costumes for the local school-children; in between, in her voyage into England, she is subjected to amnesia, a gruelling spell of hop-picking, a penniless night in Trafalgar Square with London's homeless and a period of unmitigated drudgery in a preternaturally awful private school. Orwell was not an admirer of Gissing for nothing and he clearly wanted things to be as painful as possible for Dorothy. So much so that it is hard to tell whether he appeals more to our compassion or to our sense of disgust. Take, for instance, these (visibly Joycean) sentences from the Trafalgar Square scene:

They pile themselves in a monstrous shapeless clot, men and women clinging indiscriminately together, like a bunch of toads at spawning time. There is a writhing moment as the heap settles down, and a sour stench of clothes diffuses itself. (Orwell's italics)[20]

There is clearly an element of almost sensual pleasure in misery like this; when Dorothy finally returns home, we probably feel disappointment rather than relief. Whereas hop-picking had offered her a new, if tarnished, sense of community with her fellow-sufferers, back at home she is merely stuck with her father for good, living *for* others but not *with* them. (There is the same contrast in *Nineteen Eighty-Four* between Winston's white-collar isolation and the Proles's togetherness.) Middle-class life negates communal feeling: the only true kind of 'Englishness' is the communal one. The problem for the Orwellian character is that, to attain it, it is necessary to opt out of the only social group to which he or she has any sense of belonging.

Most obviously, Gordon Comstock longs to reject his heritage of minor public school and genteel poverty:

But now it was precisely from decency that he wanted to escape. He wanted to go down, deep down, into some world where decency no longer mattered; to cut the strings of his self respect, to submerge himself – to *sink* ... He liked to think that beneath the world of money there is that great sluttish underworld where failure and success have no meaning; a sort of kingdom of ghosts where all are equal. (*Aspidistra*, p. 227)

It is not uncommon in the English novel for social disquiet to be taken out on a character's self rather than on society. The most conspicuous example is Hardy's Jude. Comstock's attitude has a powerful negative charge but he is vague about anything better than the 'decency' he rejects. When, at the end of the novel, he throws the manuscript of his poem down a drain ('*Poetry*, indeed! In 1935.' p. 268), having concluded that culture and civilisation are incompatible, it never occurs to him that poetry *might* be possible outside civilisation and without a private income. This is where Orwell differs from Lawrence. He leaves Comstock staring down opposite dead-ends. Dorothy too moves from one despair to another, as if to hammer home the point that what characterises our ordinary world is that we have to resign ourselves to it. (The fact that we have to lump it may be what makes us find a kind of attraction in it). Reading these grim – not to say masochistic – novels it can be hard to remember that it was precisely through the kind of disillusion and deprivation they depict that Orwell himself somehow became the bluff, fearless spokesman for England of popular legend. To him, patriotism came as a revelation inter-mixed with penance and even shame. It is difficult to say whether he believed in England because of England or in spite of it. Reviewing a book by his friend Malcolm Muggeridge he wrote:

It is all very well to be 'advanced' or 'enlightened', to snigger at Colonel Blimp and proclaim your emancipation from all traditional loyalties, but a time comes when the sand of the desert is sodden red and what have I done for thee, England, my England? As I was brought up in this tradition myself I can recognise it under strange disguises, and also sympathise with it, for even at its stupidest and most sentimental it is a comelier thing than the shallow self-righteousness of the left-wing intelligentsia.[21]

Such a passage should not be set down as Little Englandism. For Orwell, it refers to a larger world that he found through England, not a smaller one. It is the 'intelligentsia' which, for all its inter-nationalism, inhabits a select clique. All this, however, would not have been much compensation to Gordon Comstock. The best he can get out of England is to throw in the sponge, return to work at the advertising agency and settle down with Rosemary in suburbia with an aspidistra in the living room. One might say that characters like Gordon and Dorothy help Orwell to discover England as it really is but, in a sense, he does so at their expense. They are scapegoats and guinea pigs who are rarely permitted to share in the insights which they enable him to make. We may, for instance, take some relish from the companionship of the hop-pickers but what Dorothy is most conscious of in her time with them is back-ache. Once again, one is reminded of Hardy – all those characters who are the blind victims of a fate which the author can see coming.

To take this view is not to suggest that Orwell was a sadist to his characters (or a masochist to himself) but that he had to cut through great swathes of sentimentality in order to get to what he wanted to say about England. He makes this especially clear in *Coming Up For Air* (1939), a novel which differs from the others in having a hero who is less of a victim and in which Orwell has more complex things to do than constantly rub the reader's face in the grimness of the world as it is. George Bowling, fat and fortyish, an *homme moyen sensuel* reminiscent of Leopold Bloom, wants to escape from the monotony of suburban life and decides to return, without his wife's knowing it, to the small town of his childhood to see what it has become. (The town, Binfield, was based on Orwell's own early memories of Henley-on-Thames). Bowling's consequent feelings of loss, of the pastness of the past, are predictable and familiar; what makes *Coming Up For Air* unusual is that Orwell is able to explore his nostalgia both with ironic comedy *and* understanding. What Bowling experiences is neither sentimentalised nor underrated. He begins by realising what Dorothy's father, the Rector, had seen, that 'to live in the past is very expensive; you can't do it on less than two thousand a year' (p. 19). This connection between nostalgia and money, which drives a wedge between the English and England, had been evaded by the writers of Orwell's youth. For him, it is crucial because it brings home the fact that cultural nostalgia is out of the question for all but a small minority: however 'English' rural England may seem, it can only be English in a narrow sense, because it is really only a part of England which has been passed off as the whole, 'a leftover, a tiny corner that the bombs happen to have missed' (p. 160). This England, which Binfield seems at first to embody, is invariably the cue for a veiled conservatism. As Orwell noted in *The Road to Wigan Pier*, to a socialist 'all sentiment for the past carries with it a vague smell of heresy' (p. 177). In practice, however, he was as sceptical about the radical's future as he was about the conservative's past. This meant that what he took to be the real England was in danger of being squeezed from both ends. Bowling may be too wry about himself to fall into yet another lament for better times but he does end up deploring the drabness of democratic England in accents surprisingly reminiscent of *Howards End* or, for that matter, John Betjeman: 'And the newness of everything! The raw, mean look! Do you know the look of these new towns that have suddenly swelled up like balloons in the last few years, Hayes, Slough, Dagenham, and so forth? The kind of chilliness, the bright red brick everywhere...' (*Coming Up For Air*, p. 180). What has happened to Binfield is a disaster. The thought that this new mass-produced housing might make up for what was so lacking in Wigan never arises. But for all this, Orwell rules out any attempt to return to the past. That is what Bowling's cultured friend Porteous tries to do and he is merely a sort of well-mannered dinosaur. Bowling himself realises that it is he, not the new Binfield, that is out of joint: 'Christ! I thought, I was wrong to think that I was seeing ghosts. I'm the ghost myself. I'm dead and they're alive' (p. 196). Even so, he still finds it impossible to think of this new world as English. Visiting the 'Pixy Glen', on the site of the pool in which he used to fish as a boy, his nostalgia gives way to anger: 'doesn't it make you puke sometimes to see what they're doing to England, with their bird-baths and their plaster gnomes, and their pixies and tin cans, where the beechwoods used to be?' (p. 215). Any more authentic traditional England would, of course, be too 'expensive', a jewel behind the shop-window of its 'heritage'. Bowling's problem is that, once again, the middle-classes have taken over England and equated its culture with their own when he, like it or not, is middle-class himself. The world that repels him has clearly been built for the likes of George Bowling. For Orwell, part of being and feeling English is to be tied in precisely that sort of knot. Neither is it by chance that Bowling's mixed feelings of sorrow and anger should put one in mind of a writer as unlike Orwell as Waugh. The kind of England each rejects and fears is essentially similar. In each of them, the disgust of the satirist is hard to unravel from the loyalism of the conservative. There are still important differences between them, of course – Waugh did not have the kind of humour which would have allowed him to project his own feelings of nostalgia into someone as plebeian as Bowling – but, for both of them, the best way to define 'Englishness' was by saying what it wasn't.

To a socialist of Sturt's generation it was plainly not the cottage-dwellers themselves who wanted to preserve the picturesque way of life of village England. If he mourned the loss of the traditional crafts he still hoped that the new democratic order would offer a richer life to the craftsmen. Orwell, for all his sympathy for the working classes, was notably less confident. He feared that any social levelling down was as likely to result in cultural decline as in political improvements. He is as likely to imagine a future in which the middle-classes become working-class as one, like Sturt's, in which the workers begin to share in the culture of their 'betters'. Hence, the curiously bleak optimism of the final sentences of *The Road to Wigan Pier*: 'And then perhaps this misery of class prejudice will fade away, and we of the sinking middle-class ... may sink without further struggles into the working class where we belong, and probably when we get there it will not be so dreadful as we feared, for, after all, we have nothing to lose but our aitches' (p. 204).

This sounds more like self-chastisement than a democratic new dawn. It would be difficult to imagine anyone without 'aitches' putting it quite like this. One wonders what benefit the working-class itself is likely to derive from having the middle-class 'sink' into it. Orwell seems to have felt that the attaining of a true sense of one's 'Englishness' had to be some sort of purgatorial experience. On the last page of *Homage to Catalonia*, when he is back in England, he looks at its orderly comforts – 'the milk will be on the doorstep tomorrow morning, the *New Statesman* will come out on Friday' – and almost resents them:

Down here it was still the England I had known in my childhood: the railway-cuttings smothered in wild flowers, the deep meadows where the great shining horses browse and meditate, the slow-moving streams bordered by willows, the green bosoms of the elms, the larkspurs in the cottage gardens; and then the huge peaceful wilderness of outer London, the barges on the miry river, the familiar streets, the posters telling of cricket matches and Royal weddings, the men in bowler hats, the pigeons in Trafalgar Square, the red buses, the blue policemen – all sleeping the deep, deep sleep of England, from which I sometimes fear that we shall never wake till we are jerked out of it by the roar of bombs.[22]

These things could still stand for many people's England and they evoke a rare excursion into poetry from Orwell. Nonetheless, they represent the ideal England that George Bowling has to exorcise from his thoughts, the England that most of his class was (and is?) dependent on like a baby's bottle. But, as the genuinely strong emotion of the passage suggests, Orwell does not mock it, even if he thinks it too attractive to be real. For if it seems a mere dream after the rigours of Barcelona it also serves to commemorate his sense of home-coming. This oscillation between scepticism and attachment, each qualifying the other, was characteristic of Orwell's relation to his country. At one moment he will berate English 'intellectuals' for being 'ashamed of their own nationality' (*Lion and the Unicorn*, p. 64) and, at another, in *The Road to Wigan Pier*, we find him insisting on the shamefulness of what the English have made of England. Contradiction was his stock-in-trade. One of his main claims to be thought of as a patriot must be his vigorous debunking of most of the accepted forms of patriotism available in his time. He was usually ready with one of his hardest punches for anyone who made large claims to love their country. In 'Notes on Nationalism' (1945), he attacks the 'common figure' of 'the anglophobe who suddenly becomes violently pro-British' (Muggeridge, Waugh, Kingsmill and T. S. Eliot are all mentioned).[23] What such 'neo-Tories' have in common is that they want to think of England as in some way perfect. For Orwell, however, the ideal object is always a blemished one. What he loved in England was its very imperfection, the fact that it was real with the reality of imperfect things. He wanted to remove the pedestal from under the monument. As vivid an image for what this revealed as any he ever described was the traditional figure of the 'hanging judge':

Even hypocrisy is a powerful safeguard. The hanging judge, that evil old man in scarlet robe and horse-hair wig, whom nothing short of dynamite will ever teach what century he is living in, but who will at any rate interpret the law according to the books and will in no circumstances take a money bribe, is one of the symbolic figures of England. He is a symbol of the strange mixture of reality and illusion, democracy and privilege, humbug and decency, the subtle network of compromises, by which the nation keeps itself in its familiar shape. (*Lion and Unicorn*, p. 46)

The strength of this fine passage is that it does not confuse patriotic feeling with moral approval or put us under any pressure to admire what habit has made us tolerate. England is redeemed by its weaknesses and by the fact that it is possible to be rude about them without being whipped. Orwell's own unflagging frankness in his 'As I Please' column in *Tribune* was not unlike that of a licensed fool. He could only express his positive feelings if he could give his negative ones free rein too.

It is easy, with hindsight, to link the growing sense of solidarity with England in Orwell's writing with the infectious example of the nation's common war effort. He himself was by no means unresponsive to this spirit. Yet the struggle advocated in *The Lion and the Unicorn* is not a military one, even though it had a military context in 1941:

The heirs of Nelson and of Cromwell are not in the House of Lords. They are in the fields and the streets, in the factories and the armed forces, in the four-ale bar and the suburban back garden; and at present they are still kept under by a generation of ghosts. Compared with the task of bringing the real England to the surface, even the winning of the war, necessary though it is, is secondary. (pp. 122–3)

The 'real England' is private, not public and institutionalised. It is not something known and given, like the England to which Churchill's rhetoric appealed, but something in a state of becoming. On the last page of his book, Orwell writes, 'Nothing ever stands still' (p. 123). It is a less obvious point than it might seem. Standing still is, more often than not, just what most imaginary Englands are designed to do. Orwell's can still be won or lost.

This helps to explain why he prefers to think of 'Englishness' as something instinctive and unconscious of itself rather than as a conscious attitude. He is at pains to distinguish it both from official propaganda and the theorising of the intelligentsia. *The Lion and the Unicorn* shows him always ready to grind an axe at 'the emotional shallowness of people who live in a world of ideas' and their 'severance from the common culture of the country' (p. 63). He makes essentially the same point when he says that, 'In England, all the boasting and flag-waving, the 'Rule Britannia' stuff, is done by small minorities' (p. 42). 'Real Englishness' is less self-conscious. It is 'communal' but unofficial and half-private, centering around 'the pub, the football match, the back garden, the fireside and 'the nice cup of tea' (p. 39). Unlike churches or parliaments, we can take these things as they come, without investing them with solemn meanings: 'The genuinely popular culture of England is something that goes on beneath the surface' (p. 40). To share in it is not to subscribe to any political programme but to 'take into account its emotional unity, the tendency of nearly all its inhabitants to feel alike and act together in moments of supreme crisis' (p. 52).

It is at this point that Orwell begins to get into compromising positions. Even allowing for the fact that he qualifies this idea of 'emotional unity' by calling England 'the most class-ridden country under the sun' (p. 52), one can't help wondering what poor Gordon Comstock would have had to say on the subject. Is the 'emotional unity' unaffected by the cultural disunity which meant that you could only be a poet if you had a private income? Moreover, such 'unity' sounds uncomfortably like the 'quietism' Orwell had analysed in 'Inside the Whale'. In practice, wouldn't it be conformist and conservative? All Orwell can do to counter such doubts is to affirm his faith in the individualism of the English and his belief that their 'patriotism is finally stronger than class-hatred' (p. 103). Like Rousseau, he needs to think of the 'general will' – in England at least – as benign. At this point, his socialism enables him to take a short-cut. 'Patriotism', he says, is the 'opposite of conservatism' (p. 115) because its appeal is to something as yet uncreated: 'The England that is only just beneath the surface, in the factories and newspaper offices, has got to take charge of its destiny' (p. 85). This sudden appearance of 'destiny' – a word rich in Imperialist connotations – comes as rather a shock in Orwell's measured argument. 'Destiny' is notoriously difficult to decipher but tyrants have usually been more confident about doing so than anyone else. Will the spontaneous culture of 'the pub, the football match, the back garden' and the rest survive being enlisted under the banner of providence? How do the English 'take charge' of England and still go on reaping the benefit of being only half-conscious of it? The book which Orwell began with a prose hymn to England's 'communal' strengths finishes with words that recall the language of the most strenuous individualism: 'We must add to our heritage or lose it, we must grow greater or grow less, we must go forward or backward. I believe in England, and I believe that we shall go forward' (p. 123). It is not obvious why this sort of national self-expression should necessarily amount to anything more than the 'boasting and flag-waving' Orwell dismissed earlier. By a circuitous route he comes out closer to Churchill than had seemed conceivable.

It would, of course, be priggish not to add that this convergence has much to do with the fact that *The Lion and the Unicorn* was in part a response to the Blitz. Neither should it be assumed that the right has any sort of monopoly on patriotic rhetoric. Orwell's book, like Churchill's speeches, aspires to be non-sectarian. Nevertheless, it everywhere reminds us that patriotism is a peculiarly intractable theme for a left-winger to tackle. Customary feelings tend to be conservative whereas the desire for change tends to be divisive. The language of knee-jerk patriotism is nearly always right-wing. But, despite this, Orwell is never tempted into writing, like more partisan authors, as if he were speaking for England whilst in fact addressing only half the electorate. Some of his compromises may have been means to a broader end. At all events, he went on to repeat his uncharacteristic stress on England's 'destiny' in *The English People* which he wrote three years later:

They [the English] must have a clear notion of their own destiny and not listen either to those who tell them that England is finished or to those who tell them that the England of the past can never return.

If they can do that they can keep their feet in the post-war world, and if they can keep their feet they can give the example that millions of human beings are waiting for. The world is sick of chaos and it is sick of dictatorship. Of all peoples the English are likeliest to find a way of avoiding both ... they know that it is not possible for any one nation to rule the earth. They want above all things to live in peace, internally and externally. And the great mass of them are probably prepared for the sacrifices that peace entails.

But they will have to take their destiny into their own hands. England can still fulfil its special mission if the ordinary English in the street can somehow get their hands on power.[24]

It is embarrassing that Orwell's eloquence here makes him blind to the fact that in some countries it will seem as if he is simply recommending that, after some decades of middle-class British imperialism, the world would now be well advised to sit at the feet of the British working class for moral and political counselling. No doubt this would be to distort Orwell's tone but he is vulnerable to the charge of simply wanting to compensate for Britain's declining political power by finding it a new moral role. It is not that he is complacent about England – he hated Podsnappery as much as anyone – but he seems not to realise that, even if her 'mission' were exactly what the world most needed, it would still be coming from an unwelcome source. To give such an upbeat ending to *The English People*, and that on the very brink of Indian independence, seems at the least provincial, as if Orwell had found a way of having his cake and eating it, of being internationalist whilst remaining resolutely English.

The fact that *The English People* concludes with a passage that would have seemed inconceivable coming from the author of *Burmese Days* and 'Shooting an Elephant' ought not to make one accuse Orwell of bad faith. There is nothing doctrinaire about his position. Bernard Crick shrewdly suggests that *The Lion and the Unicorn* has been one of the most neglected of his books because its extraordinary range from revolutionary politics to emotional conservatism proved too wide to satisfy any one sectarian view of England: 'What does not fit our expectations we commonly ignore or play down.'[25] Orwell's readiness to take up contradictory positions has arguably been an important element in his appeal as a political writer. Crick calls *The Lion and the Unicorn* 'the last popular statement of [English socialism] with any literary merit written in a way that ordinary people ... could comprehend'.[26] One might add that its reflection of a wide, even contradictory, spectrum of ideas and feelings about England counts for as much in Orwell's popularity as does the celebrated plainness of his prose. He is refreshingly free of that left-wing (Robespierrian) anxiety to make his own position ideologically pure. It is necessary to distinguish between a merely stone-walling conservatism and Orwell's own more vital attachment to England's past and his concern that the present should maintain continuity with it. Orwell never succumbed to the common cant which confounds a love of one's country with a belief in its rightness. He loved England for its warts as much as for its beauties. A literary equivalent to this political pragmatism can be found in his review of Eliot's selection of Kipling's verse in which he shows himself characteristically able, at one and the same time, to respond to Kipling's literary talents whilst rejecting his politics. He even credits Kipling with producing what he calls a 'good bad poem': 'The fact that such a thing as good bad poetry can exist is a sign of the emotional overlap between the intellectual and the ordinary man ... A good bad poem is a graceful monument to the obvious. It records in memorable form ... some emotion which very nearly every human being can share.'[27] Such a paradox reminds one of his richly contradictory description of the 'hanging judge'. Yet nothing would be falser than to see such passages as examples of Orwell as Mr Facing-Both-Ways. They indicate instead his gift for acknowledging what is in front of him as it really is and not simply as he would like it to be. This is why *The Lion and the Unicorn* is that very unusual thing, a book about England that is unblemished by boastfulness or sentimentality or priggishness.

Nineteen Eighty-Four and *Animal Farm*, Orwell's most popular – or at least most widely read – books are beyond the scope of this chapter but it would be wrong not to mention them in connection with the alleged 'conservatism' of his later writings. Both have been misread and used as ammunition in the Cold War. Indeed, Isaac Deutscher, who occasionally worked with Orwell as a fellow journalist, argued that the enemies of communism had recruited *Nineteen Eighty-Four* as a 'prominent' element in 'the programme of Hate Week'.[28] Deutscher concedes that Orwell never intended this but nevertheless convicts him of naiveté and hence complicity in the book's reception. Like many other critics, he notices that the society of *Nineteen Eighty-Four* is often very like that of contemporary England. (Stephen Greenblatt points out its likeness to Orwell's description of his own prep school in 'Such, Such Were the Joys'.)[29] The problem, though, is that *Nineteen Eighty-Four* and *Animal Farm*, however much they may be based on the present, both function as predictions of society in the future and it is the revolutionary and the socialist who has invested most in imagining the future. Orwell might have been expected to make his prophecy along the lines of a book like *News from Nowhere*. Instead, both books remind us that his real solidarity was not only with ordinary folk but with the past that lay behind them and that had shaped their (often contradictory) attitudes. His belief in England inevitably modified the character of his socialism.

This, then, is the significance of his arriving in *The Lion and the Unicorn* at a position which even has some affinity with that of an ideological opposite like Waugh. Both writers felt a similar concern at the division that was opening up between England's past and its present. In both of them, this concern was so ingrained as to be virtually instinctive, operating below the conscious level on which choices of right and left are normally made. It is, in fact, precisely when an idea of England unites writers as dissimilar as Orwell and Waugh that one can begin to think of it as having some representative significance. Both writers, after all, might have been expected to create versions of England which simply cancelled each other out and yet this is not what happens when we compare them. Each of them confronts the modern world differently but they both rely on the thought of 'Englishness' as offering them a free space from which to regard that world with detachment and, sometimes, serenity. To both of them, this thought is implicitly above the realm of political ideologies. It may be that, in consequence, there is an element of the provincial in both of them but that was a price that they were willing to pay for their 'Englishness'.

NOTES

(Place of publication is London unless otherwise stated)

1 'On This Island', *Collected Shorter Poems* 1927–1957 (Faber, 1969), p. 82.
2 'Dover', *ibid.*, p. 99.
3 Quoted by Bernard Crick in *George Orwell: A Life* (Penguin, Harmondsworth, 1980), p. 533.
4 *Decline and Fall* (Penguin, Harmondsworth, 1937), p. 118.
5 *The Diaries of Evelyn Waugh*, ed. Michael Davies (Weidenfeld and Nicholson, 1976), p. 37.
6 Martin Stannard, *Evelyn Waugh: The Early Years* (Paladin, 1988), quotes his enthusiastic review of *Living* (pp. 224–5).
7 *A Handful of Dust* (Penguin, Harmondsworth, 1951), p. 18.
8 *Scoop: A Novel About Journalists* (Penguin, Harmondsworth, 1943), p. 16.
9 *Put Out More Flags* (Penguin, Harmondsworth, 1943), p. 7.
10 *Brideshead Revisited: The Sacred and Profane Memories of Captain Charles Ryder* (Penguin, Harmondsworth, 1951), p. 23.
11 *Sword of Honour* (Penguin, Harmondsworth, 1984), p. 28.
12 *Collected Essays, Journalism and Letters*, eds. Sonia Orwell and Ian Angus, 4 vols. (Penguin, Harmondsworth, 1970), IV, p. 576. See also Crick, *George Orwell*, p. 556.
13 *Coming Up for Air* (Penguin, Harmondsworth, 1962), p. 225.
14 *Keep the Aspidistra Flying* (Penguin, Harmondsworth, 1962), p. 227.
15 *George Orwell* (Fontana, 1971), pp. 16–17.
16 *The Road to Wigan Pier* (Penguin, Harmondsworth, 1962), p. 30.
17 *Ibid.*, p. 161.
18 *Inside the Whale and Other Essays* (Penguin, Harmondsworth, 1962), p. 37.
19 *Ibid.*, p. 25.
20 *A Clergyman's Daughter* (Penguin, Harmondsworth, 1964), p. 156.
21 *Collected Essays*, I, p. 535.
22 *Homage to Catalonia* (Penguin, Harmondsworth, 1966), p. 221.
23 *Collected Essays*, III, p. 221.
24 *Ibid.*, p. 55. (Although it did not appear until August 1947 'The English People' was commissioned by Collins in 1943 and written by May 1944.)
25 See Bernard Crick's introduction to *Lion and Unicorn* (Penguin, Harmondsworth, 1982), p. 8.
26 *Ibid.*, p. 29.
27 *Collected Essays*, II, p. 195.

28 In Raymond Williams ed. *George Orwell: Twentieth Century Views* (Prentice-Hall, 1974), p. 132.
29 *Ibid.*, pp. 122–3.

CHAPTER 7

Larkin, Betjeman and the aftermath of 'England'

Christopher Ricks has noticed how much of Larkin's work is 'a version of pastoral, an apprehension of poignant contraries'.[1] What is unusual about him is that his nostalgia should have been sustained by a relatively impoverished sense of history. 'An Arundel Tomb' discloses only a 'scrap' of the past to an 'unarmorial age',[2] so that all its drama is reduced to only pathos. Scott could have drawn a whole novel out of such a tomb. To what extent does the continuity established by the poem's retrospection reveal to us a living tradition? Is the culture it embodies English – or merely post-English? To explore these questions, one needs to begin obliquely, with Betjeman. There are good grounds for seeing him as Larkin's *point de repère*. Jonathan Raban, at the end of *Coasting*, loyally sees Larkin himself as the voice of the age but Larkin's own candidate for the role would probably have been Betjeman.[3]

To say 'Betjeman' today is to evoke the cuddly old reactionary who symbolised a vanishing 'Englishness' for a whole generation of television viewers. Even Larkin himself could describe the 'spirit' of this Betjeman as 'backwards, inwards and downwards'.[4] That was how he liked to think of his friend. This Betjeman, however, was and is a myth. To subscribe to it is to relegate his poetry to no higher role than that of a series of footnotes to the past that now need footnoting themselves. Larkin himself admits frankly that, 'I have sometimes thought that this collection of Betjeman's poems would be something I should want to take with me if I were a soldier leaving England: I can't think of any other poet who has preserved so much of what I should want to remember...'[5] Betjeman as a portable England for the soldier's knapsack. It is an image that is often hard to square with the reality. Readers of Bevis Hillier's *Young Betjeman* will need to set it against, for instance, the uppity undergraduate Betjeman who threw himself so madly into the social swim of 1920s

Oxford, or the hapless prep school teacher Betjeman who was more feckless than anyone in his friend Waugh's early novels. Far from sentimental, this Betjeman could be a ruthless social climber, spiky and malicious when it came to clearing his late Victorian elders out of his way. His treatment of C. S. Lewis, Field-Marshal Sir Philip Chetwode (his father-in-law to be) and, above all, his unfortunate father, might have made Julien Sorel blush. Hillier quotes a letter about Betjeman Senior's angina: 'Ernie has only got "pseudo" angina (although this can kill him, it is curable) but he also has structural disease of the heart. This means that he will die in about five years – just enough for him to wreck my life.'[6] (This was in 1927, when Betjeman was twenty-one). As one of his old friends remarked to his biographer, people would be surprised to find him so 'prickly'.[7] No doubt this prickliness subsided in later years but it never became dormant. What it signified in his Oxford days was his keen sense of belonging to a new generation. This is a feeling Betjeman understood very well and it helps to explain his popularity, despite his cult of the past of his grandfathers, as a writer who kept a vigilant eye on current taste. To think of the patina his verse conferred on the early motor-cars, the Delages, Lagondas and Talbot-Darracqs, is to glimpse his enthusiasm for the new century. He inherited such tastes from his long-suffering father as much as anybody, for he himself was a product of those rising middle-classes who were responsible for blotting out the old rural England. Not content with a villa in Surrey, Ernest Betjeman bought up a whole village in Cornwall. He made his money by manufacturing luxury craft items for Asprey's of Bond Street. By no means a Philistine, he was a kind of cross between Mr Dombey and Mr Carker. His income allowed him to spend freely and also predicated a certain *nouveau riche* good taste and both things had their effect on his son. Betjeman's sensibility was nourished on the nuances of the English class-system and that meant living imaginatively on both sides of its divides. His youthful pose of an 1890s aesthete merely masked an avid curiosity about the present. He was one of those aesthetes who need to live in the world, not one who could take refuge from it as his friend Sir Harold Acton did. This is why he never had more than one eye trained on the literary England of the Georgians. With his other eye he followed, with appalled delight, the progress of such contemporary figures as the hero of his 'Executive':

I am a young executive. No cuffs than mine are cleaner;
I have a Slimline briefcase and I use the firm's Cortina.[8]

The poet who could pin down this shark ('I do some mild developing') was in many respects more worldly than his predecessors: his concern with England was never equivalent, as it was for some of them, to burying his head in the sand.

Betjeman's reputation as a latter-day Victorian arose at first out of his preference for a Victorian prosody, based on Tennyson, Praed and Edward Lear. Yet the result was no more Victorian than Tennyson himself would have become Augustan had he written in heroic couplets. The content of the verse belies its nineteenth-century rhythms:

> Oh! Fuller's angel-cake, Robertson's marmalade,
>   Liberty lampshade, come, shine on us all,
> My! what a spread for the friends of Myfanwy
>   Some in the alcove and some in the hall.   (BP, p. 87)

Such lines ring with a different life from that in any of Betjeman's models. Their metre is a sort of rearguard strategy of seeing the modern world through spectacles which that world has actually broken. It is a makeshift way of repairing the modern lack of continuity between past and present. For this to work, both sides of the equation need to be active. In practice, Betjeman never condoned a blanket rejection of the present – not even in the case of Slough – because, at worst, he found its very vulgarities too endearing to justify an anathema. He takes even ugliness as a symptom of life:

> In labour-saving homes, with care
> Their wives frizz out peroxide hair
> And dry it in synthetic air
> And paint their nails.   (BP, p. 23)

As the dying fall suggests, the poet is not as snobbish as at first appears: 'It's not their fault they do not know / The birdsong from the radio...' (BP, p. 23). It is surprising how tolerant a satirist Betjeman could be. At such moments, his aestheticism and antiquarianism fall away like masks. At least we feel that he has actually *been* to Slough. In his book *Antiquarian Prejudice* (1939), he in fact defines 'architecture' to include even Slough, not as 'a single building or a church, or Sir Herbert Baker, or the glass at Chartres, but your surroundings; not a town or a street, but our whole overpopulated island.'[9] Larkin quotes this statement and goes on to stress Betjeman's 'fundamental interest in human life, or human life in society'.[10] This enables him to think of his characters as living their lives in relation to something larger than self: a place or a profession or a church. They are seldom isolated in the way Larkin's Mr Bleaney is as he watches 'the frigid wind / Tousling the clouds' (LP, p. 102). Even in a poem like 'Business Girls', also about the sadness of bedsitter-land, Betjeman conjures up a whole class of single women where Larkin would have homed in on just one:

> From the geyser ventilators
> Autumn winds are blowing down
> On a thousand business women
> Having baths in Camden Town.   (BP, p. 226)

Pathos does not need to be the monopoly of the 'single flower' that is 'born to blush unseen': singleness is something we have in common. Betjeman is usually thought of as a more 'lightweight' poet than Larkin, perhaps for this very reason, but his lightness is deceptive. Readers are often at a loss to explain why Larkin himself – our favourite poet of singleness – should have felt such respect for him, calling him the 'true heir of Thomas Hardy'[11] for his humanity. He stated this case in a way that made it plain that he thought of him as an 'influence' on himself: 'Can it be that, as Eliot dominated the first half of the twentieth century, the second half will derive from Betjeman?'[12] He gave him, that is, a status as crucial for his own work as Yeats or Hardy himself, albeit a status that has still to be properly recognised.

At the heart of Betjeman there is a feeling of unresolved depression that Larkin could have found in no other predecessor. It provided a precedent for such poems as 'Aubade' and 'The Old Fools' with their foretaste of the 'sure extinction that we travel to' (LP, p. 208). Yet Larkin's fears are agnostic whereas Betjeman's had their roots in religion, as when a puritan nursery-maid persecuted him with her prayers ('N. W. & N.6'):

> "World without end." What fearsome words to pray.
> "World without end." It was not what she'ld do
> That frightened me so much as did her fear
> And guilt at endlessness. I caught them too,
> Hating to think of sphere succeeding sphere
> Into eternity and God's dread will.
> I caught her terror then. I have it still.   (BP, p. 289)

The very syntax of that last line anticipates Larkin (compare the ending of 'Home is so Sad'). Yet Larkin seems more purely personal at such moments than Betjeman is. I would explain this as an indication that Betjeman came just in time to do something the younger poet was too late for: to give, as it were, a geography and an anthropology to the notion of 'Englishness'. One may not share his idea of England (over-restricted as it is by both class and place) but it remains an England that is credibly there, as actual as Sturt's, and not just a poetical England. It is that too, of course, with its 'Feathery ash in leathery Lambourne' (BP, p. 55), but its country is always too near to the town to be mythologised. Even in 'Cornish Cliffs' the 'Nut-smell of gorse and honey-smell of ling' give way to 'a usual Cornish scene' of 'Small fields and tellymasts and wires and poles' (BP, p. 296). In short, this England is inhabited, something far from common in English poetry since Housman and Thomas. Neither is it peopled only with such singular representatives of the English folk as have staked a strong claim to symbolise the spirit of the countryside like Kipling's Hobden and Thomas' Lob. For Thomas could only create a Lob but never a Bettesworth and, though Betjeman could not do Bettesworth either, he can at least gives us Bettesworth's suburban successors. Anyone seeking antecedents for the quirky English men and women who inhabit his suburbia will do better to think of Dickens than of the poets. But this is not a point that needs to be laboured. The England Betjeman bequeathed to Larkin was humanly varied; Larkin's problem was simply one of knowing how much of it could still be harnessed by a poet of the 1950s.

If one had to place the newly-weds of 'The Whitsun Weddings' in any poetic tradition it would not be alongside either Betjeman's affectionate middle-aged North Oxford wife in 'Oxford: Sudden Illness at the Bus-stop' nor the bold bride of 'Love in a Valley' who chants, 'Take me, Lieutenant, to that Surrey homestead!' (BP, p. 27). For one thing, Larkin's lovers are not as funny; for another, their sexual appetites are less frank. They are more akin to the shy lovers of Thomas's 'As the Team's Head-Brass', who emerge from the wood at the end of the poem: their love is fragile, transient but universal. David Holbrook argues, in *Lost Bearings in English Poetry*, that Larkin regards his 'girls / In parodies of fashion' with an 'air of superiority'.[13] Whether or not he is right, there is no doubt that there is a warmer fellow-feeling in poems like Betjeman's Hardyesque but quite unsardonic 'In a Bath Teashop':

"Let us not speak, for the love we bear one another –
    Let us hold hands and look."
She, such a very ordinary little woman;
    He, such a thumping crook;
But both, for a moment, little lower than the angels
    In the tea-shop's ingle-nook.   (BP, p. 129)

The touching lightness of this is deceptive; Larkin must have envied
the colloquial naturalness of that 'thumping crook'. To say that he
learnt from Betjeman, however, is not to conclude that he learnt
everything he might have done. It may be that he valued Betjeman's
verse in part for those effects he could not quite emulate himself.

Larkin's basic experience of England came early. He expressed it
through the (non-English) eyes of the heroine of *A Girl in Winter*, as
she makes her first journey in the country:

When they were out of London, she sometimes looked about her for the
England she had expected. It was difficult to see it... There was no end of
the cars. They streamed in both directions, pulled up by the roadside so that
the occupants could spread a meal, formed long ranks outside swimming
pools. Also there were innumerable hoardings, empty petrol drums and
broken fences lying wastefully about. Occasionally she saw white figures
standing at a game of cricket. These were the important things, and because
of them the town never seemed distant. Only infrequently did she see things
that reminded her of landscape paintings – a row of cottages, a church on
rising ground, the slant of a field – and she preferred in the end to watch the
road and feel the wind play around her. Everything seemed enshrined
beneath the sky.[14]

England fails to correspond with the literary image of it she has – the
twentieth century has blotted it out, as Lawrence foretold it would
– but her experience is not one of simple disillusion even so. What she
sees is still 'enshrined beneath the sky', despite the hoardings and
petrol drums, but she is obliged to re-make her England out of her
own head. It is a kind of serious tourism, similar to that implied in
poems like 'An Arundel Tomb' and 'Church Going' – both of which
seem to be written from a stance very like Katherine's. As she looks
out from a speeding car, so Larkin will later look out of his train
window to glimpse an Odeon going past, 'a cooling tower,/ And
someone running up to bowl' (LP, p. 116). Both witness England
without being able to relate to it. At the end of 'Church Going', we
don't even know what kind of church it is! Personal feeling is all he
has to fall back on whereas Betjeman, as John Sparrow has observed,
'refuses to make his poetry a medium for reflection, to commune with

himself or with his reader'.[15] The point is well taken. He finds too much to see around him to have time for introspection. The difference between the two poets is not, as many think, between the superficial and the profound but between a world that is lively and changing and one that is distant and static. In Larkin the picture seems framed and what really gives life to it is the restless visitor who doesn't quite belong in it. What is no longer there feels more vivid than anything that is present. By contrast, however 'churchy' we may find such Betjeman poems as 'Sunday afternoon service in St. Enodoc Church, Cornwall' we at least know precisely what the place is like and where it is. There is no doubt as to which England is the more real: Betjeman's art consists in remembering as much of the past as possible whereas Larkin's depends on how much he forgets.

This helps to clarify Larkin's version of modern English poetry – a version which leaves many readers at a loss. But if we can understand his anti-modernism, what are we to make of his wish to fall back on 'Englishness'? Larkin did not believe in poets devoting too much time to reading their predecessors but his own sense of tradition seems to have been so retrospective as to be wistful. Behind him there is Betjeman, then, behind him, Graves, followed by Edward Thomas, and then, still further back, A. E. Housman; behind everyone, of course, was Hardy, a Hardy who was not a 'modern' poet because no modern poet could be so 'English'. The problem with this lineage is that the further back Larkin goes in search of an authentic native tradition, the further he gets from any England of which he himself had any direct experience. In other words, his true England is on the brink of being a 'version of pastoral' from the word go. For a writer who read all D. H. Lawrence as a schoolboy, it is perhaps an understandable position to adopt – how many poets would want to go as fast as England had since the start of the century, if they had any choice in the matter? Yet what prospect of growth was there in a scenario which put nativeness firmly in the past? Larkin needed Hardy as his Katherine needed her schoolgirl memories, to supplement the England she actually found.

Somehow, the Hardy Larkin admired seemed to have eluded 'the strange disease of modern life' by dwelling in an aboriginal Wessex, innocent of Schopenhauer and Herbert Spencer. No one has seen more clearly than Donald Davie how easily admiration for Hardy can entail a 'gratuitous contraction of experience' for which the only name is 'Little-Englandism'.[16] Davie has no time for the view that

Hardy provides a 'viable insular alternative to the international "modern movement"'.[17] He sees it as a sign of the 'pusillanimity'[18] of the Movement of the 1950s, eager to write out large areas of the English experience from English history. The provinciality of this consisted in refusing to 'surrender' to what had really happened, which is represented for Davie by 'D. H. Lawrence's constant guilt and horror at what the English had made of England'.[19] Though Larkin revered Lawrence, he clearly needed to keep his insights at arm's length. In the same way, he badly needed to believe in a traditional Hardy, a Hardy whose England was pre-industrial. There is a real appreciation for the poetry in Larkin's famous essay, 'Wanted: A Good Hardy Critic', but it is nonetheless as suspect as Rupert Brooke's 'Grantchester' would be to anyone who had read *Change in the Village*. Of course, not a few English readers have never quite come to terms with precisely that contrast: for them, Larkin speaks especially clearly. Indeed, it is part of Davie's own view of Larkin that his very insularity enabled him to touch a common chord: 'we recognise in Larkin's poems the seasons of present-day England, but we recognise also the seasons of an English soul – the moods he expresses are our moods too ... the England in his poems is the England we have inhabited.'[20] In this respect, the tamer Larkin means more to us than the wilder Ted Hughes. But the implication is unavoidable: if *this* is our 'England', have we really inhabited it at all? Davie's phrase 'an English soul' deliberately begs that question. One notes that the Hardy Larkin recommends is the poet, not the novelist, and that perhaps in the long run the poet is the more provincial guide to steer by. As Charles Tomlinson once said, 'With Larkin poetry was on its way back to the middle-brow public'.[21]

Betjeman, of course, did this even more spontaneously than Larkin did and became even more popular. The interesting thing is that he achieved the same end by quite different means. He was a madcap eccentric where Larkin was the 'sober-suited' common man. Even Betjeman's strongest principles put him into the position of a rebellious licensed jester. In Larkin's words, 'the British public knows him [as] the man who is always trying to stop things being pulled down, or blocked in ...'[22] An admirable function but not altogether unconnected with what Hillier describes as 'arrested development'.[23] But if Betjeman was a 'stick-in-the-mud', like Larkin, he was an unusually exuberant one. His 'Englishness' owed more to Puck than to Mrs Wilcox. It didn't mean being dreamier and less alive. Sir

Harold Acton's memory of him is an interesting one, evoking something livelier though no less nostalgic than the 'England gone' of Larkin: 'I had only to be with him to feel certain that I was in the green heart of an Anglia besprinkled with placed church belfries. He is a genius of the *genius loci*, either pastoral or suburban.'[24] What Acton is glancing at is Betjeman's sheer vitality, the impish energy of rhythms that so spontaneously filter 'serious' matter through common forms. Davie has written brilliantly about the way Betjeman can throw away even a fine poem ('The Heart of Thomas Hardy') for the sake of a 'flippantly knowing and heartless' witticism.[25] One does not expect this poet to preserve an eighteenth-century decorum for long without needing to burst it. His wit nearly always overrides his sentimentality, except on those occasions of nostalgia when even he takes himself seriously. One such moment, over-solemn though ebullient, occurs in 'The Old Liberals':

> For deep in the hearts of the man and the woman playing
> The rose of a world that was not has withered away.
> Where are the wains with garlanded swathes a-swaying?
> Where are the swains to wend through the lanes a-maying?
> Where are the blithe and jocund to ted the hay?
> Where are the free folk of England? Where are they?   (BP, p. 229)

Even here, however, it is by no means clear whether the verse is meant to be plangent or jolly and this helps the poem to recover somewhat after this low-point. The rhythm carries it through the false sentiment. It is indispensable to his sense of the *genius loci*:

> The birch lets go
> But one brown leaf upon browner bracken below.
> Ask of the cinema manager. Night airs die
> To still, ripe scent of the fungus and wet woods weeping.
>
> (BP, p. 230)

The alliteration, for example, is no mere ornamentation.

What this comes down to is that Betjeman's most striking gift is not simply technical but spiritual. Larkin is surely right to single out his 'primitive vivacity' as what sets his verse apart 'from the verses of his contemporaries', capturing the attention 'in advance of his intellectual consent':

For Betjeman's poems, forthright, comprehensible ... are exclusively about things that impress, amuse, excite, anger or attract him, and – and this is most important – once a subject has established its claim on his attention he never questions the legitimacy of his interest. Energy most contemporary poets put into screening their impulses for security Betjeman puts into the poem.[26]

This is finely put. Betjeman may not be a major poet but by communicating this 'energy' he did much to vivify later poetry. It is partly because Larkin himself harnessed some of this energy for his own, cooler lyric manner that one values him. Finer poets, such as Thomas, may have depended on 'screening' but it was no less important to believe that 'Englishness' could sometimes be spontaneous too. So much of Larkin's own poetic feeling could not be. It remains a moot point whether any later poet will ever be able to talk about even a restricted England as naturally as Betjeman could talk about his.

What Betjeman's popularity shows is how the 'impulses' he refused to screen found an echo in readers accustomed to screening their own, readers akin to the people of his poems, like those 'people who have done nothing spectacular' whom Larkin admired Barbara Pym's novels for.[27] He enabled a whole generation to admit its 'Englishness' to itself, something most writers were keen to avoid doing. Even more important, he went on chronicling this domestic England all through a World War without relapsing into jingoism. (See the praying lady of 'In Westminster Abbey'.) Though he imitated Kipling's prosody he eschewed his Imperialistic sentiments (knowing that, to Kipling, England remained a foreign country in which he felt an outsider). Unlike Kipling, Betjeman never tired of laughing at 'Dear old, bloody old England' (BP, p. 173). In fact, his poems seldom name it at all but only its particular places, North Oxford and Leamington or Norfolk and Croydon. It is, of course, a partial England (as others are) but within its limits of class and taste and religion it is a richly specific one to which its poet really does belong. He does not need to observe it from outside as Thomas or Larkin do theirs. Perhaps, now that even this humdrum England has become another territory for pastoral, it seems more important to us than it did at the time? What P. Morton Shand, Betjeman's colleague on the *Architectural Review*, referred to as his 'xenophobia' will perhaps begin to seem like a price which we will reluctantly agree to pay for the sake of his sense of 'Englishness'.[28]

Already, by the outbreak of the Great War, Edward Thomas had understood that there were actually *two* Englands in England: one

public and orotund, that had seduced Brooke and helped his verse to
seduce a generation, and the other, quiet – even shy – England of his
own poems. The war served to expose and accentuate this divergence
(see the divided Englands of Ivor Gurney's *Severn and Somme*) but even
without the war Thomas would have needed to split England into its
public and private components in order to find a way of relating to
it (*part* of it) at all. The same might also be said, from the opposite
point of view, of the militantly self-conscious England of a poet like
Newbolt. Both clamant patriotism and quiet, elusive 'Englishness'
are, in a way, two sides of the same coin. Both depend on an appeal
to authentically English traditions. 'Drake's Drum' and the beauty
of 'When Icicles Hang by the Wall' fulfil a similar function to poets
whose present England feels increasingly problematic. Indeed,
elements of both attitudes could co-exist together in the same work,
as they do in the highly sophisticated fusion of imperial and rural
virtues that is to be found in *Puck of Pook's Hill*. (In this context, it is
intriguing to recall what a good soldier Thomas made.) Even
Lawrence, a much more radical explorer of 'Englishness', was
acutely pained by the loss of the past and understood very well those
like his Will Brangwen who longed for its preservation. It sometimes
seems to the reader of modern English writing that what we have
most in common is our nostalgia. Books as different as chalk and
cheese, *News From Nowhere* and *Howards End*, *The Dynasts* and *Wolf
Solent*, all seek to colonise the past in the interests of their own
particular version of England. What they look back to may vary;
what they have in common is the act of looking back. Nostalgia is
itself a kind of country, a focus of shared feelings through which we
can acknowledge our nationality without relapsing into mere
nationalism.

This is why Thomas's career is an exemplary one. As Jeremy
Hooker puts it, he wrote three poems called 'Home' but still 'lacked
a role in rural society'.[29] Though his poetic experience was perhaps
less febrile than Hooker goes on to claim – 'a bleeding away of
energy, that offers in return only a fugitive – and sometimes
shattering – ecstasy'[30] – it was nevertheless rooted, as it were, in
insecurity. When he claimed, in *The South Country*, that 'as far as I can
tell I am pure of history',[31] he may have been taking his eye off the
ball but it is not difficult to see why he should have wanted to. He
knew all too well what the war would do to the England his poems
tried to recover and evoke. Part of his experience of England was a

feeling of absence, a sense of loss. We find something similar in Lawrence too and it deepens in his later work. Nostalgia, in all its many forms, is the upshot of such feelings. Nor are we ourselves in any position to condescend to what we may find wistful and self-deceptive in Thomas and his contemporaries. Edwardian England has been an unconscionable time a-dying but, whatever we may have taken or rejected from it, we have surely inherited its nostalgia. For instance, the popularity of Betjeman's poems was due in no small measure to the frankness with which he admitted his nostalgia. Larkin too took such feelings as read, as in 'MCMXIV':

> Never such innocence,
> Never before or since,
> As changed itself to past
> Without a word – the men
> Leaving the gardens tidy,
> The thousands of marriages
> Lasting a little while longer:
> Never such innocence again.   (LP, pp. 127–8)

As so often ,the theme of his poetry is what he *can't* remember. There is a less plangent, more agonised version of such feelings in Geoffrey Hill too. He speaks of our need to understand and exorcise our nostalgia: 'there's been an elegiac tinge to the air of this country ever since the end of the Great War'.[32] In other words, far from being the option of the sentimentalist, nostalgia has become a living part of our culture, something that we may sometimes feel stuck with but not something we can simply wash our hands of. It is in this sense that I think it is possible to think of our England as 'the aftermath of England'.

What is original about Betjeman is that he managed to combine a Housman-like nostalgia with a puckish interest in the present. Unlike Kipling or Thomas or Gurney, his nostalgia for the past was not refracted through the folk culture and memories of *A Midsummer Night's Dream*. His quest for 'innocence' went back only as far as the Victorian period (sometimes the Regency) – a period which Carlyle and Ruskin had seen as one of the least innocent in our history. Betjeman celebrated its railways and its evangelicalism as they gave way to a world of hunt balls and motor-cars and suburban gentility. Where Sturt had listened to Bettesworth, Betjeman listened to the successors of Mr Pooter. He delighted in the middle-class world satirised in the home counties of Forster's early novels. Betjeman's England was as often as not seen from the rootless, hurrying viewpoint of a railway carriage, just as Larkin's is in 'The Whitsun Weddings' or 'Dockery and Son'. Nevertheless, Larkin called Betjeman 'the true heir of Thomas Hardy' and even liked to make him out to be more old-fashioned than he was (as when he pretends that he knew nothing about 'the modern poetic revolution').[33] The question that imposes itself is, what did Betjeman *do* with the literary England bequeathed to him by his predecessors and what use was that to Larkin when he began writing during the Second World War?

The great thing about Betjeman's England, that makes it liberating when one expects it to feel suffocating, is that he has no inhibitions either about making fun of it or at being unashamedly emotional about it. He is not, for instance, disconcerted by the fact that his 'Dear Old Village' has evolved since the days of Hardy's rustics. To his villagers:

> Nature is out of date and GOD is too;
> Think what atomic energy can do! (BP, p. 235)

In this not very serious poem the villagers get round a 'Mass Observer' with a 'Hillman Minx' to be bought drinks in their local in exchange for their tall rural tales. In another poem:

> Hodge sits down beside his wife
> And talks of Marx and nuclear fission
> With all a rustic's intuition. (BP, p. 241)

One of the lessons Betjeman taught Larkin was that it was possible to reconcile oneself to the modern world, through humour, and that to ignore its humanity in favour of the past was a form of sentimentality.

There has been little criticism which really registers Betjeman's vitality as a poet because many critics are still too embarrassed to let themselves enjoy his verse. Their usual let-out is to praise his technical dexterity (as Davie does) whilst keeping a dignified distance from his subject-matter. But unless we recognise the fellow-feeling in his poems we end by marginalising him as a lovable eccentric. It is true that Betjeman himself has abetted us in this in his television projections of himself as a sort of avuncular crank, a latter-day Mr Dick perpetually astride some pro-Victorian hobby-horse. This genial old buffer, however, was only one of his masks. As Anthony Thwaite points out, there was a 'more astringent' Betjeman too, a poet in whom 'nostalgia, fear, terror, hard-won faith and simple goodness contend'.[34] Poems like 'In Westminster Abbey' and 'Senex' may be comic but they are clearly not 'light verse'. Thwaite goes on to speak of Betjeman's 'awareness of Tradition' but here I think he begs the question: the predominantly eighteenth- and nineteenth-century character of his tradition sets it against what most earlier poets would have understood by that malleable word. His 'Tradition' has been unashamedly doctored while Mr Thwaite wasn't looking. Most of the time, it excludes both the Celtic and the European: Cowper is there but not Goethe, Cardinal Newman but not Nietzsche; France barely exists. Even the nineteenth century can seem bowdlerised when we reflect how little room Betjeman gives to Shelley or George Eliot or William Morris. (They are most likely to crop up in jokes). Neither is it a culture in which J. S. Mill or Henry James would have felt very at home. 'England', on Betjeman's terms, is only an essence, a distillation from something larger and more amorphous, even an expurgation. Within these very partial limits, however, Betjeman avidly seeks to imagine what it was like to be alive in past times. What poet since Hardy, for instance, has been as interested in *lived* English life as he has? This Dickensian interest serves us as a relief from Betjeman's nostalgia and it must have counted deeply for the Larkin who wrote 'Mr Bleaney'. That nondescript sort of life offered both of them something immediate that (as Larkin said of Hardy in contrast to Yeats) one didn't need to 'jack' one's self up to understand.[35] No wonder he and Betjeman got on like a house on fire.

What Betjeman showed Larkin was that history could be given the immediacy of the contemporary. His pictures of Victorian meeting-houses were continuous with his poems about the modern Church. The past did not have to be bathed in a kind of haze. But, if all this gave Larkin ideas, it still left one crucial question unanswered: how much of the past did Betjeman's 'Tradition' actually save from oblivion? His poetry is a constant exploration of things which are almost quaint. A poet coming after Betjeman and sensing this, as Larkin did, inevitably had less material to play with. The tentative-ness about the past of 'Church Going' (so radically unlike Betjeman's own response to churches) is an indication of this. Larkin *had* to be contemporary because that is what there was left for him to be. Nevertheless, Betjeman's influence was benign rather than intimi-dating: the oddly modern quality that came through his almost wilful old-fashionedness must have been intriguing. When Betjeman looked back it was not, as it was for the Georgians, in order to by-pass the modern world: his antiquarianism, for instance, was always a feature of his modernity. (This comes out in his ideological balancing act at the *Architectural Review* in the 1930s.) Thus, beginning from his interest in Pugin and Keble, he was able to discover the world of cast-iron girders and railway trains. Not to celebrate the latter would have been not to celebrate England's capacity to grow from a rural into an urban culture. What had to be left behind, of course, was precisely the culture out of which so much of English poetry had traditionally come. For Betjeman had to shift to find new equivalents for all the old feelings. I think this explains his mastery of the 'objective correlative', itself a trope for the newly displaced. The properties of his poems about North Oxford and Hampstead – the bus-stops and telephones and doctor's prescriptions – are in a direct line from Prufrock's coffee spoons:

> Too much, too many! so fetch the doctor,
>   This dress has grown such a heavier load
> Since Jack was only a Junior Proctor,
>   And rents were lower in Rawlinson Road.   (BP, p. 68)

Betjeman has an unerring eye for the way the genteel feel constrained to express their feelings through things and places. It is not such a big step from this to Mr Bleaney's room where 'Flowered curtains, thin and frayed, / Fall to within five inches of the sill' (LP, p. 102). For Larkin too owed much more all through his career to the Eliot of *Prufrock* than he cared to admit. Where else did those notorious bicycle clips come from if not from there? There was no better conduit from such things in the 1940s than Betjeman.

Such props as these, however, are only the ephemera of a culture and not the culture itself. If a poet fastens on them it may be because they are all he can take in. It is not uncommon, reading Betjeman, to feel that he has a much sharper eye for the small things of life than for the big ones. Large areas of Victorian England, for example, only came down to him in the form of Victoriana. As an Oxford contemporary of Sir Harold Acton and Evelyn Waugh he seems never to have had a very clear or inward sense of what Victorian 'morality' was. In any case, he distrusted antiquarians who failed to live in their own time. His best poetry began from a quite different feeling, one that was more paradoxical and not confined to either revivalism or pastiche. One way of describing it, and also of evoking

Larkin's England, is to define it as a sense of *something that was absent*: a sense of what was left when the older England was 'gone'. This feeling lurks beneath all Betjeman's historical colour and informs Larkin's self-deprecatory irony. It accounts for their displaced feeling in the present and their hankering after what went before it. It may not be the most obviously fetching aspect of their verse but it is an absence in which we can share more than in anything else in it, an absence disclosed by their keen sense of the present.

I use this word 'absence' with hesitation, aware that it may suggest simply the need to replenish an historical vacuum by giving it to nostalgia. More is involved, in Betjeman and Larkin, than a repetition of the kind of experience (or lack of it?) that is found in early Yeats, even though it is no coincidence that the author of all those poems about 'the land of heart's desire' was the major influence on the young Larkin. But both he and Betjeman began from a keen sense of place. Moreover, in the best poetry of both poets, the sense of absence tends to expand into a larger apprehension of death itself, an intimation of the void. To adapt Larkin's evocative word, the 'elsewhere' hinted at by such English places as Hull may be a foretaste of death itself, running directly counter to the conventional notion of the *genius loci*. This sense of the implicit presence of death within an English place is not easy to illustrate briefly (though it is, since Gray and Goldsmith, traditional). I think, for instance, of Betjeman's 'Sun and Fun: Song of a Night-Club Proprietress', which begins with a Soho scene on the morning after – 'The cleaning unattempted, / And a squashed tomato sandwich on the floor' (BP, p. 216) – and ends with the speaker becoming a chillingly comic death's-head:

> But I am dying now and done for,
> What on earth was all the fun for?
> For I'm old and terrified and tight. (BP, p. 217)

She is much more than just a local figure. An even better example of Betjeman's ability to write a poetry of place that is not *just* a poetry of place is 'The Metropolitan Railway: Baker Street Station Buffet'. This is the sort of poem one expects to find rather irritating: one of his over-indulgent rhapsodies on the glories of London railway stations. Yet the poem transcends its local and suburban settings ('leafy lanes in Pinner' and 'rural Rayner's Lane'). The nostalgic couple in question are (unusually where nostalgic poems are concerned) in the grip of death; it turns out that Betjeman has been rhyming about something other than the railways all along:

> Cancer has killed him. Heart is killing her.
>   The trees are down. An Odeon flashes fire
> Where stood their villa by the murmuring fir
>   When "they would for their children's good conspire."
> Of their loves and hopes on hurrying feet
> Thou art the worn memorial, Baker Street.   (BP, p. 213)

The effect of this on 'The Whitsun Weddings' will be obvious, but more striking, surely, is that phrase 'worn memorial' – direct, touching and imperceptibly comic in a way that would have been beyond Larkin. Nonetheless, Larkin did learn from Betjeman's ability to evoke nothingness from a carefully observed sense of place, particularly in some of his last poems. I don't suppose that one could fully understand 'The Old Fools' without having seen inside an old people's 'home' but it certainly isn't just a poem about old people. 'The Building', also from *High Windows*, works both as circumstantial description of a big hospital and as one of his most symbolic poems. Here is its ending (its *written* quality is something Larkin builds up to very slowly):

> All know they are going to die.
> Not yet, perhaps not here, but in the end,
> And somewhere like this. This is what it means,
> This clean-sliced cliff; a struggle to transcend
> The thought of dying, for unless its powers
> Outbuild cathedrals nothing contravenes
> The coming dark, though crowds each evening try
> With wasteful, weak, propitiatory flowers.   (LP, pp. 192–3)

Larkin is more eloquent than Betjeman and more 'serious' (to quote his own, to me, suspect word from 'Church Going') but less successful at finding tangible ways of expressing a sense of emptiness. Betjeman doesn't, for instance, need to move into top gear at the end of 'The Metropolitan Railway' as Larkin does here. Nevertheless, Larkin is clearly after a quiet sense of nothingness, even if some of his effects are a shade noisy.[36] To look closely at the poems both he and Betjeman wrote about death, whilst still writing about 'England', poems like 'Devonshire Street W.1' and 'Aubade', is to see how Betjeman helped introduce Larkin to an area that was rich for meditation though ungrateful to the rhetorician.

To talk, as Thwaite does, of Betjeman's 'awareness of the Tradition'
– as if we all still knew what that was – is to raise unanswered
questions. Which tradition? How much of the past is a particular
poet alive to? How deeply is he in touch with that past? These
questions imply a test which, in ways, Betjeman passes better than
Larkin does. He is genuinely nourished by the past because he is so
interested in it *for itself*. That is, he finds an independent life in it that
is capable of standing for our own. This is why the past he writes
about is just within hailing distance of living memory, not so far off
as to be romanticised in the *Eve of St Agnes* fashion. (This is also true
of the best Scott novels.) But he never treats the past with kidgloved
reverence; his nineteenth century is as funny as his twentieth. When
one thinks of his architectural enthusiasms in particular, it is apparent
that past and present in fact knitted together in his imagination into
one (often revivalist) crusade. Larkin's case seems a very different one
from this. He has very few poems specifically about the past and one
of the best-known, the early (1950) 'Deceptions', which sets out as a
dramatisation of a passage of Mayhew, ends up by enforcing a
distinctly 1950s moral. In his book on Hardy, Donald Davie finds
Larkin's refusal to measure the present against the past, as the
'nostalgic' Betjeman does, 'thoroughly refreshing'.[37] This may be so
but I find it hard not to connect it with something Davie himself
complained of repeatedly in Movement writing: a 'conspiracy to
pretend that Eliot and Pound never happened'.[38] As *All That Jazz*,
with its extreme selectiveness, makes especially clear, there were parts
of the immediate past which Larkin simply preferred to ignore. The
fact that one of his earliest works, *A Girl in Winter*, take such a cool,
hard-bitten view of England might suggest that, in casting the same
wary eye on the past as on the present, Larkin's natural attitude to it
would be that of a debunker. His real position was subtly different
from that. He writes as someone who neither knows nor wants to
know the past as Betjeman does but who would be only too willing to
rely on it, as a sort of crutch, if only he knew how to. If he is unable
to imagine himself back into any past age he can still look back with
envy as well as scepticism, discerning a 'world we have lost' without
being sure what that loss entails. Such thoughts may appear merely
negative but they conduce as easily to a romantic view of the past as
to a disillusioned one. Indeed, Larkin's feelings of disillusion were
increasingly directed to the present (as in 'Going, Going', for
instance). It is not surprising that a poet writing in the 1950s, when

all the pink on the map of the world began to drain away, should have entertained the idea of England through mainly negative feelings, nor is it surprising that that negative idea should have harboured a much rosier one inside itself. What *is* less expected is that when Larkin does try to suggest an older England – as in 'An Arundel Tomb' – he should actually seem very at home with the feelings it calls up.

'An Arundel Tomb' is, of course, one of Larkin's best-loved poems, though I suspect this is not a little owing to its touching subject-matter and the way it gives one a sentimental illusion of communing with the past whilst actually keeping it at arm's length. I can't myself help feeling that the poet is not interested enough in the medieval tomb for the poem to be as much of an epiphany as it would like to be. It remains, for me, an enjoyable and moving poem but scarcely a 'great one'. It attempts above all to give a more formal (doctored?) version of the feeling of England as an absence, the feeling Katherine has at the start of *A Girl in Winter*. But one's first impression is neither of the symbolic nor the monumental but of the domestic affection of what might be any couple, intimate under their 'jointed armour, stiffened pleat':

> his left-hand gauntlet, still
> Clasped empty in the other; and
> One sees, with a sharp tended shock,
> His hand withdrawn, holding her hand.

> They would not think to lie so long.
> Such faithfulness in effigy
> Was just a detail friends would see:
> A sculptor's sweet commissioned grace
> Thrown off in helping to prolong
> The Latin names around the base. (LP, p. 110)

This seems more graceful than imaginative. At least, it seems to want us to believe that the couple's medieval 'friends' would feel the same about the sculptor's 'detail' as a Movement poet does. The 'Latin names' are treated in the same betraying way, almost as if they too were only there as 'commissioned grace'. Larkin is not very interested in what the tomb has to tell about their world. He is more interested in the 'plainness of the pre-Baroque' (LP, p. 110) though personally, as someone who has seen the tomb many times, I suspect that what has struck him most is the opportunity of handling his verse stanza in a way that offers an equivalent to the simple and smoothly flowing

lines of the sculpture itself. The appropriateness of the verse
movement seems to me the most successful thing in the poem though,
even so, to turn to the tomb itself is to be reminded also of a rough,
eroded texture to the stone's smoothness. The poem glosses this over
in arriving at its 'final blazon' (LP, p. 111). A 'blazon' seems rather
formal after Betjeman's 'worn memorial'. Whether or not Larkin's
poem manages to evoke the Middle Ages does not perhaps matter too
much – though I find the way it secularises the meaning of the tomb
rather dated – but its sense of time involves more than just histori-
cism. The poem is not like, say, Browning's 'The Bishop Orders His
Tomb', based on love and curiosity about the past, so much as a sort
of costume version of 'Church Going': it seeks to explore the poet's
bemused and self-deprecating modernity. One reason for its popularity is that it manages to find a moral for the present in the past:
'What will survive of us is love' (LP, p. 111). Will it? Many readers
seem to have felt that it will though all that survives in the poem is the
'love' of the stone effigies (if Larkin is right in imputing 'love' to
them) – the poet says nothing about our or his own love. The word
'us' in the last line comes in with a train of assumptions behind it.
Moreover, it might be felt that 'love' is not exactly what has survived
in Chichester Cathedral either; the poem itself is actually more
eloquent on the survival of art. But perhaps 'art' is no better a word
for what the poem is about than 'history' is? Either way, its past
functions mainly as a touching and romantic back-drop for the
poem's final statement. The intimations of time feel a little poetical:

> Rigidly they
> Persisted, linked, through lengths and breadths
> Of time. Snow fell, undated. Light
> Each summer thronged the glass.   (LP, p. 110)

In the end, the effigies, like history itself, are moving because they are
other: the only thing we can share with them is 'love' and that, for
all we know, is a projection. The 'fidelity' they 'hardly meant'
echoes our 'almost-instinct':

> Now, helpless in the hollow of
> An unarmorial age, a trough
> Of smoke in slow suspended skeins
> Above their scrap of history,
> Only an attitude remains:
> Time has transfigured them into
> Untruth.   (LP, p. 111)

Not every reader will find that the poem says enough about 'love', whether in history or in 'an unarmorial age', to make even this paradoxical transfiguration convincing. The effigies only represent love because the bereft and doubting speaker clearly lacks it. The poem is really about absence – the kind of absence that is to be found in the past-dominated present. Only its sense of atmosphere and the elegance of its phrasing disguise the fact.

To criticise 'An Arundel Tomb' is not, necessarily, to criticise Larkin's poetry in general. The poem has a 'one-off' quality, as if the poet had been over-intent on working up a special effect. Set it beside 'Mr Bleaney' or 'Dockery and Son' and it seems to have an air of false nobility. Larkin seems to have felt this himself. In his interview with John Haffenden he says of it (just after a spirited defence of 'The Whitsun Weddings'):

> Well, that is rather a romantic poem; there's even less reservation in that. I don't like it much, partly because of this; technically it's a bit muddy in the middle – the fourth and fifth stanzas seem trudging somehow, with awful rhymes like voyage/damage. Everything went wrong with that poem: I got the hands wrong – it's the right-hand gauntlet really – and anyway the hands were a nineteenth century addition, not pre-Baroque at all.[39]

It would be unfair to criticise Larkin for making an art-historical blunder, even if it turned out that the emotional focus of the poem really came from the same century as Little Nell. That only matters if one feels that the whole picture of the earl and countess is sentimental anyway. What is potentially more damaging in Larkin's remarks is his feeling that the fourth and fifth stanzas of the poem are 'trudging'. I would say that they contain a certain amount of filling, in comparison with the opening stanzas. Neither the 'old tenantry' nor the 'litter of birdcalls' nor the 'endless altered people' seem inevitable enough. Yet, as Larkin must have realised, these stanzas are crucial in taking the reader from the opening picture of the tomb to the poem's final diapason. In both their phrasing and their movement one feels the poem slowly and deliberately building up for the climax. Larkin's word 'trudging' is blunt but perhaps it has the effect of brushing what is rhetorical and calculated in the lines under the carpet: if anything, 'An Arundel Tomb' feels *too* accomplished, not laboured.

Larkin's memories of writing the 'Whitsun Weddings' were much happier. He told Haffenden: 'You couldn't be on that train without feeling the young lives all starting off, and that just for a moment you were touching them. Doncaster, Retford, Grantham, Newark, Peterborough, and at every station more wedding parties. It was wonderful, a marvellous afternoon. It only needed writing down. Anybody could have done it.'[40] The poem does feel more spontaneous (save perhaps for its ending), as if Larkin had been unusually possessed by his material. 'Just for a moment you were touching them' nicely suggests its mixture of wonder, excitement and pathos. Elsewhere, he tends to be more clearly either the excluded onlooker ('Afternoons'), the wry self-examiner ('High Windows') or a simpler combination of the two as in 'Poetry of Departures' or the posthumously published 'Letter to a Friend About Girls'. In 'The Whitsun Weddings' there is a more fertile tension between feeling alone and fellow-feeling. The poet is both at home in his own country ('someone running up to bowl' etc.) and yet sees things 'all again in different terms', as if he were a traveller in a foreign land. His deepest impressions are fugitive and the life they imply goes on beyond his ken. He is, of course, quite consciously the poet as bachelor; his stance might be described as having been sired by 'Prufrock' and early Yeats out of Keats. He avoids any mention of his own social place, after placing the couples and their families so precisely. He was 'late getting away' but we neither know where from nor where he is going to. Both the poem's vicarious elation and its ostensibly sober way of mulling the experience over depend on our sense of the speaker as a rootless observer. It is quite possible to read the poem *either* as mainly descriptive *or* as self-communing. How could there be any more ordered response to the events of the journey? They are merely a series of sublimely gratuitous happenings that impinge too briefly on his thoughts to do more than hint at a meaning, leaving him half-dazzled and half-bemused by a life he hardly shares even in imagination.

The core of this experience was already clear in the two novels Larkin wrote after he left Oxford: *Jill* (1946) and *A Girl in Winter* (1947). Both are about people trying to adapt to living in unfamiliar surroundings. Katherine, in *A Girl in Winter*, is a foreign exile in England; John Kemp, the green northern scholarship boy hero of *Jill*, feels like a foreigner in Oxford. Both feel equally cut off from 'home' (indeed, we hear oddly little about Katherine's home at all and are never quite sure where it is). In Larkin, 'home' is usually either somewhere one has left or that one dislikes or a mixture of the two. The idyllic home counties England of her pre-war holiday with the Fennels is a kind of home to Katherine, the only past she ever thinks about. Trapped by the war in a bleak northern city, she feels like an exile. Yet she never thinks of her southern holiday as a time of fulfilment. Her memories are rather of what failed to happen there – of her elusive, still-born love-affair with her host Robin Fennel, who punted her romantically down the Thames but never really came to the point. At the end of the novel Robin returns, a gatecrasher from a less innocent world, in the lumbering shape of a tipsy soldier who needs somewhere to be put up for the night. Katherine perfunctorily allows him to seduce her, not because she hopes to savour some return to *le temps perdu* but to bring herself finally down to earth. In succumbing to Robin she exorcises the past of its charm without making any real contact with it. The lonely feeling of being a foreigner overlaps with her sense of the common disappointingness of things: there is nothing in *A Girl in Winter*, nor is there very much in *Jill*, to make one feel that living in England is really any different for those who are *not* foreigners. This is presumably why Larkin was able to compress so much of the experience he was later to explore in his poems in a novel about an expatriate. In fact, both of his novels seem to me more mature and more successful than he himself thought they were – so much so that one wonders if there weren't more truth in them than he later cared to admit. In some respects, both books look at traditional images of England in a more intelligently critical way than some of his later poems do. To think, for example, of the sweet coating of 'love' applied to the ending of 'An Arundel Tomb' is not to think the ending of *A Girl in Winter* either less honest or less mature.

This does not mean that to be without illusions is automatically the same thing as being 'mature'. That would be too easy. When readers complain that reading Larkin can be an unduly lowering experience, what they are resisting is probably not so much his unblinking wisdom as a feeling that his poems are too repetitious, that they tend to end up saying the same thing. To complain of the way they constantly defeat our expectations of life is not necessarily to wish that they were more romantic. They offer no more scope for tragedy than they do for romance. Even the bleak 'Aubade' gets much of its effect by constantly rubbing the same point in. Larkin famously remarked that 'deprivation' was for him 'what daffodils were to Wordsworth' and one takes his point[41] – he wrote about what he could write about – but the polarity the remark sets up is a false one. If there is more joy in Wordsworth there is also far more pain. The levelness of tone and the emotional consistency of Larkin's best poems is what is most striking about them. The fact that their irony often plays with the contrast between an ideal and a realistic attitude to experience does not mean that it is used to dramatise sharply contrasting emotions. In 'Wild Oats', for instance, a very characteristic performance, both the defeatism and the romanticism of the speaker are viewed in the same wry way. Both sides of his nature are equally thwarted:

> I was too selfish, withdrawn,
> And easily bored to love.
> Well, useful to get that learnt.
> In my bosom there are still two snaps
> Of bosomy rose with fur gloves on.
> Unlucky charms, perhaps.   (LP, p. 143)

The humour only works if we realise that he has not really 'learnt' much at all. Similarly, there seem to be two distinct Englands in *A Girl in Winter*, one poetic and southern and the other dour and northern, but by the end of the novel Katherine turns out to have had the same experience in each. As in so many of the poems – 'Poetry of Departures', 'Reference Back', 'Sunny Prestatyn' among them – the essential Larkin experience is the sense of what has *not* been experienced. Moreover, if fulfilment is possible at all in Larkin's world it often seems more on the cards the further he is from his ordinary, waking world: even 'real life' is not very real. 'The Importance of Elsewhere', for example, gives a surprisingly positive account of his own experience of being abroad:

> Lonely in Ireland, since it was not home,
> Strangeness made sense. The salt rebuff of speech,
> Insisting so on difference, made me welcome:
> Once that was recognised, we were in touch.   (LP, p. 104)

But 'Living in England', where the poem is being written, is another matter. The speaker's feelings are blocked by his 'customs and establishments': 'Here no elsewhere underwrites my existence' (LP, p. 104). In other words, what is especially difficult 'in England' is to be English in other than a conventional, self-thwarting way.

To say this is merely to put into abstract terms what a poem like 'Mr Bleaney' puts in inimitably precise and vivid images. That poem captures both the routine greyness of Mr Bleaney's England and the sad, disenchanted self-contempt of the speaker as memorably as anything Larkin ever wrote. Although its speaker can place his predecessor so unerringly ('I know his habits') he of course shares his bachelor *bovarysme* and the same experience of seeing life's highpoints dwindling into ordinariness:

> He kept on plugging at the four aways –
> Likewise their yearly frame: the Frinton folk
> Who put him up for summer holidays,
> And Christmas at his sister's house in Stoke. (LP, p. 102)

The deadness of this is intensely alive. Most of the poem consists of the (even more?) lonely speaker speaking about Mr Bleaney's life, but there is nothing putative about it. It is in earnest in a way that a poem like 'Church Going' is not. Larkin clearly knows much more about what it is like to live in a bed-sitter than to be in a church. Beside 'Mr Bleaney', 'Church Going' seems like a prolonged effort to discover a meaning in an experience which has never quite seemed meaningful. The fact that the poet always ends 'much at a loss like this, / Wondering what to look for' (LP, p. 97), together with his falsely flip donation of an Irish sixpence, suggests a certain embarrassment at not knowing what to feel. For a while the poem tries to explore this feeling critically, rather in the way the speaker's own feelings are explored in 'Mr Bleaney', but Larkin seems too uncertain about the 'accoutred frowsty barn' to do this other than speculatively. Instead of telling us anything about the speaker, 'Church Going' concludes by building up to a kind of spiritual 'high'. The last stanza has been widely admired though it seems to me only to be saved from seeming simply 'purple' by the understatement of its last two lines:

> A serious house on serious earth it is,
> In whose blent air all our compulsions meet,
> Are recognised, and robed as destinies.
> And that much never can be obsolete,
> Since someone will forever be surprising
> A hunger in himself to be more serious,
> And gravitating with it to this ground,
> Which, he once heard, was proper to grow wise in,
> If only that so many dead lie round. (LP, p. 98)

Too many of the words here are poetic diction: 'serious', 'blent', 'compulsions', 'robed as destinies' and so on, straining after profundity. The lines do have some of the even, sustained music and the spun-out syntax of the end of 'Mr Bleaney' but not the same sense of bringing the whole poem to an emotional head. The tone (beautifully maintained) is rather mannered and, in a discreet way, homiletic. Far from being the Gray's 'Elegy' of our age, Larkin's poem seems to me to be 'churchy' without being religious.

To generalise for a moment, Larkin writes about England in two main ways: in the first he has a keen eye for the actual texture of English life ('Mr Bleaney') but in the second ('Church Going') he often falls into an unfocussed spirituality. The slow, appalled self-realisation at the end of 'Mr Bleaney' continues the description of the room and the view from the room. There is nothing ruminative about it:

> But if he stood and watched the frigid wind
> Tousling the clouds, lay on the fusty bed
> Telling himself that this was home, and grinned,
> And shivered, without shaking off the dread

> That how we live measures our own nature,
> And at his age having no more to show
> Than one hired box should make him pretty sure
> He warranted no better, I don't know.   (LP, pp. 102–3)

There is surely much more going on in these lines than in the last stanza of 'Church Going'. They may not be quite free from the poetical and the self-pitying – 'frigid', the dying fall of 'I don't know' – but the scene is much nearer to being placed and understood. For instance, there is a dead-pan comedy to the speaker's solemn glumness ('how we live measures our own nature') which, at the end of 'Church Going', we would have had to take straight. It is its wit and economy that makes the poem more than just a piece of 1950s realism. 'Frinton', for instance, manages to suggest more than just Frinton itself – it resonates, where 'robed in destinies' was hollow. In Larkin, the real often becomes the symbolic like this ('Sunny Prestatyn' is a good example). It is not the richly layered realism of the novelist, the sort of thing that made James call *Middlemarch* a 'treasure-house of detail':[42] Larkin's art consists in being telling with as *few* details as possible. In his later poems especially – most famously in 'Annus Mirabilis' – social history tends to crystallise into epigram. (Betjeman's spry vignettes of English social life inevitably come to mind.) The related impression one has of Larkin's trying, as it were, to put England into a nutshell also helps to explain the limits of his interest in the socially particular for its own sake. There is not much diversity in his England. As he says of his hometown: 'Nothing, like something, happens anywhere' (LP, p. 32). He does not have Lawrence's (or even Betjeman's) sense of the 'spirit of place' – what strikes him in particular things is not their differences but what they have in common.

It is tempting to think of Larkin as a representative of *l'homme moyen sensuel*, taking the pulse of the egalitarian, welfare state England which has displaced the hierarchical culture of the past. An American critic has saluted him as the 'poet of the common man';[43] he himself once said that 'everyday things are lovely to me'. Yet a love of the commonplace is different from a love of the common people. In Larkin, it did not imply even a liberal political position. It came as a shock to many admirers that this presiding bard of the comprehensive school – today's students have often read 'Church Going' more reverently than *Paradise Lost* – should have backed C. B. Cox's Black Papers on education. While teachers evangelised their flock with 'Mr Bleaney' its author was composing jaundiced epigrams on the decline of British education – for instance:

> When the Russian tanks roll westward, what defence for you and me
> Colonel Sloman's Essex Rifles? The Light Horse of L. S. E? (LP, p. 172)

This squib, published by Cox, reminds one of what a bad influence Amis was on Larkin. It also recalls the beleaguered philippics which Donald Davie despatched from the radical hotbed of Wivenhoe Park in 1968. Moreover, as a university librarian, Larkin was charged with guarding one of the key buildings that 60s radicals sought to occupy. No wonder he insisted that he was not the popular poet – 'a sort of cut-price Betjeman'[44] – that many of his readers took him for. If his early poems seemed almost Wilsonite it became clear, by the 1980s, that his political convictions had been formed before 1945. He claimed to feel more at home with Mrs Thatcher than with any politician since Sir Stafford Cripps.[45] During the 1966–70 Labour administration he was moved to protest at the fact that spending on education had surpassed that on defence. More than just wryness moved him, in poems like 'Annus Mirabilis', to present himself as a voice from a pre-permissive, pre-Beatles England. (Stan Smith is one of the few critics who try to analyse his politics.)[46]

Ever since Dr Johnson, the poetry of disillusion has been more conservative than liberal. This was implicit in the Movement from the start, before Suez and within earshot of the Cold War. *The Less*

Deceived belongs to the same moment as Robert Conquest on Stalinism and the anti-high-brow little Englandism of *Lucky Jim*. Larkin himself was notoriously uninterested in 'abroad', and most of the Movement rejected the work of Charles Tomlinson and with it that of its American and European contemporaries. The only Movement writer to get beyond such attitudes was Davie, for instance in his championing of Basil Bunting. Larkin rarely mentioned such cosmopolites. Thus, although The Movement was a shaping influence of the late 50s, it was quite distinct from the radical writing of the period – non-Oxbridge, working-class writers like Osborne, Wesker, Braine and David Storey. It comes as a surprise to think of Larkin as being of the same generation as Albert Camus. By contrast, Movement writers like Amis and Wain look increasingly like pseudo-rebels who were actually engaged in constructing new little myths for a new little England. The crucial fact is how quickly they all 'made it', how much nearer to the centre of the metropolitan culture they went than such great outsiders as J. C. Powys, Leavis and Bunting.[47] They all had an undoubted nose for the axes on which this culture moved, the Sunday papers and the weeklies (Anthony Hartley puffed them shamelessly in *The Spectator*) and the Third Programme. Wain, for example, quickly cut out John Lehmann and used the B. B. C.'s main poetry programme to promote The Movement. These few young writers effected a sort of *coup d'état*, not of the means of production but of the means of communication. This process, manifestos apart, was never a simple triumph of the ordinary as Larkin seems to have liked to think. Rather, it was the Movement's gift to *seem* ordinary, to be wolves who went dressed as sheep. They managed, for instance, to brand Leavis as an illiberal 'élitist' even as they purveyed a watered-down version of his 'standards'. As Amis showed especially clearly in the 60s, when he was one of the few British intellectuals to support the Americans in Vietnam, what underlay the belief in the common man was often common or garden reactionary politics. Anyone who doubts the relevance of this to Larkin should read *All That Jazz*, his reviews from the *Telegraph*, to see how he virtually judged records according to whether they were made before or after about 1934. These reviews may be amusing but it is remarkable how confident Larkin was in the role of arbiter; hardly ever did he feel obliged to argue for his judgements. It was easy for the alert reader to hitch a ride with this new metropolitan clerisy. The only one of the Movement writers who grew uneasy with this inviting stance was Davie (the only one of them to have been deeply influenced by *Scrutiny*). The others gladly took their new parochialism for urbanity. Only Davie saw that the England of Amis and Larkin could easily turn into a mere happy hunting ground for conservatives.

In 'If my Darling', which opens *The Less Deceived*, Larkin ponders what it would be like 'to hear how the past is past and the future neuter' (LP, p. 41). The line sums up his England – a succession of moments or snapshots, what the French call 'clichés', rather than an organic sequence through time. He feels tradition most keenly when he feels cut off from it. What marks him out from earlier poets like Hardy and Thomas is that the past seems to reach him quite unmediated, either by religion, by history, or even by Betjeman on television. The past lies alongside his present without being part of it, not as its life-blood but as a back-drop or stage-set. This makes it all the harder to tell what really lies below the tamed surface of affection and pathos which Larkin gives his 'Englishness'. One is never quite sure how to take the angry contempt which can sometimes break through the habitual decorum ('Sunny Prestatyn', 'This be the Verse'). Larkin knows that the culture he builds on is only skin-deep, as removable as clothes. Even when he posits a meaning in its community, as in 'the Whitsun Weddings', he remains poised to disavow it, ready to retreat into social bachelordom. His poetry is so often about communal feelings which he himself cannot share. As Holbrook points out, his imagination is non-participatory. This need not be a criticism; as the young Flaubert said in *Novembre*, if you want to write about being drunk the best way to do it is to remain stone-cold sober yourself. Moreover, there is a kind of 'Englishness' in a reluctance to participate in any common rituals. The nearest Larkin went towards joining in was in a late poem like 'To the Sea':

> Still going on, all of it, still going on!
> To lie, eat, sleep in hearing of the surf
> (Ears to transistors, that sound tame enough
> Under the sky), or gently up and down
> Lead the uncertain children, frilled in white
> And grasping at enormous air, or wheel
> The rigid old along for them to feel
> A final summer, plainly still occurs
> As half an annual pleasure, half a rite.   (LP, p. 173)

What is touching here is not just the bathers but the fact that the poet
only observes this rite and never quite shares in it. 'To the Sea' is a
poem about communion as witnessed from outside. Larkin watches
the scene as from some high breakwater off-stage.

The poem usually felt to epitomise this stance is 'The Whitsun
Weddings'. How problematic its England is! Do we feel we belong
with the wedding parties or with the observing poet? One can hardly
side with both at once, even though Larkin does try to share in the
general elation. The poem succeeds because it doesn't try too hard to
call up too many of the ghosts which inhabit our notion of England.
But if 'The Whitsun Weddings' celebrates ordinariness, poems like
'Homage to a Government' and 'Going, Going' express a wistful
desire to see Britain 'great' (whatever that means). They versify
Thatcherism as early on as the days of Wilson and Heath. I find both
poems frankly embarrassing now. Their main interest is to demonstrate that, in Larkin, the everyday England and the England of
English politics never quite came together. This makes his verse both
suggestive and frustratingly difficult to pin down. What strikes one
most is Larkin's virtuosity in keeping the same balls turning round in
the air. Poems like 'The Whitsun Weddings' almost deliberately let
both England and the reader off the hook. It is important to listen to
the way the poem moves:

> Now fields were building-plots, and poplars cast
> Long shadows over major roads, and for
> Some fifty minutes, that in time would seem
> Just long enough to settle hats and say
> *I nearly died,*
> A dozen marriages got under way.
> They watched the landscape, sitting side by side
> – An Odeon went past, a cooling tower,
> And someone running up to bowl – and none
> Thought of the others they would never meet
> Or how their lives would all contain this hour.
>
> (LP, pp. 115–16)

What is most striking here is the smoothness with which Larkin
makes his transitions and the snapshot precision that accompanies it.
Unlike Eliot, in *Four Quartets*, he takes his England as given, not as a
theme for meditative exploration. Perhaps this is because he knows it
better, and can depend on our knowledge of it too, but it surely also

suggests that he simply could not find *enough* to explore in the idea of England.

In a few late poems about ageing and death Larkin did go deeper and it is within this theme that he finally crystallised his feelings about England. For what the word 'England' conjured up most potently for him was another England that was absent. In 'The Old Fools', for instance, an unblinkingly bleak late poem, the subject is not just dying but the remembering of what is no longer accessible: 'an air of baffled absence, trying to be there / Yet being here' (LP, p. 197). It was to this realm that England itself had begun to retreat for Larkin. The country has become a kind of nursing home, full of echoes. (Not for the first time. One thinks of Shaw's *Heartbreak House* and, more recently, of David Storey's *Home*.) This is why the experience of dying gave Larkin his most characteristic subject: death corroborated the distance he had always needed to write poetry from. His final note, in the final stanza of 'Aubade', with its frank admission of fear, is the thought of extinction and of the world going on without him – just as the past had:

> Slowly light strengthens, and the room takes shape.
> It stands plain as a wardrobe, what we know,
> Have always known, know that we can't escape,
> Yet can't accept. One side will have to go.   (LP, p. 209)

It was to this domain that Larkin increasingly restricted his England, a starkly modern England without a past. There could be no finer instance of what I have called the 'aftermath' of England than this surprisingly Beckettian late Larkin.

'Going, Going', however, gives us only the flip-side of 'Aubade', not a sense of *lacrimae rerum* but a familiar kind of self-protective cynicism. The poem is not one of Larkin's best but it sums up one side of him (the side that was dazzled by Amis):

> I thought it would last my time –
> The sense that, beyond the town,
> There would always be fields and farms,
> Where the village louts could climb
> Such trees as were not cut down;
> I knew there'd be false alarms
>
> In the papers about old streets
> And split-level shopping, but some
> Have always been left so far;
> And when the old part retreats

As the bleak high-risers come
We can always escape in the car.

Things are tougher than we are, just
As earth will always respond
However we mess it about;
Chuck filth in the sea, if you must:
The tides will be clean beyond.
– But what do I feel now? Doubt?

Or age, simply? The crowd
Is young in the M1 café;
Their kids are screaming for more –
More houses, more parking allowed,
More caravan sites, more pay.   (LP, p. 189)

A poem about the condition of England turns into a complaint of the middle-aged poet as he looks with rueful envy at the young. Larkin disowns the energies of the screaming 'kids' and cultivates a tired wistfulness:

It seems, just now,
To be happening so very fast;
Despite all the land left free
For the first time I feel somehow
That it isn't going to last.   (LP, p. 190)

There is an almost unmanageable amount of self-pity in that plangent 'so' – indeed, Larkin can only control it by taking his customary refuge from emotion in colloquialism:

before I snuff it, the whole
Boiling will be bricked in
Except for the tourist parts –
First slum of Europe: a role
It won't be so hard to win,
With a cast of crooks and tarts.

And that will be England gone,
The shadows, the meadows, the lanes,
The guildhalls, the carved choirs.
There'll be books; it will linger on
In galleries; but all that remains
For us will be concrete and tyres.   (LP, p. 90)

The common touch does not tap any real common feeling here. It is not even clear what the poet is referring to. Are the 'crooks and tarts' the cast of the Profumo Affair or not? The 'meadows' and 'lanes' seem to have come from some guide-book rather than from any real countryside. It is all very well to speak of 'England gone' but was the

England Larkin laments here really there for him in the first place? The 'M1 café' seems to have more vitality. Despite the poem's desponding rhythms, one hardly knows whether England's passing is tragic or simply a case of 'good riddance'. The 'guildhalls' and 'carved choirs' are merely the stage properties of 'Englishness'. There is no living sense of the tradition the poem purports to defend. Its England has the spiritual tiredness of an old people's home, an England where Georgianism finally comes to rest. Larkin's only course from it was retrenchment, as in the self-consciously traditionalist 'Show Saturday' (a poem born out of Betjeman by way of *A Girl in Winter*). But this poem is surely one of the least interesting he ever wrote about England, a rhythmically dull, over-long attempt to describe an England which, unlike Betjeman, he never knew.

> Grey day for the Show, but cars jam the narrow lanes.
> Inside, on the field, judging has started: dogs
> (Set their legs back, hold out their tails) and ponies (manes
> Repeatedly smoothed, to calm heads); over there, sheep
> (Cheviot and Blackface);   (LP, p. 199)

Larkin tries to see the show as an ancestral celebration of 'regenerate union' but when he really does confront the traditional, as here, his verse has the beat of tired prose. It only comes to life in the grim, cultureless world of the contemporary.

An obvious case in point is 'Homage to a Government', one of the few poems where Larkin's tone is radically uncertain. This poem is a clever piece of versified editorialising written in protest at the second Wilson government's closing down of British military bases in South East Asia. It is hard to believe that Larkin felt very passionately about this theme although he speaks like some ashamed ghost sadly visiting the scene of its former glory:

> It's hard to say who wanted it to happen,
> But now its been decided nobody minds.
> The places are a long way off, not here,
> Which is all right, and from what we hear
> The soldiers there only made trouble happen.
> Next year we shall be easier in our minds.   (LP, p. 171)

Whether these listless rhythms are meant to convey irony or depression or both isn't clear. How could it be? We are not even told where the 'places' the troops are leaving actually *are*. Neither does Larkin risk mentioning that they were sent there in the first place to safeguard British money – that is, for the same reason they are now being withdrawn. The poem is really just another moan over the present, disguising itself as public comment. It is as bankrupt politically as rhythmically. Seldom has moral decline been castigated in accents so weary and inert. The fact is that by the end Larkin had little in common with his actual England and only an increasingly helpless irony with which to fend it off. When one compares a poem like 'Homage to a Government' with his really fine late work – 'Aubade', 'The Building', 'The Old Fools' – it becomes clear that, as Edward Thomas also realised, the best writing about England is that which avoids rolling the word 'England' around its mouth. Larkin wrote most deeply about it when he did not need to write about it literally.[48]

NOTES

(Place of publication is London unless otherwise stated)

1 *The Force of Poetry* (Oxford University Press, 1987), p. 278.
2 *Collected Poems*, ed. with introd. by Anthony Thwaite (Faber, 1988), p. 111. (Future references will be incorporated in the text as LP.)
3 *Coasting* (Pan Books, 1986), pp. 260–8.
4 *Required Writing: Miscellaneous Pieces 1955–1982* (Faber, 1983), p. 208.
5 *Ibid.*, p. 214.
6 *Young Betjeman* (John Murray, 1988), p. 203.
7 *Ibid.*, p. xvii.
8 *Collected Poems: Enlarged Edition*, comp. with introd. by the Earl of Birkenhead (John Murray, 1984), p. 385. (Future references will be given in the text as BP.)
9 *Antiquarian Prejudice*, p. 207.
10 *Required Writing*, p. 207.
11 *Ibid.*, p. 211.
12 *Ibid.*, p. 218.
13 *Lost Bearings in English Poetry* (Vision Press, 1977), p. 168.
14 *A Girl in Winter* (Faber, 1975), p. 80. See Seamus Heaney's brilliant essay on 'Englishness' in Larkin (and Hughes and Hill) in *Preoccupations: Selected Prose 1968–1978* (Faber, 1980), pp. 150–69.
15 Preface to *Selected Poems by John Betjeman* (John Murray, 1948), p. xix.
16 *These the Companions: Recollections* (Cambridge University Press, 1982), p. 123.
17 'Hardy's Virgilian Purples', *The Poet in the Imaginary Museum*, ed. Barry Alpert (Carcanet, Manchester, 1977), pp. 221–35.
18 *Ibid.*, p. 72.
19 *Thomas Hardy and British Poetry* (Routledge and Kegan Paul, 1979), p. 68.

20 *Ibid.*, p. 64.
21 'Middle-Brow Muse', *Essays in Criticism* 7 (April, 1957), 209.
22 *Required Writing*, p. 208.
23 *Young Betjeman*, p. 67.
24 Quoted *ibid.*, p. 165.
25 *Thomas Hardy*, p. 110.
26 *Required Writing*, p. 209.
27 Quoted by Charles Monteith, 'Publishing Larkin', *Larkin at Sixty*, ed. Anthony Thwaite (Faber, 1982), p. 42.
28 *Young Betjeman*, p. 393.
29 Jeremy Hooker, *Poetry of Place: Essays and Reviews* 1970–1981 (Carcanet, Manchester, 1982), p. 30.
30 *Ibid.*, p. 34.
31 *The South Country*, introd. by Helen Thomas and new preface by R. George Thomas (Dent, 1984), p. 5.
32 See *Viewpoints: Poets in Conversation with John Haffenden* (Faber, 1981), p. 89.
33 *Required Writing*, p. 209.
34 *Poetry Today: A Critical Guide to British Poetry* 1960–1984 (Longman, 1985), p. 7.
35 *Required Writing*, p. 175.
36 See 'The Novels of Barbara Pym' in *Required Writing*, for an example of such quietness.
37 *Thomas Hardy*, p. 65.
38 *These the Companions*, p. 152.
39 *Viewpoints*, p. 31.
40 *Ibid.*, p. 32.
41 *Ibid.*, p. 38.
42 *The House of Fiction: Essays on the Novel by Henry James*, ed. Leon Edel (Mercury Books, 1962), p. 259.
43 Lolette Kirby, *An Uncommon Poet for the Common Man: A Study of Philip Larkin's Poetry* (Mouton, The Hague, 1974).
44 *Viewpoints*, p. 41.
45 *Required Writing*, p. 52.
46 See Stan Smith, *Inviolable Voice: History of Twentieth Century Poetry*, (Gill Macmillan, 1983), p. 161.
47 For a detailed account of the 'Movement' writers and their highly revealing careers see Blake Morrison's *The Movement: English Poetry and Fiction of the* 1950s (Methuen, 1980).
48 Donald Davie's *After Briggflatts* (Carcanet, Manchester, 1989) appeared after this chapter was written. The reader will find much of value in it on subjects tackled here. It was also too late for me to profit from Tom Paulin's cogent account of Larkin's 'Englishness' in *Minotaur: Poetry and the Nation State* (Faber, 1992), pp. 233–57.

CHAPTER 8

Geoffrey Hill and the 'floating of nostalgia'

Although Hill gives the impression of feeling England in his bones he also thinks of it as lying outside himself, at a remove. Writing about his own part of England he begins with a pondered deliberateness, as if it were only imaginable through meditation:

> So to celebrate the kingdom: it grows
> greener in winter, essence of the year;
> the apple-branches musty with green fur.
> In the viridian darkness of its yews
>
> it is an enclave of perpetual vows
> broken in time.[1]

The 'kingdom' is disclosed gradually, as if one's eyes were slowly becoming accustomed to the dark and beginning to make things out in it. Hill is not from the same part of England as A. E. Housman for nothing but the many-layered, unfathomed quality of his 'kingdom' makes Housman's look rather simple. His music is richer, with more pith and sinew, like a dark baritone to Housman's tenor:

> Oh tarnish late on Wenlock Edge,
>   Gold that I never see;
> Lie long, high snowdrifts in the hedge
>   That will not shower on me.

The poignancy of these lines attaches more to the poet's feelings than to their object: Wenlock Edge seems precious because it is so little known. It is Housman's distance from his image of England that gives *A Shropshire Lad* its lyric simplicity. He never gets near enough to Shropshire to complicate this image with a living complexity.[2] Hill, by contrast, is always trying to edge nearer the past, to press beyond poetical assumptions about it. What gives depth to his England is that, though it is never finally knowable, he feels drawn to pursue it even as it eludes him. He is as stimulated by its mysteriousness as by the (numerous) things he does know about it. A static symbol of lost beauty, like Housman's Wenlock Edge, could not satisfy this need, because it is a need to recover a relation to the past and not simply a desire to make plangent celebrations of its pastness.

The sensation of being drawn to your roots though cut off from them is, of course, a particularly modern one. Hill himself has been especially conscious of it in connection with the written word, which may be why he has sometimes sought, as in *Tenebrae*, to write in the accents of earlier poets. But it is as if English civilisation no longer benefits from the continuity it once had. In a recent essay on Tyndale and the Revised English Bible, Hill maintained that modern 'education and communication' have 'destroyed memory and dissipated attention'.[3] In the same essay he claimed that for us 'The doctrine, the faith, of Luther and Tyndale are an alien tongue.'[4] The consequence of this has been 'irreparable damage inflicted, during the past eighty years or so, on the common life of the nation'.[5] England has become 'alien' to the English because of their obsession with their own modernity (in this case, with modern versions of the Bible). Such views are no doubt 'conservative' but they are also anti-establishment (Hill gives short shrift to the Anglican hierarchy). He is not interested in the past as a stick to beat the present with. He no more takes the 'common life of the nation' for granted in its history than he can in his own times. To participate at all in such 'common life' the poet has to recreate it for himself by a slow process of conscious effort. He knows very well that, if the English are, as it were, spiritually amputated, their plight can hardly be rectified by wishful thinking. This is why his poems about English history deliberately focus on passages in our history that most of us have forgotten about. It is because of this forgetting that *Funeral Music* and *Mercian Hymns* can be seen as poems about what it is like to live in twentieth-century England too.

To begin from Hill's preoccupation with the past may be misleading. Most poems about the past are wistful and elegiac whereas Hill's are terse and direct. For him, the act of retrospection is seldom an excuse for leisurely musings about 'battles long ago'. The first thing that strikes one about his poems (it also helps to explain their cryptic quality) is their lack of preamble, their ability to begin from the front line:

> I love my work and my children. God
> Is distant, difficult.   ('Ovid in the Third Reich' HP, p. 61)
> There is a land called Lost
> at peace inside our heads.
>
> ('Two Chorale-Preludes', I, HP, p. 165)

Openings like these throw us off balance, plunge us without more ado into some new experience. They are quite free of that tone of rumination which lowers the temperature of so much recent verse. The words are crisp and definite, chiselled words that demand attention. Even when they seem obscure there is nothing hazy about them. When Hill writes about the past, he makes us feel as if we were living *in* it, not simply looking back on it. It is more important to him that history should be capable of shocking us than that it should be picturesque. It is as immediate to him as his present is.

In the important interview he gave to John Haffenden in 1981, Hill repudiated the suggestion that, in writing about the past, he had been prompted by nostalgia. What had motivated him was the desire to exorcise the nostalgia that struck him as endemic to twentieth-century England:

If one writes lyrics of which nostalgia is an essential element, naive or malicious critics will say that the nostalgia must be one's own. There are, however, good political and sociological reasons for the floating of nostalgia: there has been an elegiac tinge to the air of this country ever since the end of the Great War. To be accused of exhibiting a symptom when, to the best of my ability, I'm offering a diagnosis appears to be one of the numerous injustices which one must suffer with as much equanimity as possible.[6]

Hill may be a too self-conscious St Sebastian here to the arrows of his critics but he is entitled to feel stung by their complaints. The past he dwells on is more often a snare or a bad dream than a consoling refuge. It is pain that solicits him, more than pleasure:

> Poetry as salutation; taste
> Of Pentecost's ashen feast. Blue wounds.
> The tongue's atrocities. Poetry
> Unearths from among the speechless dead
>
> Lazarus mystified, common man
> Of death. The lily rears its gouged face
> From the provided loam.   ('History as Poetry' HP, p. 84)

Violence and death are the only soil in which the spirit can truly grow. Thus, *Funeral Music* unremittingly undermines any nostalgia or glamour we may still project onto the blood-stained history of the

Wars of the Roses. The sequence is able to explore religious feelings only because it always keeps in mind what the sixth sonnet calls 'the world's real cries' of pain and despair. Hill interrogates the ghosts of the fifteenth century as if they enabled him to perform an especially testing series of spiritual exercises. Every sonnet is tight-lipped with suffering. The verse remains lapidary and chillingly concise, refusing to pull out all its rhetorical stops as one expects it to do:

> Recall the cold
> Of Towton on Palm Sunday before dawn,
> Wakefield, Tewkesbury: fastidious trumpets
> Shrilling into the ruck; some trampled
> Acres, parched, sodden or blanched by sleet,
> Stuck with strange-postured dead. Recall the wind's
> Flurrying, darkness over the human mire.   (HP, p. 71)

There is no attempt to force contemporary meaning onto the grim scene, no wish to provide the twentieth-century excursionist with a guided tour of one of the more colourful landmarks of history. The reader is no more spared the meaningless horror than are the poem's speakers themselves. What survives of Towton, in the words of Hill's short essay on *Funeral Music*, is 'a florid grim music broken by grunts and shrieks'(HP, p. 199).[7] To come to terms with history as human experience the poet has to recognise its otherness. The last thing Hill offers us is an opportunity to make believe we are medieval.

Nostalgia, on the other hand, likes to pretend that the past is really there just to feed itself. It makes it into a repository for feelings it is unable to indulge in the present, projecting them onto it until they mask what it really was. (Thus, the traditional Western film – all those open spaces and shoot-outs laid on for suburban America – is a classic example of nostalgia.) By contrast, in Hill's poems, we are directed to the invisible and larger part of the iceberg of the past and not to its obvious emotional high-points above the surface. He is not interested in our received ideas about England but either in Englands of which we are ignorant or in seeing the Englands we do know from an unexpected angle. What strikes one most in Hill's treatment of history is his acute sense of the painfulness of life in the past. Life is not a whit less hard in medieval England than it is in poems like the 'Two Formal Elegies' in *For the Unfallen* which he dedicates 'For the Jews in Europe'. The past he writes about is never *over*. In his moving essay on St Robert Southwell, the Jesuit martyr tortured under Elizabeth I, Hill puts himself on the rack too, both repelled and drawn by the thought of the poet's terrible end. It is as if he himself were implicated in the guilt for such horrors and felt doomed to re-live Southwell's agony. History guarantees neither an attitude of objectivity nor a means of escaping from the self.

Referring to his sonnet sequence *An Apology for the Revival of Christian Architecture in England*, Hill reminded John Haffenden that it is as important to deplore what happened in the past as to celebrate it. One good reason for not being nostalgic is the thought of the countless ordinary people who suffered in the creation of England's greatness:

I think the sad serenity and elegance of the eighteenth century country house landscape was bought at a price: not only the sufferings of English labourers but also of Indian peasants... The celebration of the inherited beauties of the English landscape is bound, in the texture of the sequence, with an equal sense of the oppression of the tenantry.[8]

This feeling for the unsung classes which political and artistic history ignore is a constant in Hill's work. (Not for nothing did he choose to write at length about a poet like Charles Péguy, who came from peasant stock.) Even at its loveliest, the past can weigh on Hill like some beautiful incubus. One finds such feelings in one of the first things he ever published, a student piece written at Oxford:

One might think that the great strength and appeal of Oxford lay in its tradition; that an awareness of this would grant a sense of peace and security. But one has found tradition as cold a shadow here as in Westminster Abbey. There is small comfort in being crowded out by ghosts. Under the chill salty-smelling stone of the great Tudor gate-houses, beneath the high rows of portraits in the halls, thin lipped prelates, all evil-looking old men, you are brow-beaten by the past.[9]

Hill's fascination with history has always been accompanied by feelings of exclusion. It is this that has drawn him to a poet like Ivor Gurney who felt so bitterly his lack of recognition from the country on whose behalf he had written.[10] The only way Hill has ever been able to express a full-throated, unembarrassed love of country has been indirectly, through the French poet Charles Péguy's commitment to his 'terre charnelle'. In his own voice, he has never been certain of *which* England his poems invoke. Indeed, speaking of *Mercian Hymns*, he describes Offa as a 'tyrannical creator of order and beauty' who serves him as 'an objective correlative for the inevitable feelings of love and hate which any man or woman must feel for the *patria*.' Offa represents 'the ambiguities of English history in general'[11] – that is, an England that can never be so defined that it evokes only one emotional response. It is an illusion to imagine that, because one is English, one knows what England is.

Hill's claim to diagnose the 'elegiac tinge' of modern Britain might be taken to mean that he sees himself as a physician bent on lancing some infected growth. But he is less puritanical about nostalgia than such a description suggests. His attitude to it is by no means simply hygienic. In the essay on Southwell, for instance, he speculates that, as early as the Tudors, a nostalgia for lost innocence was already present in English culture. Such emotions are not automatically spurious or self-deceiving; indeed, Hill finds a certain nobility in them, as he does in their literary equivalent: 'there's a real sense in which every fine and moving poem bears witness to this lost kingdom of innocence and original justice. In handling the English language the poet makes an act of recognition that etymology is history. The history of the creation and the debasement of words is a paradigm of the loss of the kingdom of innocence and original justice.'[12] For the poet who uses a fallen language there are two ways of imagining the past, one nostalgic and the other redemptive, but they are too complementary to be easily told apart. The interview with Haffenden makes this clear by both disclaiming nostalgia and, in the same breath, acknowledging its central place in poetry. Hill begins by describing the 'failure to truly grasp experience and substance' as no less than 'one of the characteristic failings of human nature':[13]

If critics accuse me of evasiveness or the vice of nostalgia, or say that *I* seem incapable of grasping true religious experience, I would answer that the grasp of true religious experience is a privilege reserved for very few, and that one is trying to make lyrical poetry out of a much more common situation – the sense of *not* being able to grasp true religious experience. I'm accused of being nostalgic when I'm in fact trying to draw the graph of nostalgia. The painter Francis Bacon said somewhere that he was 'trying to paint the track left by human beings like the slime left by a snail', and it seems to me that in poetry also one is trying to trace the track left by human beings, which is full of false directions and self-pity and nostalgia as well as lust, wrath, greed and pride.[14]

The diagnostician is not simply bent on keeping himself pure from some emotional malady. He recognises nostalgia as a part of his humanity, something more deep-seated than the sort of modern vice which a critic like D. W. Harding tended to treat it as.[15] To be able to draw its graph a poet must first of all feel it in himself. One lesson we can learn from Hill is to be suspicious of any English writer, coming this late in the country's history, who claims to be free of nostalgia. It is a salutary lesson for there have been few periods when more writers have pretended to be aloof and immune to their own 'Englishness' and free to judge it dispassionately than the last twenty years. Condescending analyses of Edwardian and Georgian patriotism have, for example, been the stock-in-trade of many writers on the Left who never trouble to expose their own feelings about England to a similar scrutiny.[16] Their attitude to nostalgia is very different from Hill's: he can claim to chart it because he has felt it himself, whereas they reject it because they cannot quite believe it to be real. As his essay on Ivor Gurney makes clear, it has not been just the sentimentalists among us who have yearned for the England before the Great War. It needs no ghost come from the dead to remind us what deep feelings have been sharpened by that watershed, severing for good what continuity had been left untouched by a rampant industrialism. It is, in fact, arguable that, without nostalgia, for many of us the past might not exist at all. The malady is not simply deep-seated – it may even be necessary.

Hill's verse at times can give the impression of having discarded the fleeting liveliness of modern speech for a weightier idiom culled from the past. It often has a curiously timeless feeling about it, as if it would be as much at home in the age of Wordsworth or the seventeenth century as with the glib intimacies of contemporary poetry. This is not to say that its music is archaic but his scrupulosity with words is a more musical scrupulosity than is usual.[17] He listens for the right word like a musician listening for the right note. It is this which gives his language its special precision. The effect would be beyond a simple Parnassian stylist. It aims at power, not fastidiousness. *Funeral Music*, for instance, has a grave underswell that probably owes more to the English of the King James Bible than any of Hill's contemporaries do, though it does not read like imitation. Witness the plain dignity of these lines from the seventh sonnet, describing the bloody battle of Towton in 1461:

> 'At noon,
> As the armies met, each mirrored the other;
> Neither was outshone. So they flashed and vanished
> And all that survived them was the stark ground

Of this pain. I made no sound, but once
I stiffened as though a remote cry
Had heralded my name. It was nothing ... '
Reddish ice tinged the reeds; dislodged, a few
Feathers drifted across; carrion birds
Strutted upon the armour of the dead. (HP, p. 76)

This is so grim because it is shorn of rhetoric. In many ways, its
rhythms are prose rhythms – they refuse to catch fire, to sing. The
witness of the battle is cut short in mid-sentence and his voice
swallowed up in an eerie silence. The last three lines of the sonnet feel
almost clinical in their unremitting pursuit of the *mot juste*. Yet the
overall effect is far from being simply austere. What makes *Funeral
Music* unusual is its union of intensity and detachment, as of fire and
ice. Far from being a means of disengaging himself from the carnage
of Towton, Hill's neutral tone is a way of bringing out the enormity
of the scene. It is striking how vivid a picture of the battle's violence
the sequence conjures up whilst treating that violence with a sort of
guarded reticence. Of course, Hill is less interested in a drama of
action in *Funeral Music* than in the silence of its aftermath. This is why
he avoids giving his sequence any coherent narrative (though his
essay on the poem hints at one). The real drama takes place between
the reader and the unrehearsed anguish of the victims as it carries
across the centuries. Hence the voice heard in sonnet VII, measured
like the speech of yesterday but direct as a contemporary's.

Funeral Music never offers the compensatory thought of time the
healer (as *Little Gidding* does): Hill's object seems to be to direct us to
an exposed wound in our history to make sure that it stays exposed.
He refuses to mediate the anguish of Towton through any sort of
hindsight. The battle, or what glimpses we have of it, is presented as
raw experience, not as a stage in any larger historical pattern. Its
victims are denied the option of viewing their fates with detachment:

I believe in my abandonment, since it is what I have. (HP, p. 75)

And:

Then tell me, love,
How that should comfort us – or anyone
Dragged half-unnerved out of this worldly place,
Crying to the end 'I have not finished'. (HP, p. 77)

Such suffering is irreducible, without hope of transcendence. Its only
lesson is in its sheer acuteness. With other Hill poems in mind (for

example, 'Four Poems Regarding the Endurance of Poets' in *King Log*) it might be argued that the sufferers in *Funeral Music* undergo a kind of martyrdom (Hill has always been drawn to martyrs) but it is not possible to say what their martyrdom might be *for*. The many religious allusions in the sequence feel studiously agnostic. What matters seems to be the suffering *as* suffering. But why rake over the faded coals of history and fan them back into heat, only to walk barefoot over them? Should we see *Funeral Music* as at bottom an elaborate penitential exercise? In fact there are twentieth-century parallels for Towton but Hill is careful not to imply that its bloodshed is evoked merely to symbolise more recent holocausts. To make Towton's suffering stand for something else would be to make it less actual by providing a way of intellectualising its horror. Hill's poetry is often accused of being over-cerebral but, characteristically, it works very close to lived experience – in *Funeral Music*, uncomfortably close. His vigilant attention to the suggestions of its every word strikes me as stemming not primarily from either self-consciousness or academic ingenuity but from an anxiety not to falsify or doctor that experience. Thus, one of the most constant effects of *Funeral Music* is its habit of punctuating its own rhetoric with unmusical, vernacular cries of pain. It is as if the poet needs to remind himself that what he has made into a poem had another, quite unliterary origin:

> Blindly the questing snail, vulnerable
> Mole emerge, blindly we lie down, blindly
> Among carnage the most delicate souls
> Tup in their marriage-blood, gasping 'Jesus'.   (HP, p. 72)

The word 'Jesus' is deliberately ambiguous – sacred and profane – and, coming where it does, with an unexpected spontaneity as well as with finality, its ambiguity undercuts the meditative assurance of the lines that lead up to it. Whether the word is said in prayer or as an expletive its effect is to sabotage the carefully cadenced music of the poem's conclusion. This sort of sniping at our aesthetic satisfactions is a reminder that there was something in the horror of Towton which could not be sublimated into art. Similar scruples can be found both in Hill's first book, *For the Unfallen*, overshadowed by the modern holocaust, and in later things like his tragi-comic treatment of the death of Péguy at the Battle of the Marne. All through his career he has been drawn to make poetry out of pain and violence and suspicious of his own motives for doing so.

Usually, when writers re-create the past, they seek to bring it back to life for a while as if we belonged in it. This is not how Hill proceeds. The nameless speakers of *Funeral Music* may voice an intense experience but that experience always seems truncated, eked out in an abbreviated and edited way. The sequence even leaves us uncertain as to when Suffolk, Worcester and Rivers – its putative protagonists – are being referred to: we are never on speaking terms with them. The voices we hear seem to belong to everyone and no one, a chorus of anonymously individual cries of pain. History remains foreign and impenetrable, a puzzle to which we possess only a few of the clues. The poet adjures us to remember events which we have no means of reconstructing, a past which leaves us face to face with a kind of redoubtable blank:

> Recall the cold
> Of Towton on Palm Sunday before dawn,
> Wakefield, Tewkesbury: fastidious trumpets
> Shrilling into the ruck; some trampled
> Acres, parched, sodden or blanched by sleet,
> Stuck with strange-postured dead. Recall the wind's
> Flurrying, darkness over the human mire.   (HP, p. 71)

As the neutral 'stuck' suggests, the picture of the battlefield is alienating as well as appalling. Windswept and amorphous, it offers no purchase to our desire for a human narrative. It is as if the sequence had only created a sense of tragedy in order to reveal that there is nothing in the scene for tragedy to attach itself to. History affords only a succession of unanswered questions. There are no clearly shaped tragic destinies to be found in the 'human mire' of Towton. When the third sonnet refers to 'England crouched beastwise beneath it all' (HP, p. 72) one takes it that, whatever 'England' may be, it is something too hidden and primitive to be interpreted by the rational patterns of the historian. Hill takes us only a step inside this remote past and then the line goes dead and we are left to conjecture. But this is not simply a way of reflecting our limited knowledge of the history of the fifteenth century. More is known about Towton than Hill chooses to divulge. The drive of *Funeral Music* is towards a rigorous selection from history – so much so, that the sequence leaves us to guess who was fighting and who won. Not that Hill is merely teasing his readers. Keeping us in the dark is a way of reminding us that history is never there for the asking, just because it is our own. *Funeral Music* is one long caveat against our desire to explain the past:

> If it is without
> Consequence when we vaunt and suffer, or
> If it is not, all echoes are the same
> In such eternity.

(HP, p. 77)

Hill unflinchingly refuses to prise a meaning out of such echoes.

Hill's originality becomes clearer if one compares him with a writer like Sir Walter Scott, who was equally absorbed by the past. For instance, in *Old Mortality*, one of Scott's finest novels, the story is mediated through the strange figure of Old Mortality himself as he travels the length and breadth of lowland Scotland renovating the gravestones of the old Covenanters. His chisel, like Hill's pen, serves as a reminder of mortality, of all the deaths that constitute what we call history. But Scott uses Old Mortality as a means of underlining our fellow-feeling with the dead. If the faces of the Covenanters begin by seeming as blank as their gravestones the novelist fills those blanks in. This is precisely what *Funeral Music* refuses to do.[18] If it invites sympathy for the victims of Towton at one moment, it fends it off the next. What shapes up as a drama keeps turning into a kind of ritual which, though moving, keeps us at arm's length:

> For whom do we scrape our tribute of pain –
> For none but the ritual king? We meditate
> A rueful mystery; we are dying
> To satisfy fat Caritas, those
> Wiped jaws of stone.

(HP, p. 71)

Whoever is speaking here, Hill is speaking through them. This is why the lines appear to be standing back with grave composure from the suffering in which the speakers are trapped. The poignancy of the verse has none of that warming sense of fellow-feeling that characterises Scott. The object of the solemn meditation, 'fat Caritas', is far more vivid than those who are dying for it. That is, the undoubted intensity of *Funeral Music* remains a rather cold intensity. For instance:

> Our lives could be a myth of captivity
> Which we might enter: an unpeopled region
> Of ever new-fallen snow, a palace blazing
> With perpetual silence as with torches.

(HP, p. 73)

Such lines seem to hold themselves aloof from us, just as the past Hill describes does.

The remoteness of the speakers in *Funeral Music* is of a special sort. They are also very much at the poet's disposal. One feels that they say just so much and no more, according to the overall shape of the poems they appear in. By not naming them, Hill makes it easier to control them. There is something placed about his people, as if he had asked them to stand still and hold their pose while he photographed them. The stained-glass saint of 'In Piam Memoriam' is a famous example of a figure pinned down in an attitude that assists and never distracts the poet who is communing with him. Other characters in Hill's poems are pinned down by death – he has little of Hughes's delight in creatures that move. Even Péguy, a man whom no one could silence in life, is virtually dispossessed of his voice in *The Mystery of the Charity of Charles Péguy*. I do not suggest that these things are at all inappropriate in context (Hill has a keen sense of poetic decorum) but that they imply a component of mastery in his writing, a will that needs to keep every element of a poem in its grip. And this is what his vigilant alertness to possible puns, his tightness of structure and his weakness for over-finical footnotes also imply. His habit of holding himself morally responsible for every word he writes is itself in part an expression of his feeling for power over what he creates.[19] The desire to leave nothing to chance can also denote an unusually insistent sense of purpose. The pared-down economy of *Funeral Music* portends something very similar, a writer who is unusually conscious about what he is trying to do. In each of Hill's major sequences his calculated abridgements of his story leave one contrasting his control over his material with one's own uncertainties about it. What we know about Sebastian Arrurruz or Offa or Péguy feels more salient than complete. Any coldness is clearly related to the reduced opportunity for empathy that such selectiveness entails. To describe Hill's writing as cryptic is really to point out the ways in which it keeps emotion at bay, rather than its more obvious tendency to tease the intellect.

A critic who takes a similar view of *Funeral Music* to this is C. H. Sisson. Though he praises its 'indubitable directness' he is troubled by the way it draws attention to itself as an artifact: 'something worked towards and built, which suggests a growing distance between the poetic impulse and the words which finally appear on the page – a gain in architectonics, perhaps, but at a price which is so often paid, by all but the greatest writers, in a loss of immediacy. '[20] Sisson describes the intensely written quality of Hill's verse as a form of self-protection: 'There is in Hill a touch of the fastidiousness of Crashaw, which is that of a mind in search of artifices to protect itself against its own passions. '[21] This may be so but another upshot of Hill's fastidiousness is found in his gift for stamping his own identity on whatever he deals with. There is nothing random about the speakers in *Funeral Music*, no sense of their forming a chorus of jarring and disparate voices: every voice we hear in the poem has the solemnity of the poet's own voice. That is presumably part of the subject's attraction to Hill. The dead, like the past itself, cannot answer back. We can impose ourselves upon them as we wish or need to. However, the fact that we are always conscious of Hill's fashioning of his material does not mean that his sequence is an 'artifact' merely in the technical sense, as, say, a clock is the product of the clock-maker's craft. Hill is evidently as much drawn to his subject by the moral as by the technical demands it makes on him; the sort of 'difficulty' he deals in is a matter of both. What Sisson does put his finger on is the sense that Hill has laboured and laboured his lines and, unlike the Yeats of 'Adam's Curse', is prepared to let that labour show. But Hill is a more dogged poet than Crashaw. It is easier to imagine him chipping painstakingly away at his words than as having the leisure to elaborate them with a flourish of fancy. In the end, the Hill Sisson conjures up sounds too flamboyant and not sufficiently concentrated in feeling to have written *Funeral Music*.

A fuller description of the kind of control Hill has over his subject matter in *Funeral Music* is supplied by Merle Brown (one of his most perceptive critics). He draws attention to the tenacious, heuristic movement of the verse: 'Even though it seems magnificent when read as both sequential and simultaneous, it is always edged with a problem in painful need of solution, so that it does not move like a broad and deep river, but twists and turns, swerves or shrinks. '[22] This captures well Hill's gift for keeping his reader on the *qui vive*, never letting any one emotion take over more than briefly. The poem shapes the feeling, not the feeling the poem. Hill's later work may be less jagged and sudden in movement than *Funeral Music* but it remains every bit as controlled. John Silkin argues persuasively that in the later poems this control declines into a literary manner. Unlike poems where 'the directness comes in the character of expressed experience, for which there is no finer, more delicate intermediary

than directness, the simplicity [in *Tenebrae*] is one of style. There is
nothing to compose from conflicted response into directness. There is
no apprehension.'[23] Certainly, anyone turning from the earlier to the
later volume will come upon verse which seems liturgical and
aesthetic, as if the intensity had been shaped out of it:

> And you, who with your soft but searching voice
> drew me out of the sleep where I was lost,
> who held me near your heart that I might rest
> confiding in the darkness of your choice:
> possessed by you I chose to have no choice,
> fulfilled in you I sought no further quest.   (HP, p. 172)

These lines from 'Tenebrae' are so finished, so poised in their
antitheses, that their beauty, though moving, feels artful. The very
smoothness of the movement seals it in upon itself. It is as if an
aesthetic emotion were keeping an actual one at bay.

This is not to imply that *Funeral Music* itself is always innocent of
the sounding phrase and ringing cadence. Its rhetoric can be equally
written, as in sonnet 5:

> So many things rest under consummate
> Justice as though trumpets purified law,
> Spikenard were the real essence of remorse.
> The sky gathers up darkness. When we chant
> 'Ora, ora pro nobis' it is not
> Seraphs who descend to pity but ourselves.   (HP, p. 74)

The difference between these lines and those from 'Tenebrae', is that
their rhythm is skilfully arrested whenever it seems about to become
too swelling (for example, after 'remorse'). The final cry of the
speakers may be moulded by Hill's taut syntax but it still has the force
to break free of it:

> Racked on articulate looms indulge us
> With lingering shows of pain, a flagrant
> Tenderness of the damned for their own flesh.   (HP, p. 74)

The shock sprung by that last line is rarer in *Tenebrae*. This is not
because Hill has more control over his material than in the earlier
sequence but that his control has become more striking than that
which is being controlled. The final section of 'Tenebrae' underlines
this:

Music survives, composing her own sphere,
Angel of Tones, Medusa, Queen of the Air,
and when we would accost her with real cries
silver on silver thrills itself to ice.   (HP, p. 174)

This is immaculate but hardly unobtrusive. The poetry too inhabits its 'own sphere' where those 'real cries' seem elegantly to freeze. In *Funeral Music* it is the sound of such cries that we remember.

One of the epigraphs to Hill's *Collected Poems*, a line from Pound, seems especially pertinent to his treatment of history: 'In the gloom, the gold gathers the light against it'. Hill clearly wants to plunge his reader into this darkness so that he can let him slowly become accustomed to seeing in the half-light. Thus England itself, which history discloses and conceals, lies not on the surface of our lives but buried like treasure trove, as in poem XIII of *Mercian Hymns* where Offa's 'masterful head emerges, kempt and jutting, out of England's well'. (HP, p. 117) It is from this 'well' that the speakers of *Funeral Music* come. One of the most fascinating aspects of the sequence is the sense it gives of raw human experience suddenly looming towards us out of the remote past. The silence in which it seems enveloped is itself part of the drama. A well has to be deep. It is as though Hill sees life most clearly when he sees it at a distance.

This is why the dead of *Funeral Music* are faceless and undefined, without the bravado of tragedy. Hill infers their suffering but never presumes to share it. Their cries never quite come from centre-stage. Moreover, Hill distrusts the modern myth which chooses to see the poet as occupying some perilously exposed outpost on the frontier of 'Reality'. He has written more than one poem about the holocaust whose burden is the inadequacy of poetry to describe such a subject. It is not, to his mind, so easy to live on the front line as some poets have made out. The point is made in his essay on Yeats when he quotes from Czeslaw Milosz (a favourite of Ted Hughes's). In Milosz's view, 'only those things are worth while which can preserve their validity in the eyes of a man threatened with instant death'. In Hill's view, this is to glorify an 'arbitrary fire':

The passage purports to establish new terms of the utmost purity: things and moments. What it does, in fact, is to elevate the man-of-the-moment. However humbled one may be by this, it is still necessary not to be bullied by its absolutist élitist tone. For those who detect the élitism, yet remain humiliated by their implied failure to live up to such demands, the poem of rigorous comfort is Yeats's 'Easter 1916'.[24]

One of the things for which Hill prefers Yeats's poem is what he calls its 'artifice', 'the tune of a mind distrustful yet envious, mistrusting the abstraction, mistrusting its own mistrust'.[25] If it achieves such 'intellect', poetry need not be either 'confessional' (a word Hill uses with distaste) or self-consciously bent on outstaring the Gorgon's head. But if Hill's patiently reconstructed history, his peering down 'England's well', seems vicarious in comparison with the front-line activity of Milosz (or Hughes) that does not mean that its end-product is less intense. Hill's indirections in *Funeral Music* give rise to an unsettling directness. If this is not the tension Milosz recommends it is at least comparable to it.

Hill's ambition to chart our nostalgia is a way of claiming a public role for his work. His concern with the power poets wield issues naturally in a concern with the way power operates in politics itself. Both kinds of power are aspects of the same thing, notably so in many of the writers he has been drawn to write about – Southwell, Swift, Péguy, Yeats and Pound among them. Writing is a political act. The literary conscience requires a commitment to the language which, in turn, implies a commitment to the community that the language embodies. A poet has more than just himself to express, rather in the way Leavis thinks of Bunyan as a spokesman for a whole culture. This does not mean, of course, that a poet can take the continuity of his culture as guaranteed. Taken on trust, the language of the past becomes a barrier to the new. A crucial element in the literary conscience is the power to transform language in the light of new experiences. But if poetic creation begins at this nexus of past and present so too do its dangers. Creativity entails responsibility and responsibility all too easily entails guilt. It is this fraught region that most of Hill's essays (like his poems) set out to explore.

To possess a literary conscience is also to possess a sense of power, though the two senses sometimes clash. In 'Our Word is Our Bond', a complex meditation on this theme, Hill begins from the 'treason' of Ezra Pound which he defines as a poetic as well as political treason. Pound's fatal error was to confuse the two spheres. As the Washington hearing put it, his alleged crime was 'closely tied up with his profession of writing' (LL, p. 158), so much so that he ended up believing that poets were also 'legislators' (LL, p. 159). Hill's own position, on the other hand, is like Sir Philip Sidney's: 'for the *Poet*, he nothing affirmeth, and therefore never lieth'. In wanting to be a poet *and* to affirm (legislate) his views Pound stands condemned according to the rigour of his own search for the *mot juste*: by keeping a foot in both camps he ceases to be *juste* in either sense. In Wittgenstein's words (quoted by Hill in his essay on Empson): 'Ethics and Aesthetics are one.'[26] The power Pound abused was inseparable from the power on which his poetic 'technique' depended.

Hill himself sometimes takes Wittgenstein's aphorism to an extreme where his own literary conscience begins to look neurotic:

> It seems to me one of the indubitable signs of Simone Weil's greatness as an ethical writer that she associates the act of writing not with a generalized awareness of sin but with specific crime, and proposes a system whereby 'anybody, no matter who, discovering an unavoidable error in a printed text or radio broadcast, would be entitled to bring an action before [special] courts' empowered to condemn a convicted offender to prison or hard labour. (LL, p. 8)

Hill concedes that this could seem 'obsessional' but seems not to notice how near such an inquisition comes to censorship if put into practice. It is not the writer's rights that concern him. Nonetheless, the sense of guilt may not always be as existentially purifying as Weil claimed. In Hill's case, it is also the spur to a self-regardingness whose literary fruits are inhibition, equivocation and sheer fussiness. Some of his notes to his own poems are guarded enough for a libel trial. More seriously, his penchant for double-meanings, which Christopher Ricks makes so much of, also has its roots in his sense of guilt.[27] But responsibility is a source of power as well as anxiety. The author of *Funeral Music* has agonised over his words in the interest of a final directness, not from a taste for casuistry. The music he converts his anxiety into is not itself anxious: 'poetic utterance is nonetheless an utterance of the self' (LL, p. 17). It is precisely within this area – between 'personal utterance' and 'responsibility' – that books like *Mercian Hymns* and *Tenebrae* find their subject. So too does their understanding of history as the main arena where individual will and obligation coincide, in Saxon Mercia as in the British Raj. We are never mere observers of our past, as the child of *Mercian Hymns* discovers, because we are implicated in history ourselves.

To think of Hill's version of history as a sort of substitute for more immediate political concerns is to ignore this capacity it has to involve us morally. The past is too much a part of us to be merely optional. There may, in our century, be two Englands, one past and one present, rather than one – that is something Philip Larkin increasingly felt – but whether they can still connect is the question Hill's poetry addresses. A sequence like *An Apology for the Revival of Christian Architecture* needs to keep a foot in both worlds to have meaning at all, to confirm that the language we inherit from the past can still create poetry in the present. 'Ethics' and 'aesthetics' remain inseparable but the modern poet is unsure of how far his power extends. This is the sense Hill shares with his predecessors and is drawn to explore in his criticism: though implicated in the Romantic notion of the writer's role he yet feels morally unable to share it. How can a poet have the prophetic authority of a Victor Hugo if he has the literary conscience of a Flaubert? Unlike the writers of Flaubert's and Baudelaire's generation, Hill does not seek to divorce art from politics. On the contrary, he finds them indissoluble. Hence the exemplary importance of Péguy. As the heir of Hugo rather than Mallarmé, Péguy was one of the last poets to lay claim to a genuinely public authority. In this respect, he could hardly be more different from Hill himself: an embattled polemicist, outside the pale of the university, the intransigent editor of *Les Cahiers de la Quinzaine*, Dreyfusard, antinomian, ex-communicate catholic, patriot in defiance of conventional patriotism, a sort of French version of the Coleridgean *clerc*, an intellectual with a conscience no institution could silence. A great figure, certainly, but also a curiously nineteenth-century mind for a modern poet. His quixotic distaste for any ivory tower during the Dreyfus Affair marked him out as a survivor from another world. It is precisely those qualities which make him noble in Hill's eyes which also mark the difference between them. But if I emphasise this difference it is as a way of underlining just how crucial their common sense of literary and political conscience is. The nature of the poet's responsibility is exactly the point at which Hill chooses to begin his *Mystery of the Charity of Charles Péguy*:

> Did Péguy kill Jaurès? Did he incite
> the assassin? Must men stand by what they write
> as by their camp-beds or their weaponry?　　(HP, p. 183)

The place Hill himself stands in is lonelier, though less exposed, but conscience is not all he has in common with Péguy. They are both faced with the problem of finding some continuity between their past and their present. In fact, the watershed that gives a shape to the life and death of Péguy, the Great War, is the same one that is crucial for Hill, the time from which the nostalgic bent of English culture since then derives. Péguy's words may have reverberated in a more public theatre but already their author had begun to seem a sort of noble misfit. No other solution would have been so fitting as his heroic death *pour la patrie*. As the case of Pound underlined so ironically, the problem of the writer's responsibility – so crucial to writers like Yeats and Lawrence at just this time – was simply that society had no use for it: it preferred to do without a conscience. This is what Pound failed to understand and what makes us think of Péguy as belonging to another age than our own. Hill, if he could, would like it both ways but fears that it is precisely that that is impossible.

Péguy was a lifelong socialist but also a declared enemy of that Progress for which most of his generation was so ready to tell lies. Furthermore, he was the kind of socialist who felt no qualms about taking over the right wing's rhetoric of 'la patrie', 'la vieille France' and so on. (The *anti-Dreyfusards* claimed to have a monopoly on patriotism.) What 'la vieille France' came down to in practice was something like a Catholic version of the 'organic community'. Some of the finest passages of Hill's poem on Péguy are evocations of precisely that. Hill's own interest in Tory radicals like Richard Oastler or the Southern Fugitives chimes closely with this side of Péguy. It enables him to refer to England when he is ostensibly writing about France. But, as one would expect, Hill is more sceptical about the past than Péguy was. He never takes it on trust. What is more, unlike Eliot, he can see tradition as threatening as well as benign. He thinks of words as coming down to the poet with a built-in 'inertial drag' (LL, p. 87) to them, inviting what I. A. Richards called 'stock responses'. Such words tell us what to think rather than allowing us to think through them. They may seem to propose a continuity that is 'organic' but, in reality, the poet needs to resist them. Only by resisting this 'inertial drag' in language do a few poets change its course enough for past and present to be brought together. Continuance is arrest and disjunction growth. This problem of actually making poetry creative takes us to the heart of Hill's work as a critic, to his essay 'Redeeming the Time' and, at its centre, the example of Wordsworth.

It may, however, help to begin from a simpler essay, the one on 'The Poetry of Swift', because it makes clear that what Hill is saying is not confined to Romantic poetry. Swift is praised for his 'capacity to be at once resistant and reciprocal' (LL, p. 67), for renewing the clichés that are his raw material by an 'energy' which seems 'to emerge from the destructive element itself' (LL, p. 81). One of the ways poets conserve their past is by seeming to erase it. Hill's own problem is very similar, though, as Merle Brown saw, it takes a more acute form. Brown defines Hill's poetry as 'a return home' via a 'deracinated language miraculously rooted anew', a return that mirrors England's post-war political situation: 'bound up with present-day English English, a language which had gradually come to be identical with the world on which the sun never sets, and, then, precipitously contracted into the language of but one small island.'[28] This helps to explain how verse as condensed and enigmatic as Hill's should result from writing in the shadow of a long poetic tradition. Yet this was by no means a new crisis in Hill or even Eliot. Walter Jackson Bate wrote a classic study of it in the eighteenth century in his *The Burden of the Past*. Its more recent crises find their model for Hill in 'Redeeming the Time', first published in *Agenda* in 1972–3, in a discussion of a famous passage of Wordsworth. None of Hill's essays is closer to his own poetic practice or more suggestive of the dilemmas he inherited from earlier poets.

The essay hinges on the not uncommon belief that the nineteenth century ushered in a radical change in English life. For poets, this change took the form of a new, quickened 'tempo' (LL, p. 84) of living, although only the greatest of them, Wordsworth and Hopkins in particular, were able to assimilate this new 'tempo' into their verse. Hill himself is alerted to it by a famous remark from Hopkins on the 'magical change'[29] of rhythm between stanzas eight and nine of the 'Immortality Ode', a change he too regards as one of the great moments of modern poetry:

> Full soon thy soul shall have her earthly freight,
> And custom lie upon thee with a weight,
> Heavy as frost, and deep almost as life!
>
> ix
> O joy! that in our embers
> Is something that doth live,
> That nature yet remembers
> What was so fugitive!

The cumulative impact of Wordsworth's change of key is lost in so short an extract but the scope of the change is still breath-taking. Here is Hill's response to it, as prompted by Hopkins's letter to Canon Dixon:

Wordsworth's strategy of combining a pause with a change of time-signature within the 'merely iambic' prevailing rhythm overrides both the propriety and the pressure. It could be suggested, in response to C. C. Clarke's criticism, that the Ode is being broken but that the break, far from being an injury sustained, is a resistance proclaimed. If language is more than a vehicle for the transmission of axioms and concepts, rhythm is correspondingly more than a physiological motor. It is capable of registering, mimetically, deep shocks of recognition. (LL, p. 87)

Hill no more sees this moment as merely technical than Hopkins did, though both locate its 'magic' in Wordsworth's technique. The technique is a spiritual one. It enables the poet to foresee something of 'the developing life-crisis of the nineteenth century'. Here, the 'shock' of the new is 'redeemed by the silence' between the two stanzas: 'Wordsworth transfigures a fractured world'. It is what Hill's own poetry aspires to do. Certainly, if one doesn't find profundity in Wordsworth's pauses one won't find it anywhere. It seems natural that Hill should spend the rest of his essay in explaining just how 'magical' the 'change' in the *Ode* is. What makes it modern, however, is that it breaks 'continuity', it is not an 'organic' change in the normal sense of the word. This is why it would have been beyond a writer like George Eliot who was still committed to a traditional form of organicism.

What Hopkins learnt from Wordsworth's 'Ode' was the possibility of bridging a similar spiritual hiatus in his own time. The essay shows Hill trying to learn from Hopkins as Hopkins learnt from Wordsworth. He begins from two poems in sprung rhythm which most readers would find unpromising successors to the 'Ode'. Both come in the class of instructive failures:

In 'Harry Ploughman' the man is in stride, his craft requires it; and the poem itself, in its rhythm and 'burden lines', is the model of a work song. In the companion piece, 'Tom's Garland', the dispossessed are thrown out of work and out of stride and the piece is, both discursively and rhythmically, perhaps the harshest, most crabbed, of all Hopkins's poems. It is as though the poet is implying that, because the men cannot work, therefore the poem itself cannot ... [but this] does not diminish the respect that is due to him for encompassing in his rhythm not only 'the achieve of, the mastery of the thing' but also 'the jading and jar of the cart'. 'Tom's Garland' is a failure, but it fails to some purpose; it is a test to breaking point of the sustaining power of language. (LL, p. 98)

What makes this profound criticism, worthy of Hopkins on the 'Ode', is that its perceptions about rhythm are grounded in the historical, what Hill calls 'the underlying ambiguity of nineteenth century society' (LL, p. 98). Prosody is not, as it usually is, shunted off into a fenced-off area called 'technique'. 'Redeeming the Time' and redeeming words are the same thing. Even in failure, Hopkins found a rhythm to reflect the shocks of change in his society.

Even so, Hill is almost as interested in those Victorian writers who failed to redeem their time as in the few who did. Indeed, he needs their example to explain fully what Wordsworth achieved. To do this he is not afraid to apply the word 'decadence' (LL, p. 103) to precisely those Victorians whom we usually see as standing for the organic transmission of traditional values: George Eliot and Matthew Arnold. Though Hill admires both writers, he argues that both failed to relate their sense of the past to their response to the present and the future. Neither was capable of Wordsworth's quantum leap into a new world. Hill's example from George Eliot is a fine passage from the late *Theophrastus Such*, a passage that celebrates the idea of the 'organic community' so central to all her work. He proceeds to contrast it with her highly rhetorical *Address to Working men by Felix Holt* of 1868. Without casting a slur on her 'fine sense of traditional rhythmic life' (LL, p. 88) in a book like *Adam Bede*, he judges the 1868 pamphlet a 'blatant, disingenuous compounding' (LL, p. 89) in which the author's would-be Radical speaker is really 'Felix Holt the Conservative' (LL, p. 90), as an early critic put it. George Eliot's fault is political *and* aesthetic: it lies in 'rhythmic gerrymandering', in excluding from her argument its necessary 'cross-rhythms and counterpointings', 'the antiphonal voice of the heckler' (LL, p. 90). She forgets to provide just that quality which gives her novels their depth. Taking a phrase from Coleridge, Hill calls it 'the drama of reason' (LL, p. 90). It is also very much the quality Arnold praises Burke for in his famous 'return' on the French Revolution in *Essays in Criticism*. Nonetheless, both he and George Eliot could respond to the crisis of their times by ignoring it, stand for disinterestedness and continuity and yet fail to notice when they were flouted in their own work. As Hill points out, the Felix Holt pamphlet 'betrays the priorities' of *Theophrastus Such* but 'with no sense of contact or coherence between them' (LL, p. 103). It was against that approach that Hopkins, both as poet and priest, fought with 'dogged resistance' (LL, p. 103).

As one would expect, Arnold is convicted of a rather more Hellenic lapse into 'decadence' (one that has often been singled out in recent years): the brilliant comic passage in 'The Function of Criticism at the Present Time' where he teases the hapless Mr Roebuck by repeating the words '*Wragg is in custody*'. But this piece of indignation against the middle classes fails to save Arnold from a spectacular lapse of his own. He turns from 'Wragg' herself, and the insensitivity of calling her merely that, to the vulgarity of the name itself: 'by the Ilissus there was no Wragg, poor thing!'[30] It is a conspicuous instance of how 'culture' is, at best, a mixed blessing. It is almost as if Arnold is as sorry for her name as because she is '*in custody.*' As Hill says, 'the critic who has warned against catch-words is caught by a word ... righteous anger and unrighteous taste become compounded'. The indignation ends up as a 'whinny of petty revulsion' (LL, p. 94). Arnold did not see that this contradiction clashed with his own praise of Burke's 'disinterestedness'. A writer who was clever enough could still project *mauvaise foi* as a kind of urbanity.

Hill is really making a passionate plea against the flaw of the age itself, not simply against writers whom in other ways he admires. What he underlines is the price that has to be paid when a culture so reveres its own past that it neglects to focus its intelligence on its present. He knows how close to home such criticisms can come, just as he sympathises with George Eliot's vision of England even as he sees how it could make her language go dead on her just when it most needed to come alive. As Hopkins said, 'Victorian English' was often a 'bad business'[31] and had to be resisted by poets who refused to be decadent with a decadent age. All this does not rule a Tory Radical like Oastler, with whom 'Redeeming the Time' begins, completely out of court. To pretend to ignore the past is as bad as to sentimentalise it. Oastler reminds us that not all harking back to our past is a cover for reaction. In difficult times, as an agrarian culture gave way to an industrial one, he realised how difficult looking back was. His predicament still reminds us, as it does Hill, that to look back at the past can be our safeguard against rhetoric and sentimentality, nostalgia and false optimism, and not a way of indulging them. The high wire that any good writer has to tread between his present and his past, narrow as it is, remains the only route to a real sense of

'England'. In this respect, what will matter to a poet, as it did to Wordsworth, will not be any national abstraction or slogan but the chance of a living rhythm. This is what is meant in *Mercian Hymns*, where King Offa and the child keep exchanging roles: the poet thereby finds new ways of voicing what he has to say about the past.

Geoffrey Hill's poems are full of direct speech but the people they speak to are nearly always dead, Péguy, Mandelstahm, the Jews of Auschwitz and King Offa among them. He invokes their shades across the centuries, addressing rather than talking to them: Thus, to Péguy:

> So, you have risen
> above all that and fallen flat on your face
> among the beetroots. (HP, p. 187)

Unlike Dante's Virgil, this dead poet does not answer back or engage in dialogue. What Hill values and explores is his silence (there are many silent poets in his work). Offa was one of the most powerful of the Saxon kings, the only ruler in Europe 'to deal on equal terms with Charlemagne',[32] but nearly everything we hear of him seems to originate in the thoughts and fancies of the book's speaker himself who is a kind of more articulate sub-Offa. Hill begins from his distance from the king himself because what matters is less the archaeological truth about Mercia than how it is perceived from the present. The invocation conflates historical periods and turns the real king into 'the presiding genius of the West Midlands' (HP, p. 201):

> King of the perennial holly-groves, the river sand-
> stone: overlord of the M5: architect of the his-
> toric rampart and ditch, the citadel of Tamworth,
> the summer hermitage in Holy Cross: guardian of
> the Welsh Bridge and the Iron Bridge: contractor
> to the desirable new estates: saltmaster: money-
> changer: commissioner for oaths: martyrologist:
> the friend of Charlemagne.

> 'I liked that,' said Offa, 'sing it again.' (HP, p. 105)

History is a patchwork though Offa's relish of power makes him lap up these disparate titles. He also has a cheeky vanity in his tone which is oddly reminiscent of Hughes's Crow and is enough in itself to dispel any expectation of getting an historically accurate portrait of him. In

fact, *Mercian Hymns* chronicles an apparition which finally turns out
to be a vanishing act. The final poem (XXX) – again reminiscent of
Crow, this time of the analogous poem 'A Glimpse' – is curt even for
Hill:

> And it seemed, while we waited, he began to walk to-
>   wards us   he vanished
> he left behind coins, for his lodging, and traces of
>   red mud.   (HP, p. 134)

Hill's drama lies in what the speaker makes of these 'traces'. By
choosing West Mercia he forestalls our preconceptions about the
past. When Offa's son Ecgfrith was anointed king of the Mercians it
was, according to Sir Frank Stenton, 'the first recorded consecration
of an English king' and the first to include a 'religious element',[33] but
few people remember that now, or that the coins Offa left behind
mark the beginning of the English currency. We may hail from that
England – as a West Midlander, Hill presumably does – but it is
difficult for us to *see* it. Such knowledge as we are given is mostly the
result of excavation. Poem XII, one of the richest of the hymns, seems
to describe the discovery of a 'hoard' by workmen 'paid to caulk
water-pipes'. Its fascination with what lies underneath the earth is
characteristic of the whole sequence:

> It is autumn. Chestnut-boughs clash their inflamed
>   leaves. The garden festers for attention: telluric
>   cultures, enriched with shards, corms, nodules, the
>   sunk solids of gravity. I have raked up a golden
>   and stinking blaze.   (HP, p. 116)

Excavation, of course, recalls the digging games of children and, in
poem XIX, we learn that the child of *Mercian Hymns* plays in 'a
kitchen-garden riddled with toy-shards, with splinters of habitation'
(HP, p. 123). Indeed, the children there 'shriek and scavenge, play
havoc' (HP, p. 123) like frantic warriors from the England that made
the 'shards' in the first place. But when the past does illuminate the
present its brightness is always set off against the darkness it comes
from. As the opening of poem XIX has it:

> Behind the thorn-trees thin smoke, scutch-grass or
>   wattle smouldering. At this distance it is hard
>   to tell. Far cries impinge like the faint tink-
>   ing of iron.   (HP, p. 123)

There is more than one place these faint cries may come from.

Offa's appearances at first seem oddly similar to those of the Saxons and Romans who appear to the children in *Puck of Pook's Hill*, except that Kipling's *revenants* bring news of what history was *really* like whereas Offa comes in the guise of a question mark. *Mercian Hymns* is not one of those poems, like *The Triumph of Life* or *Little Gidding*, where the dead communicate with the living. Offa's clearest message is his silence. The child may exchange roles with him in fantasy but the significance – even location – of such exchanges eludes us. Though the poet has 'invested in mother-earth' and bided his time 'where dry-dust badgers thronged the Roman flues, the long-unlooked-for mansions of our tribe', and though this is also 'Child's play', as one England is uncovered and another buried, it is 'hard to tell' which England is which (HP, p. 108). If Hill offers a variant on all those Victorian juxtapositions of past and present he refrains, as the Victorians did not, from saying what the juxtapositions are *for*.

What makes this salutary rather than puzzling is that Hill has prevented us from reading our familiar notions of 'Englishness' into our own history. Mercia confronts us with a culture-shock, a reminder of our exile from the past and not of our belonging to it. Even 'mother-earth' has no finality: it is 'the crypt of roots and endings' (HP, p. 108), but Hill is careful not to say where the roots go or come from and when the endings are or were. Not all our history is recoverable. Moreover, Mercia itself is only partially 'English', as the commentators were quick to note. Vincent Sherry, tracing an allusion from the Romans to Thor, points out that 'England enters history as a Roman colony and is becoming, in Offa's time, increasingly a focus for Danish and Viking interests.'[34] Martin Dodsworth presses home this 'amused irony at the expense of "Englishness"' by observing that 'this Offa who is so much part of our ideal England ... actually claimed to come from continental Anglia'.[35] Who is to say where 'England' begins? If links between Saxon and contemporary England exist, their recognition arises from ignorance and guesswork and expresses itself as surprise. Offa's funeral, for instance, is a surreal gathering of ancient and modern:

> 'Now when King Offa was alive and dead', they were
> all there, the funereal gleemen: papal legate and
> rural dean; Merovingian car-dealers, Welsh mercen-
> aries; a shuffle of house-carls. (HP, p. 131)

Poem XXVII here should be compared with poem IX, a more modern
and personal burial amid an 'eldorado of washstand marble' which
yet turns out to be a 'saga' too (HP, p. 113). Is the present past or the
past present or either distinct from the other? It is precisely as the
reader asks such questions that a more spectral but bloodier
apparition emerges, deeper than Offa's world of *realpolitik* and
touched by religion. Until this point the tone of poem XXVII is clipped
and witty but now the rhythm opens out and wit converts into
gravity and wonder:

> After that shadowy, thrashing midsummer hail-storm,
>   Earth lay for a while, the ghost-bride of livid
>   Thor, butcher of strawberries, and the shire-tree
>   dripped red in the arena of its uprooting.   (HP, p. 131)

The further back we get towards our roots the more foreign they
become. There is no need to unpick these intensely vivid words here,
save to remark that they show Hill's poetry reaching an intensity that
is beyond the anguish and guilt which his work starts from. The blood
is richer than that. It is also rich enough to reveal how strange the
past is, far stranger than our obsessive nostalgia would have it. A long
history can sometimes illumine or terrify as well as simply over-
shadow those who come at the end of it.

   The glimpses of Offa's kingdom that *Mercian Hymns* affords are not,
then, merely a way of enacting our uncertainties about the past. If
Hill travels backward in time he also travels inwards into a
psychological space where the child of the poem explores his own
mind by dreaming of Offa:

> Exile or pilgrim set me once more upon that ground:
>   my rich and desolate childhood. Dreamy, smug-faced,
>   sick on outings – I who was taken to be a king of
>   some kind, a prodigy, a maimed one.   (HP, p. 109)

The child is masterful and vindictive as well as lonely (see poem VII)
and he dreams especially of Offa's power. But his dreams are not
mere daydreams of history. They are also a delving into his self, a sort
of psychological archaeology that is analogous to the process whereby
Offa's famous coin-hoard was brought patiently into the light:

> Trim the lamp; polish the lens; draw, one by one, rare
>   coins to the light. Ringed by its own lustre, the

masterful head emerges, kempt and jutting, out of
England's well. Far from his underkingdom of crin-
oid and crayfish, the rune-stone's province, *Rex
Totius Anglorum Patriae*, coiffured and ageless,
portrays the self-possession of his possession,
cushioned on a legend. (HP, p. 117)

Hill makes a fuss in his notes explaining that Offa never used this
grandiose title himself but it is quite clear that his dominion in the
poem is imaginative as well as political. Offa was the first king to
claim authority over the whole country. His England, though, is a
'well', hidden beneath the Englands we know, a 'coiled entrenched
England' below a 'primeval heathland spattered with bones of mice
and birds' (HP, p. 124) that recalls the England of *King Lear*. This is
where the coins are drawn from and what the child dreams of in his
kitchen garden. He may be a 'prodigy' but what he is doing parallels
those later generations who have unconsciously built on the same
land and named their houses after forgotten Saxon battles: 'Ethan-
dune', 'Catraeth', 'Maldon', 'Pengwern'. 'Steel against yew and
privet. Fresh dynasties of smiths' (HP, p. 124). These smiths
perpetuate the Mercian craft of metal-work without remembering
the work of their forbears. Sometimes traditions can be forgotten *and*
continued. That is where the child, modern yet attuned to the
ancient, has his opportunity.

It may seem, then, that Hill's Mercia is nearer to the England of
Hughes's 'Pike' than his antiquarian bent might suggest. When
Offa, the forerunner of more modern rulers, divides his realm, 'an
ancient land, full of strategy', what looms out of it comes from a dark
world of myth and pre-history: 'a reliquary or wrapped head, the
corpse of Cernunnos pitching dayward its feral horns' (HP, p. 119).
But what balances this shuddering apparition, as it would not in
Hughes, is that Offa still governs his realm to some purpose, as the
'masterful head' on his coins attests. Hill celebrates the arts of
Mercia, the way human power can be creative and not merely
violent. Such arts have become the roots of the region. Thus, the
three poems about 'Opus Anglicanum', in which a modern poet
salutes the 'Englishness' of Saxon art, combine evocations of it with
allusions to nineteenth-century cottage industry. One of the things
that connects us with our past is work and, particularly, craft. As
'Redeeming the Time' makes clear, it is a lesson Hill learnt from the
George Eliot of *Adam Bede* (another book about Mercia). Poem

xxviii, a meditation on the 'Processes of generation', provides an especially haunting example:

> Tracks of ancient occupation. Frail ironworks rust-
>   ing in the thorn-thicket. Hearthstones; charred
>   lullabies. A solitary axe-blow that is the echo
>   of a lost sound.
>
> Tumult recedes as though into the long rain. Groves
>   of legendary holly; silverdark the ridged gleam.   (HP, p. 132)

Is the distant past becoming more or less visible and audible here? Is it the present or the 'lost' axe-blow whose sound dies away in that fading rhythm? It is when the scene is quiet that a 'gleam' is cast from some (pagan?) past. But one thing at least is clear: the traces that remain bespeak not only Mercia but (like *Remains of Elmet*) the past of early industrial England. What preserves this immediate past is not simply its crafts but the pain that accompanies their practice. As always in Hill, the past's achievements are never without their price. The third of the 'Opus Anglicanum' poems commemorates the sufferings of the poet's grandmother in the 'nailer's darg', her 'face hare-lipped by the searing wire' of which the nails were made (HP, p. 129). (Nail-making is a traditional industry of the West Midlands.) The poem is one of the most passionate in the book, especially read by Hill himself, who brings redoubled intensity to the reprise of the opening verset at its conclusion. The tone is of someone who is determined to remember and preserve the past, though more as an admonition than out of nostalgia. Here is its opening:

> Brooding on the eightieth letter of *Fors Clavigera*,
>   I speak this in memory of my grandmother, whose
>   childhood and prime womanhood were spent in the
>   in the nailer's darg.
>
> The nailshop stood back of the cottage, by the fold.
>   It reeked stale mineral sweat. Sparks had furred
>   its low roof. In dawn-light the troughed water
>   floated a damson-bloom of dust –
>
> not to be shaken by posthumous clamour.   (HP, p. 129)

It is a measured poem, for all its anger and compassion, and Hill keeps his eye firmly on the grimness of the place. This grimness frames the poem's one moment of beauty, reminding us that even the 'damson-bloom of dust' is another source of pollution. Nevertheless, the poem celebrates the courage as well as the vulnerability of those who worked in such conditions. As in the poems about English history in *Tenebrae*, the legacies and the curses which the past bestows on us are inextricable. England's history is both hidden and frighteningly near.

When Hill read *Mercian Hymns* on Radio 3 in 1973 he prefaced poem X, in which Offa exchanges gifts with the 'Muse of History' while the child indulges in 'mild dreams', with a note saying that in it the King and the child 'interchange roles'. In so far as the sequence has an action, this 'interchange' is central to it. Nonetheless, the images of Offa driving a sports car or the child enjoying fantasies of kingly power which follow from it are comically incongruous. Such forced connections betray a fundamental discontinuity. Hill's concern is not to make Offa's England too easy for his reader to imagine. Thus, the child's fantasies are interrupted by the mundane details of his domestic life (for example, in poem XXIX he enters 'the last dream of Offa the King' to the sound of 'his dice' whirring in 'the ludo-cup' (HP, p. 133). Hill is guarded about the chances of one historical period's understanding another. Continuity is merely an hypothesis; it is by no means in the bag. This doubt is at the heart of *Mercian Hymns*. For instance, in Hill's notes to the book one finds a studiously non-committal reference to Offa's 'dominion enduring from the middle of the eighth century until the middle of the twentieth (and possibly beyond)' (HP, p. 201). Precisely what is meant by 'possibly beyond' is never made clear although, putting two and two together, the second date appears to pull Hill's own life asunder, divorcing the child from the man. It is unclear why this putative disjunction should be located in the 1940s rather than a century earlier, say, where Sturt put it. I think it is possible to be this precise about the date because hardly any of Hill's contemporary references come later than this. The book reveals a covert nostalgia for the period of the poet's own childhood. Thus, although Hill aspires to probe the deracination of modern life, the light he casts on it is actually an oblique one. It is not 1971 that he is contrasting with the eighth century. Like *Adam Bede*, *Mercian Hymns* leaves us just on the far side of the present, in a kind of historical limbo that neither quite enters into the past nor is quite resigned to the present. The half-legible 'traces of red mud' with which it ends pinpoint this sense of spiritual hiatus which is its keynote. The clipped, unflowing rhythms of Hill's language, restraining the reader from over-glib connections, curtailing lyricism, enact the same dilemma.

Mercian Hymns has been more admired than any of Hill's books and
its brilliant combination of the incisive with the sensuous makes it
easy to see why. What has been less noticed is the way its very
exactness sometimes constricts the life it depicts. Hill puts his finger so
unerringly on what he wants to say that his words can seem too
finished to allow his subject to breathe. The drawback of his verbal
polish is that it sometimes seems to exist only to reflect itself. The short
second hymn is a good example of how Hill's language sometimes
seems to be preening itself on its own chiselled phrasing:

> A pet-name, a common name. Best-selling brand, curt
> graffito. A laugh, a cough. A syndicate. A specious
> gift. Scoffed-at horned phonograph.
>
> The starting-cry of a race. A name to conjure with.   (HP, p. 106)

What such compacted economy suggests is a poet whose diction and
rhythmic movement may have been arrived at too consciously. The
writing is fastidious, rather in the way a dandy might be over-
conscious of his dress. Not that this impression is simply an aesthetic
one. The tightness of Hill's grip on his rhythms is also an index of a
certain kind of power, somewhat akin to the child's power to fashion
a world of his own in his dreams of Offa. (A writer one might
compare Hill to is Walter Pater, who listened equally attentively to
his own well-honed cadences.) But if *Mercian Hymns* is insistently
written, its effect is as much a moral as a literary one. Even so, some
of his readers have felt that he buys his precision – both of language
and conscience – at too high a price. Geoffrey Thurley (writing before
Mercian Hymns) complained that Hill was too anxious to 'load' every
rift with 'significance': 'What Hill proves in the end is that the
Empsonian obsession with consciously exploited ambiguity is ulti-
mately stultifying: he succeeds in making room for the ambiguities at
the expense of expression ... '[36] Thurley sees Hill as a laboriously
academic poet partly because he fails to notice the taut, withheld
passion beneath the intellectual surface of his verse. He perceives the
consciously willed side of his writing and takes that part for the whole.
Peter Levi, writing in *Agenda*, makes a similar point in a more
nuanced way:

One is conscious in sentence after sentence of a complete exactness, and
there is no way of articulating the gaps between sentences or stanzas: it is
filled with a kind of reverberant humming, it invites attention to what is

specific but not to itself... in these poems the context of language is used to the bone, very exactly, and this means that each stanza completely fills the surrounding silence.[37]

For Levi, the impression that Hill's poetry is cerebral is deepened by its inability to unfold organically in its reader's mind: 'It is like a tree with fruit and branches, perfectly alive, but without leaves.'[38] This captures very well Hill's dual gift for pinpointing his subject without robbing it of its mystery. *Mercian Hymns* fuses moments of illumination with a keen sense of where illumination turns into uncertainty. It's language is tailor-made for probing an England that is problematic and concealed.

Mercian Hymns is in many respects a meditation on the history of the English race but it is also a very personal poem which construes past and present in private terms. The child's identification with Offa is the cue for Hill's recognition of himself as the 'staggeringly-gifted child' (HP, p. 133) of the penultimate hymn. This recognition is not, however, one which the reader can share in and neither is it, strictly speaking, a response to history *as* history. It seems to be no part of Hill's purpose to celebrate the continuous history of his part of England as it survives in the popular imagination. Child and poet might both be described as adepts, privy to secret knowledge. The poetic childhood in question is 'rich and desolate' (HP, p. 109) and, as such, removed from ordinary life. Thus, Offa in a way becomes as much Hill's *alter ego* as a pure apparition from the past:

> 'A boy at odds in the house, lonely among brothers.'
> But I, who had none, fostered a strangeness; gave
> myself to unattainable toys.
>
> Candles of gnarled resin, apple branches, the tacky
> mistletoe. 'Look' they said and again 'look.' But
> I ran slowly; the landscape flowed away, back to
> its source. (HP, p. 110)

It is natural for such a child, in search of substitutes for the companionship he lacks, to confound his present with his past. The promise of vicarious living has always been one of the things that draw us to the past. There is nothing novel in the fact that *Mercian Hymns* seeks to annex a corner of English history for the exploration of personal rather than communal feelings. Neither Offa nor the child are endearing spokesmen for 'Englishness' but that is part of their point. Patriotism need not be morally estimable, as Shakespeare understood when he gave the most patriotic lines in *King John* to the Bastard. Hill is content for his reader to remain at a distance from the main drama of the book because he knows that his own relation to it as a writer is vicarious too. By implication, the lonely child's fantasies about Offa are comparable to the sense which other English people have of their own past.

For some poets the dramas of the past have already been consummated, so that they can be looked back on in a mood of 'calm of mind, all passion spent'. In 'Little Gidding', for instance, Eliot exorcises the divisiveness of English history by sealing it off from the present:

> We cannot revive old factions
> We cannot restore old policies
> Or follow an antique drum.

Though Hill owes a great deal to Eliot's example he never treats the past like this, as if it were over. For him, its conflicts are neither reconciled nor extinguished. His poetry proposes more than one past for us to relate to, more than one England that claims our allegiance. He never allows the achievements of English civilisation to obscure the price that has been paid for them, often by one class on behalf of another. This awareness informs the sonnet sequence *An Apology for the Revival of Christian Architecture in England* in *Tenebrae*. In 'the Laurel Axe', for instance, Hill both voices and undercuts our nostalgia for the world of the country house:

> Platonic England, house of solitudes,
> rests in its laurels and its injured stone,
> replete with complex fortunes that are gone,
> beset by dynasties of moods and clouds.
>
> It stands, as though at ease with its own world,
> the mannerly extortions, languid praise,
> all that devotion long since bought and sold,
>
> the rooms of cedar and soft-thudding baize,
> tremulous boudoirs where the crystals kissed
> in cabinets of amethyst and frost.   (HP, p. 160)

The house's aura of serenity is partly a sham: it has been raised by corruption and maintained by arrogance. Yet its elegance is no less real for this admixture of guilt. Unlike the England of 'Little

Gidding', this one has not been simplified and ironed out by time. The crispness of the poem's phrasing is a token of this, combining suggestiveness ('dynasties of moods and clouds') with ironic judgement ('the mannerly extortions, languid praise').

If history is never over for Hill it is because it teaches us a compunction that it would be evasive to repress. The three sonnets entitled *A Short History of British India* dissect the 'heroic guilt' (HP, p. 155) that underlies the pomp of Empire. The Raj cannot be put out of mind by blackening its memory. If it raped and desecrated India it also aspired to bring to it 'the clear theme of justice and order' (HP, p. 157). History rejects black and white resolutions and demands to be swallowed whole, even at the cost of splitting our sympathies in irreconcilable ways. A poem which puts this tension in a nutshell is 'The Herefordshire Carol' (alluding perhaps to old Herefordshire carols set by the very 'English' Vaughan Williams):

> the squire's effigy bewigged with frost,
> and hobnails cracking puddles before dawn.
> In grange and cottage girls rise from their beds
>
> by candlelight and mend their ruined braids.
> Touched by the cry of the iconoclast,
> how the rose-window blossoms with the sun!   (HP, p. 164)

By now, the iconoclast is as much a part of our sense of the Gothic as the stained glass which he threatened. It is even implied that the rose-window is more beautiful because of his violence. Only in history can we see all parties from their own point of view, the squire and the peasant in hobnails. History quivers inside us like an array of exposed nerves. We are unable to keep our distance from it because it is never really finished. Nostalgia is a red herring. We experience history as part of the present.

Critics have not paid much attention to Hill's strong sympathy with the oppressed masses who made possible the England of his colonial administrators and Plantagenet kings. Yet he studies power with an appalled fascination for the price it extorts from its victims, whether in the Middle Ages or the Third Reich. The strong swing between tenderness and indignation in the Mercian hymn about his grandmother is characteristic, both a valediction and an incantation designed to keep anger hot. Unlike Eliot's, his England discloses a perpetual tension between Gentlemen and Players. This emphasis (reminiscent of the Tory Radicalism of Disraeli who supplies one of

the epigraphs to *An Apology*) comes out especially clearly in Hill's
highly personal F. W. Bateson lecture on Ivor Gurney. He sees
Gurney as someone who came from below to seek recognition from
those above him, a plebeian anxious to attract the notice of the
establishment. Despite his pastoral love-affair with his native
Gloucestershire he was radically at odds with England as he knew it.
His *Severn and Somme*, superficially modelled on the verse of the
patrician Rupert Brooke, strikes Hill as 'a determined bid to wrest
the 'English manner' from the hands of the officer-class'.[39] Moreover,
Hill sees Gurney's master, Edward Thomas, for many readers the
epitome of that vague halcyon England of the years before the Great
War, as the victim of a society riddled with 'social injustice': he
quotes Frost to the effect that Thomas 'was suffering from a life of
subordination to his inferiors'.[40] In the twentieth century, culture
and power have occupied separate spheres of action. Hill's Ivor
Gurney is another denizen of the 'nailer's darg', someone whose love
of England is equalled only by his resentment towards it. Out of such
conflicting emotions, a poet has to discover an England complex
enough to include both. The value of Gurney's poetry is that it helps
us to diagnose more precisely those divisions which most of us would
prefer to believe can be healed by time. Both Gurney and Thomas are
the victims of a specific kind of unjust society, not the unscarred
celebrants of some timeless 'Englishness'.

The anger that flashes out in the poem about the 'nailer's darg'
seldom comes right up to the surface of Hill's work. Not for him the
more simply alternative version of English history that contents Tony
Harrison. It is perhaps the judiciously equivocal character of *An
Apology* which has prompted Jon Silkin and others to accuse it of
being *too* consummately written. Yet Hill surely apes this quality in
order to undercut it. His commandeering of Pugin's solemn and
wordy title is itself enough to imply that the sequence is not merely
one more lament for the 'Platonic England' (HP, p. 160) of myth.
Hill's guilt and anxiety over English history undercut his desire to
celebrate it. In the sonnet entitled 'Loss and Gain', for instance, self-
deception is presented as an integral part of the dream of 'England':

> Platonic England grasps its tenantry
> where wild-eyed poppies raddle tawny farms
> and wild swans root in lily-clouded lakes.
> Vulnerable to each other the twin forms
> of sleep and waking touch the man who wakes

> to sudden light, who thinks that this becalms
> even the phantoms of untold mistakes.   (HP, p. 158)

This is a more honest way of coping with nostalgia, admitting yet
resisting its force, rather than pretending to be exempt from it. There
would be no point in dwelling on the past if it were nothing more than
an exploded myth. Hill admits that the myths remain real to us even
as we try to demystify them. It is a part of the strength of his poetry
that it does not try to shrug the past off or to settle its account with
it.

A critic who avoids reading *An Apology* as a kind of historical
pastoral is Jeffrey Wainwright, in an article in *Agenda*. In his view,
Hill is engaged in diagnosing a myth rather than propping one up.
He 'affects' a 'nostalgia for an old past England' that appears to be
'organically at one with its largely comfortable, domesticated natural
surroundings' but was actually always a myth. The real England the
poems reveal is a 'suppered, gently decaying and surviving England'
and the real subject of *An Apology* is 'the affective ideology of a whole
area of English mind and culture, and of its muddled dreaming.'[41]
Hill offers a means of analysis. Not the solace of lyrical outpouring.
He invests the past with a beauty that feels fragile and precious (for
example, 'tremulous boudoirs where the crystals kissed / In cabinets
of amethysts and frost'). Such an overtly poetical past silently shuts
us out as it turns in upon itself. Its very perfection makes one uneasy
about what it excludes. Nor is nostalgia a possible response to evils
that still beset us; looking backwards brings us round to where we
already are. To this extent Wainwright's reading of *An Apology* is a
true one. Where I find him misleading is when he suggests that the
myths about 'England' can one day be disinfected altogether. For all
their irony, the poems surely celebrate *as well as* undermine them:

> radiance of dreams hardly to be denied.
> The twittering pipistrelle, so strange and close,
>
> plucks its curt flight through the moist eventide;
> the children thread among old avenues
> of snowberries clear-calling as they fade.   (HP, p. 159)

If that is nostalgia, for all its precision, only a prig could fail to
succumb to it. There is a stronger desire in *Tenebrae* to capture such
moments than Wainwright allows. Though Hill asks us to include
iconoclasm in our image of England he is no mere iconoclast himself.

If we need to break free of our past and come to terms with it we may also find a meaning to our own lives by calling it back to mind. Hence Hill's sympathy for an antagonist of the modern world like Charles Péguy, a poet who, far from being a dreamer, lived in the thick of events as few modern poets have.

Hill's feeling for the Péguy of *The Mystery of the Charity of Charles Péguy* is of a paradoxical sort: there are as many differences between them as similarities. At some moments, Péguy seems to figure as Hill's *alter ego*, at others he is like his anti-type. He enables Hill to dramatise his own concerns and also to look at them with the detachment that Péguy's more simple convictions ask for. Péguy was remarkable as a writer for the intensity of his commitment, whether to Dreyfusisme or socialism, 'la vieille France' or to God, and he had the courage never to temporise over these convictions. Though Hill shares his religious seriousness and his allegiance to the past (and possibly more of his socialism than meets the eye) he is clearly a more subtle – not to say equivocal – poet than Péguy is. It is difficult to think of him saying, as Péguy does, that 'Toute situation double est une situation fausse. Toute situation double est une situation déloyale.'[42] In so far as it entertains conflicting views of Péguy *The Mystery* might be said to express a 'situation double'. This is not to say that Hill fails to admire the courage of Péguy's stand against the modern world but, coming after 1914 himself, he finds that sort of heroism rather anachronistic. Hill's poem concentrates much more on Péguy the editor of *Les Cahiers de la Quinzaine*, the political and religious gadfly of the age, than on Péguy the poet. Though there are occasional allusions to his poetry (which its English readership would perhaps be unlikely to pick up) the poem makes no sustained attempt to give Péguy a voice of his own. Hill prefers to apostrophise him. Like most of the other poets he has written about, his Péguy is an exemplary figure, as much moral symbol as individual artist.

This contention becomes more plausible if one considers how different Péguy's poetry is from Hill's own. *Le Mystère de la Charité de Jeanne d'Arc*, for instance, is a vast, undulating drama about the saint's dawning vocation, set some years before Orléans and the martyr's fire. Its music is steeped in the grandiloquent rhythms of Corneille and Hugo, its favourite figure of speech a kind of oratorical repetition that gives it a momentum both incantatory and pulsating. Péguy's delight in sonorous speech is such that anything that is well-said once will sound even better to him when said twice. Here is a brief example, describing Christ in his father's workshop:

> Car il avait travaillé dans la charpente, de son métier.
> Il travaillait, il était dans la charpente.
> Dans la charpenterie.
> Il était ouvrier charpentier.
> Il avait même été un bon ouvrier.
> Comme il avait été un bon tout.
> C'était un compagnon charpentier.
> Son père était un tout petit patron.
> Il travaillait chez son père.
> Il faisait du travail à domicile.[43]

Words are held in the mouth and savoured like wine. It is hard to get beyond their chiming. The poetry, to my ear at least, is in danger of being muffled by the clang of rhetoric. It is prolix where Hill's is succinct and taut; Hill's every word and cadence feels as if it had been tested like glass, to make sure there were no cracks in it. Péguy's very eloquence dates him. Presumably, part of his usefulness to Hill was as a representative of an emotionality in poetry which, to a modern English poet at least, seems no longer possible. This would explain why it is often so difficult in reading *The Mystery* to tell whether Hill's tone comes down on the side of irony or admiration for Péguy.

These differences between Hill and Péguy are perhaps more of temperament than belief. Péguy has always been a contradictory figure for those who like to put people in ideological boxes: a socialist who was a nationalist and a Dreyfusard who became a militant Catholic. It is not surprising that the Right tried to claim him for its own or that his mystical Gallic nationalism found favour with General de Gaulle. Yet Péguy saw the Dreyfus Affair as a socialist struggle to wrest a genuine patriotism away from reactionaries who had perverted it. (Gurney's patriotism comes to mind.) A recent historian has placed him in 'la vieille tradition patriotique de la gauche française de la Révolution'[44] and he described himself as 'un vieux républicain ... un vieux révolutionaire'.[45] None of this by itself offers much of a foothold to an English poet but, despite their dissimilar political traditions, the French and the English often adopted a very similar attitude to those features of the modern world common to both of them. Though a socialist, Péguy had no time for the great nineteenth-century faith in 'Progress' and he loathed positivism. The philosopher who influenced him most was Bergson, with his emphasis on intuition and organicism. Coupled with this went a profound attachment to 'la vieille France', to the peasantry as opposed to the bourgeoisie. He came from peasant stock himself and his allegiance was to the France of Joan of Arc rather than the France of Descartes and Voltaire. Patriotism was an intuitive spiritual force to him, not prudential but not merely passive either. As he said, 'Tout commence en mystique et finit en politique.'[46] In *Notre Patrie*, he thinks of the French people's realisation of the menace of Germany as 'une nouvelle venue de l'intérieur', from the depths, like Victor Hugo's music or a Bergsonian memory, a 'voix de mémoire engloutie'.[47] It is this patriotism, like his religion or his poetry, that sets Péguy against the modern world.

Much of this might seem to take us a long way from Geoffrey Hill but some of it will sound surprisingly familiar. For Péguy is another Tory Radical, riven by the same conflicts between past and present that have drawn Hill to the English nineteenth century. His feeling for the 'terre charnelle' has more than a little in common with the 'organic community' depicted in *Adam Bede* and *Silas Marner*. Thus, in writing about Péguy, Hill is able both to pursue such preoccupations and, at the same time, distance himself from them. The difference of nationality is not crucial because neither Hill nor Péguy is nationalist in a chauvinistic sense and the problems they confront have anyway a European dimension. Even in *Mercian Hymns* Hill found that one way of defining England was by reference to Offa's relations with Charlemagne. Similarly, it is a tacit hypothesis of *The Mystery* that something not unlike the France Péguy stood for must once have existed in England too. There is nothing far-fetched in this. In a way, the divide between past and present made by the Great War was greater and more traumatic than any divide between England and France was before it. Moreover, Hill's most obvious reason for choosing to write about Péguy was surely that he died in that war. It would be difficult to think of the battle of the Marne as either a merely French or a merely English event.

Péguy's France, like Coleridge's 'old Platonic England', may seem irretrievable to Hill but *The Mystery* never presents it as an idyll. From its opening lines Hill ponders the responsibility of the writer for what he writes (a polemic of Péguy's may have inspired Jaurès's assassin). He takes history more for a bed of nails than a pillow on which to lay a nostalgic head. *The Mystery* may be in part an evocation of a lost world but it admits how difficult it now is to conceive that world, even in imagination. In this respect, Péguy himself stands for everything in European civilisation that failed to survive the war. We can only guess at what he was really like:

> he commends us to nothing, leaves a name
>
> for the burial detail to gather up
> with rank and number, personal effects,
> the next-of-kin and a few other facts.   (HP, p. 195)

The coolness of Hill's tone is a reminder of how little of history survives, how much of it is lost voices and feelings about which we can only conjecture.

The pastness of the past is one of the great subjects of English poetry but where Hill's handling of it is unusual is in his strict avoidance of any emotional diapason. He deliberately breaks and halts his music, as if his song had to carve out a way for itself through the resistance of language, the tailored syntax: a lyricism with the terse elegance of the epigram. However much his poetry expands it never loses its tightness:

> At Villeroy the copybook lines of men
> rise up and are erased. Péguy's cropped skull
> dribbles its ichor, its poor thimbleful,
> a simple lesion of the complex brain.   (HP, p. 195)

This is an epitaph but it sounds like satire. The precision keeps Péguy's tragedy at a distance. Lamentation ('poor thimbleful') is stiffened by wit. To an ear attuned to earlier poets who also celebrate the past, like Tennyson and Milton, Hill's restraint may appear calculated. Their music can flow through long periods and then break like a wave, unashamed of rhapsody:

> O that 'twere possible,
> After long grief and pain,
> To find the arms of my true-love
>   Round me once again!

To Milton the thought of what is irremediable, so sobering to Hill, offers purgation and even a chance for grandeur:

> Or whether thou, to our moist vows denied,
> Sleep'st by the fable of Bellerus old,
> Where the great Vision of the guarded mount
> Looks towards Namancos, and Bayona's hold;
> Look homeward, Angel, now, and melt with ruth:
> And, O ye dolphins, waft the hapless youth.

The thrilling pause after 'Bayona's hold' – where the verse breaks like the sea on the 'guarded mount' – highlights Hill's ascetic rigour. The thought of the past and the death of the past brings a note of sourness into his voice that is not heard in Tennyson or Milton. There is scarcely a lyrical passage in *The Mystery* which is not checked and framed by irony:

> This is your enemies' country which they took
> in the small hours an age before you woke,
> went to the window, saw the mist-hewn
> statues of the lean kine emerge at dawn.
>
> Outflanked again, too bad!   (HP, pp. 186–7)

The rather awkwardly colloquial 'too bad!' seems like a deliberate device for sabotaging the pathos. I am not sure why Hill should want to ration the poetry's emotion at this point but he does seem to need to emphasise Péguy's gritty sense of being beaten by history. In the words of the poem's epigraph (omitted in the *Collected Poems*): 'Nous sommes les derniers. Presque les après-derniers. Aussitôt après nous commence un autre âge, un tout autre monde, le monde de ceux qui ne croient plus à rien, qui s'en font gloire et orgueil.'[48] By choosing to write about Péguy, Hill avows his own alienation from this 'autre âge'. He writes from a position that is neither of the past nor of the present, as cut off from modern England (one surmises) as from Péguy's France. *The Mystery* thus becomes a poem about patriotism by a poet who no longer lays claim to a living *patrie* himself.

The France Péguy celebrated was a France of the folk, deeper than the France touted by the bourgeoisie, that went back to the time of Saint Louis, long before the world of the nineteenth-century nation-state. As such, his mystical Gallic nationalism could offer Hill an oblique equivalent for his own sense of a vanishing 'Englishness'. Thus he addresses Péguy more as a tragicomic casualty of history than as a brother. It is precisely Péguy's conviction that he finds dated and naive:

> You know the drill,
> raw veteran, poet with the head of a bull.
>
> Footslogger of genius, skirmisher with grace
> and ill-luck, sentinel of the sacrifice.   (HP, p. 184)

This astringent tone is never absent for long from the *The Mystery* and it hovers behind all of Hill's most eloquent evocations of Péguy's 'vieille France'. On first reading, the poem's rhythm may strike the

ear as a sort of grand droning – all those impeccable quatrains one
after the other! – but, as the character of the verse becomes clearer,
one starts to notice the unusual commerce in it between lyrical feeling
and ironic concision. Lines like:

> So much for Jaurès murdered in cold pique
> by some vexed shadow of the belle époque.   (HP, p. 187)

turn out to be variations on the same tune heard in very different
lines:

> The chestnut trees begin to thresh and cast
> huge canisters of blossom at each gust.   (HP, p. 194)

Whether epigrammatic or sensuous the verse has a clipped, pinpointed beauty. It is what one might expect from a poet whose
sympathy for his subject is necessarily conditional. This does not
prevent Hill's poetry from achieving real power but it does preclude
the kind of homemade spontaneity that one finds in a book like
Hughes's *Moortown*, the sense of life done *sur le vif*. It is part of Hill's
point in *The Mystery* that that sense cannot be had for the asking. His
arrested lyricism is, among other things, a confession of his distance
from Péguy's eloquence.

This distance sometimes makes Hill moralise too much over Péguy.
Though he wryly describes him as 'Truth's pedagogue' he is a
pedagogue himself. But the poem would not work if all the charity
were Péguy's and Hill can also make us *feel* his mystical feeling for
rural France:

> There is an ancient landscape of green branches –
> true tempérament de droite, you have your wish –
> crosshatching twigs and light, goldfinches
> among the peppery lilac, the small fish
>
> pencilled into the stream. Ah, such a land
> the Ile de France once was. Virelai and horn
> wind through the meadows, the dawn-masses sound
> fresh triumphs for our Saviour crowned with scorn. (HP, p. 194)

The nostalgia of this is frankly admitted and grounded in definite
perceptions. It makes no pretence of being more than wistful.
Elsewhere, however, Hill's music can be brassier and his eloquence a
thought browbeating:

> Dear lords of life, stump-toothed, with ragged breath.
> Throng after throng cast out upon the earth,
> flesh into dust, who slowly come to use
> dreams of oblivion in lieu of paradise,

> push on, push on! – through struggle, exhaustion,
> indignities of all kinds, the impious Christian
> oratory, 'vos morituri', through berserk fear,
> laughing, howling, 'servitude et grandeur'... (HP, p. 193)

This pulls out the stops in a suitable Péguy-like way but its grandeur veers into clangorous rhetoric. At the climax of the passage Hill imagines the soldiers of France:

> expecting nothing but the grace of France,
> drawn to her arms, her august plenitude. (HP, p. 193)

War memorial pomp? The phrase 'august plenitude' sounds too consciously written. It has an empty ring, like something translated from Chateaubriand which would sound better in French. The rhythm of the lines about the 'ancient landscape of green branches' is more supple. Hill's picture of the 'grace of France' seems official by comparison. Perhaps the grand language is deliberate, a sly dig at the expense of a doomed heroism? Perhaps it is simply the consequence of trying to be inward with the patriotism of a foreign country?

There is a more tender tone in the poem as well, a tone that manages to be valedictory without loss of intimacy:

> Woefully battered but not too bloody,
> smeared by fraternal root-crops and at one
> with the fritillary and the veined stone,
> having composed his great work, his small body... (HP, p. 195)

This has dignity without being in full fig. The risk Hill runs is that the gravity of such moments, extended over a hundred quatrains, will come to seem sententious and homiletic. For a poet writing with the hindsight of history the form lends itself to the kind of epigrammatic certainty that is only possible *after* the event. Sometimes Hill can't help savouring his epigrams a little too much:

> The brisk celluloid clatters through the gate;
> the cortège of the century dances in the street;
> and over and over the jolly cartoon
> armies of France go reeling towards Verdun. (HP, p. 183)

This is too well phrased for its own good. It suffers from the fact that only someone who was *not* at Verdun could be so pithy about it. Sometimes Hill gives the impression of being able to see all round Péguy too easily. His *ad hominem* tone impales him like a butterfly. It leaves Péguy lost for an answer – a position no one was able to put him in in his lifetime. In his note to the poem, Hill describes him as 'one of the great souls, one of the great prophetic intelligences, of our century' (HP, p. 207) but he never really attains that stature in the poem because Hill can't resist setting down his historical judgement of him. What he is better at evoking is the France for which Péguy was fighting:

> in the fable this is your proper home;
> three sides of a courtyard where the bees thrum
> in the crimped hedges and the pigeons flirt
> and paddle, and sunlight pierces the heart –
>
> shaped shutter-patterns in the afternoon,
> shadows of fleur-de-lys on the stone floors.
> Here life is labour and pastime and orison
> like something from a simple book of hours...   (HP, p. 185)

The picture depends on a quiet clustering of sensuous perceptions. There is nothing consciously edifying about it. The France of the patriot for a moment becomes real:

> Yours is their dream of France, militant-pastoral:
> musky red gillyvors, the wicker bark
> of clematis braided across old brick
> and the slow chain that cranks into the well
>
> morning and evening. It is Domrémy
> restored.   (HP, p. 186)

A small sign of how fully Hill's imagination has entered into this France and found in it a correlative for England is the naturalness with which he slips that Shakespearian 'gillyvor' into the picture. Part of our pleasure is to see how, enriched by a French poet, another country, Hill goes on drawing his inspiration from its English roots. Moreover, it is clear that Péguy's France can also stand for a pre-industrial England. The feeling of homesickness may be displaced but it is no less profound for all that.

I have stressed what is guarded in Hill's attitude to Péguy but his poem can be impersonal in a less negative way. Particularly in its fifth section, he expresses a feeling of joy in recapturing the past that is too intense to dismiss as nostalgia. The Péguy evoked in the following lines, like Proust, is a disciple of Bergson who seeks to bring the past back, not a man pining helplessly for 'the good old days':

> Or say it is Pentecost: the hawthorn-tree,
> set with coagulate magnified flowers of may,
> blooms in a haze of light; old chalk-pits brim
> with seminal verdure from the roots of time.

Landscape is like revelation; it is both
singular crystal and the remotest things.
Cloud-shadows of seasons revisit the earth,
odourless myrrh borne by the wandering kings.

Happy are they who, under the gaze of God,
die for the 'terre charnelle', marry her blood
to theirs, and, in strange Christian hope, go down
into the darkness of resurrection,

into sap, ragwort, melancholy thistle,
almondy meadowsweet, the freshet-brook
rising and running through small wilds of oak,
past the elder tump that is the child's castle.

Inevitable high summer, richly scarred
with furze and grief; winds drumming the fame
of the tin legions lost in haystack and stream!
Here the lost are blest, the scarred most sacred. (HP, pp. 188–9)

Where this differs from the way the past is conceived in many modern
poems is in its ability to imagine it as a continuous accumulation of
human experience rather than as just one particular period in history
for which the poet feels wistful. The feeling which underpins the
exhilaration is one of mortality and loss: 'seminal verdure' springs
from 'the roots of time'. There may be nostalgia in the passage but it
is a nostalgia which includes the thought of death rather than the
more common kind which seeks to circumvent it. Death, moreover,
is something greater than either France or England and one effect of
section five is to broaden the poem's subject beyond that of Péguy's
particular kind of patriotism. There is nothing exclusively French
about Hill's 'high summer, richly scarred / with furze and grief'.
Indeed, Grevel Lindop has rightly pointed out how much of the
imagery of the passage can, as in *Mercian Hymns*, be descriptions of
Hill's own childhood.

It may nonetheless be objected that, whether or not Hill is writing
about England in the guise of France, his poetry has shown too little
interest in *contemporary England*. It tells us more about the world we
come *from* than the world in which we live. No one would want him
to write like Betjeman or Larkin but some critics – Silkin and Lindop,
for example – detect an evasion of lived experience in his preference
for imagining life from a distance. Lindop sees the impersonality of
The Mystery as partly a failure of nerve, a reluctance on the poet's part
to communicate his emotion directly:

it is hard not to feel that there is an element of pastiche about the poem. This is a danger Hill has courted repeatedly, and is perhaps the besetting risk for any poet who combines great technical skill with a reticence that makes him unwilling to apply his resources to direct statement of his personal concerns.[49]

Lindop's complaint is that Hill has obscured his own intention in writing about Péguy: 'What, after all, does Charles Péguy mean to him? Is it sufficient for Hill to hold him up to us as a bundle of brave paradoxes?'[50] Perhaps Hill allows us to see round Péguy too easily – to judge him before we understand what he felt? Is Péguy just too far away from Hill to put his own assumptions to the test? There are moments in the poem when we seem to be witnessing a kind of costume drama, a story reassuringly over. One therefore needs at least to acknowledge the possibility that history may sometimes be for Hill a convenient screen behind which to shelter from the present.

However many parallels one draws between Péguy and Hill, it remains the case that Hill scarcely lets him speak with his own voice. This may well have been deliberate (to underline the fact that Péguy was one of the last of his kind) but it contributes to the feeling that *The Mystery* sometimes seems a less passionate poem than it was meant to be. It may even be that what is being defused is simply *England* itself, the England that Hill refrains from writing about directly but that one surmises as a hidden presence behind every line. Péguy's fate is moving but, to an English audience, what happened to Owen and Gurney and Edward Thomas would have felt more tragic. Hill inevitably pays a price for the extra subtlety and scope that he achieves by writing about a surrogate England. Of course, the problem can't be reduced merely to the question of 'Englishness'. It also entails something diagnosed earlier by C. H. Sisson: a verbal fastidiousness that impedes the poetry's expressiveness. Yet this is as much a moral and psychological matter as an aesthetic one. One cannot separate the impeccably written quality of Hill's verse from his anxious Puritan scrupulosity with telling the truth. Even his notes show someone who *wants* what he says to be clear. Where uncertainty arises is when one asks what the precision conceals. Hill's verbal accomplishment, which Christopher Ricks lavishly praises him for, is not at issue but it is nonetheless possible to wonder if it sometimes becomes an end-in-itself, a way Hill has of hiding himself from himself.

It seems to me that the only conclusion one can reach about *The*

Mystery of the Charity of Charles Péguy is that it is two poems. One is a profound meditation on French, and by extension English, national feeling; the other takes 'Frenchness' and 'Englishness' as a pretext for covert and surreptitious introspection without ever coming clean about why Charles Péguy should be an appropriate objective correlative for Geoffrey Hill. The poem is unusual in that it offers an impersonal account of a personal subject-matter and yet is seldom dramatic in its approach. Indeed, there are some passages (usually of polished irony) where Hill seems more taken up with the sound of his own voice than with reaching his readers. Yet despite such criticisms *The Mystery* remains a remarkable poem, very private but also much more public in import than has yet been recognised. What is especially interesting about it is that it finds a way of addressing the issue of 'Englishness' without making it into a purely provincial and local obsession. England, that is, only has a meaning if it is considered as part of Europe. It is, that is, a far cry from Edward Thomas.

Hill's verse has, of course, been widely praised already and critics as influential as Harold Bloom and Christopher Ricks have referred to it as great poetry.[51] Such praise has its place and there is no intrinsic virtue in the more two-edged approach adopted here. But it seems to me very difficult to regard Geoffrey Hill's poetry with unmixed feelings, however much one admires it, and this is why I prefer to conclude this account of it on this side of Poet's Corner, in the knowledge that there is clearly so much of it which we still need to understand much better than we yet do.[52]

NOTES

(Place of publication is London unless otherwise stated)

1 Geoffrey Hill, *Collected Poems* (Penguin, Harmondsworth, 1985), p. 164. (Subsequent references to this edition will be incorporated into the text as HP.)

2 Hill himself points out that 'it's entirely due to the fact that Housman was hardly ever in Shropshire that the atmosphere of his literary 'Shropshire' is so curiously clear yet remote'. See *Viewpoints: Poets in Conversation with John Haffenden* (Faber, 1981), p. 80.

3 'Of Diligence and Jeopardy', *Times Literary Supplement*, November 17–23 (1989), 1274.

4 *Ibid.*, p. 1275.

5 *Ibid.*, p. 1275.

6 *Viewpoints*, p. 93.

7 This two page essay is as condensed as the poems are: it tantalises as much as informs its reader.

8 *Viewpoints*, p. 93.

9 Quoted by Henry Hart in *Geoffrey Hill: Essays on His Work*, ed. Peter Robinson (Open University Press, 1984), p. 12. (This book provides a helpful introduction to Hill's verse though it tends to take his importance for granted.)

10 See his F. W. Bateson Memorial Lecture 'Gurney's "Hobby"' in *Essays in Criticism*, vol. 34, no. 2 (1984), 97–128.

11 *Viewpoints*, p. 94.

12 'The Absolute Reasonableness of Robert Southwell', *The Lords of Limit: Essays on Literature and Ideas* (André Deutsch, 1984), p. 22. (Given hereafter as LL.)

13 *Viewpoints*, p. 88.

14 *Ibid.*, p. 89.

15 'A Note on Nostalgia', *Scrutiny*, vol. 1, no. 1 (1932), 8–19. Leavis often cited this short essay as a *locus classicus* on the subject.

16 This applies to Colls's and Dodd's otherwise valuable *Englishness: Politics and Culture 1880–1920* (Croom Helm, 1986). The impress of the politics and culture of the 1980s tends to be implicit in it but unanalysed. Yet the contemporary disabused attitude to nationalism and jingoism is surely a constant feature of 'Englishness' and not just a fruit of post-Suez realism. For an interesting study of our sense of our past see Patrick Wright, *On Living in an Old Country* (Verso, 1985).

17 Hill's twin sense of the moral and aesthetic qualities of rhythms and cadences is to the fore in his essay on Tyndall and in 'Redeeming the Time' in *The Lords of Limit*. See also his Clark lectures, *The Enemy's Country: Words, Contexture and Other Circumstances of Language* (Clarendon Press, Oxford, 1991).

18 This does not mean that Scott therefore has the deeper sense of history. We have first to ask whether *any* modern writer is close enough to the past to bring it to life as warmly as Scott did. One implication of *Funeral Music* may be that an *Old Mortality* is no longer possible.

19 See particularly 'Our Word is Our Bond' in *The Lords of Limit*. For instance, 'the dyer's hand, steeped in etymology if nothing else, is, by that commonplace, craftsmanlike immersion, an infected hand' (LL, p. 153).

20 'Geoffrey Hill', *Agenda*, vol. 13, no. 3 (1975), 26.

21 *Ibid.*, p. 27.

22 *Double Lyric: Divisiveness and Communal Creativity in Recent English Poetry* (Routledge and Kegan Paul, 1980), p. 45.

23 'War and the Pity' in Robinson ed. *Hill: Essays*, pp. 115–16.

24 '"The Conscious Mind's Intelligible Structure": A Debate', *Agenda*, vol. 9, no. 4 and vol. 10, no. 1 (1971–2), 22.

25 *Ibid.*, p. 27.

26 'The Dreams of Reason', a review of the Empson 'Special Number' in *The Review* (June 1963), *Essays in Criticism*, vol. 1, no. 1 (1964), 96.

27 See his contribution to Robinson ed. *Hill: Essays* and the two long essays in *The Force of Poetry* (Oxford University Press, 1987), pp. 285–355. Ricks has been a subtle and persuasive advocate for Hill but he sometimes projects his own cleverness onto the poems in a way that draws attention away from their own intensity.

28 *Double Lyric*, p. 19.

29 *The Correspondence of Gerald Manley Hopkins and Richard Watson Dixon*, ed. C. C. Abbott (London, 1935), p. 148.

30 *The Complete Prose Works of Matthew Arnold*, ed. R. H. Super (Ann Arbor, Michigan, 1962), III, p. 273.

31 *The Letters of Gerald Manley Hopkins to Robert Bridges*, ed. C. C. Abbott (London, 1935), pp. 265–6.

32 Sir Frank Stenton, *Anglo-Saxon England* (Clarendon Press, Oxford, 3rd edition, 1971), p. 215. Stenton's account of Offa helps to flesh out many of Hill's allusions.

33 Stenton, *Anglo-Saxon England*, pp. 218–19.

34 *The Uncommon Tongue: The Poetry and Criticism of Geoffrey Hill* (Ann Arbor, 1987), p. 136.

35 In Robinson ed. *Hill: Essays*, p. 51.

36 *The Ironic Harvest: English Poetry in the Twentieth Century* (Edward Arnold, 1974), p. 154.

37 'Geoffrey Hill', *Agenda*, vol. 9, no. 1 – vol. 10, no. 1 (1971–2), 100.

38 *Ibid.*, p. 100.

39 'Gurney's "Hobby"', pp. 104–5.

40 *Ibid.*, p. 117.

41 'An Essay on Geoffrey Hill's *Tenebrae*', *Agenda*, Geoffrey Hill Special Number, vol. 17, no. 1 (1979), 10–11.

42 *Notre patrie* (Gallimard, Paris, 1945), p. 83.

43 *Oeuvres poétiques de Charles Péguy*, ed. François Porché (Gallimard, Paris, 1948), p. 85.

44 Eric Cahm, *Péguy et le nationalisme français: de l'affaire Dreyfus à la grande guerre* (Cahiers de l'Amitié Charles Péguy, Paris, 1972), p. 126.

45 Quoted by Cahm, *Péguy et le nationalisme,*, p. 124.

46 Quoted by Bernard Guyon, *Péguy* (Hatier, Paris, 1960), p. 25.

47 *Notre patrie*, pp. 123–4.

48 *The Mystery of the Charity of Charles Péguy* (André Deutsch, 1983).

49 'Myth and Blood: The Poetry of Geoffrey Hill', *Critical Quarterly*, vol. 26, nos. 1 and 2 (1984), 152–3.

50 *Ibid.*, p. 153.

51 Bloom's influential view of Hill can be found in his 'Introduction: The Survival of Strong Poetry' in Hill's *Somewhere in Such a Kingdom: Poems 1952–1971* (Houghton Mifflin, New York, 1975).

52 Hill's most recently published poetry is 'Scenes With Harlequins', *Times*

Literary Supplement, 9–15 February (1990), 137. Although these six poems are concerned with the Russia of Aleksandr Blok their way of imaging the past has distinct affinities with Hill's earlier work. The 'Geoffrey Hill Sixtieth Birthday Issue' of *Agenda* (vol. 30, nos 1–2, 1992) includes four new poems (pp. 5–8).

Afterword: A homemade past

The fact that English writers have written so often about their 'Englishness' does not mean that one necessarily gets any general sense of England from their work. The private country of the mind and the real country are split as seldom before. This baffled a sympathetic American critic like Hugh Kenner who found plenty of writers here but no 'literature' in the old sense:

there's no longer an English literature. Talent has not been lacking, not at all; but, a center absent, talent collects for itself the materials of some unique cosmos. As never before, good poets are dispersed round the land; as never before, each commands a personal readership, including with good luck a perceptive critic (thus Hill stirs the eloquence of Christopher Ricks); as never before, no talk, however extensive, about any of them need cause you to mention another. You *think* of them quite separately, and that is a symptom. Larkin was perhaps the last poet whom 'everyone' had heard of, and the 'Movement' he was connected with soon didn't contain him. Nothing ever contained, or can account for, so disparate a quartet as Hill, Jones, Charles Tomlinson, Basil Bunting: nothing save a common devotion, in utterly disparate idioms, to the past of England. That's a symptom too, that need to reclaim – affirm – a past. Pasts are homemade now.[1]

Kenner may well be right about the lack of any standard for judging these writers but his position as an outsider shows in his anxiety to draw a line between the past and the present. It may be that our pasts have always been 'disparate'. In practice, he makes little distinction between 'where the main currents run' and his own opinions.[2] But he at least recognises that a literature is more than just the best writers taken together, picked like a football team by the reviewers. As Kenner sees, there is a gulf between our past and our present and 'Englishness' has become a name for the effort to bridge it. It condemns us, as Santayana predicted, to the diagnosing of our own nostalgia.

Nostalgia has, in fact, become part of our staple cultural diet, as available as takeaway food. In *Coasting*, his suggestive record of a voyage around the British Isles in pursuit of 'Englishness', Jonathan Raban is brought up against the thought that, in some places, England has actually *become* its own past. Especially telling is his account of Rye, the quintessentially 'English' retreat of Henry James:

Its very failure as a town had emerged as a marketable commodity for which there was an apparently unlimited international demand. Stagnation and decay, smartly painted and packaged, were selling like hot cakes. Looking at the Rye town model, I thought how horribly well it might be made to work as a representation of Britain at large.[3]

Modern England is in danger of becoming a museum of itself. Nothing could be more foreign in spirit from, say, the 'coiled, enwreathed England' of Hill's *Mercian Hymns* but Raban makes no mention of Hill. The poet who sums up the country for him and gets pride of place at the end of the voyage is his old teacher, Philip Larkin, whom he whisks off to a Lebanese restaurant in Hull, near where all the trawlers used to be. Larkin's death just three years later ('I hadn't grasped how much he was loved in England')[4] makes a watershed in *Coasting*, the demise of England as it was:

> It seems, just now,
> To be happening so very fast;
> Despite all the land left free
> For the first time I feel somehow
> That it isn't going to last. (LP, p. 190)

Raban's book concludes with the symptoms of this new England: the end of the 'Falklands War', the miners' strike and the oil boom in Aberdeen. Needless to say, even there the echoes of the past haunt the present in the old, familiar way. Even the strike 'looked at first as if it must be some kind of historical reconstruction put on by the Tourist Authority'.[5] When the future does *happen*, to use Larkin's helpless word, it bears 'Victorian values' with it.

Raban never suggests that *all* England is like Rye but his decision to end *Coasting* in the north is a pointed one. There are grounds for thinking that the axis of 'Englishness' has moved northwards over the century, from Belloc's South Downs, through Lawrence's Nottinghamshire, to places like Tony Harrison's Leeds. Harrison identifies his poetry with the city of his birth but he is not a regional poet in the way William Barnes was. To be regional implies the existence of a centre which Harrison no longer has. For all its local problems and distinctive language, his Leeds is a microcosm for what is happening in England as a whole – the real, as opposed to the tourist England, that is. This is partly because Harrison has a gift for hitting the nail on the head of basic English concerns like language, class and the past but also because he looks back at Leeds as someone who has left it, as Barnes never left Dorset. He may not have found any centre as solid elsewhere but he has come to see the city through a cosmopolitan culture that lies beyond it. The fact that he cherishes his Yorkshire vernacular underlines this. What is interesting in his verse is that although the context is new the emotion is often familiar. A great industrial city becomes the source of a nostalgia previously reserved for the rural 'South Country'. Many of Harrison's poems are twin-elegies for his parents and the Leeds that has disappeared along with them but some of them link urban to 'natural' change. The sonnet 'Dark Times', from *Art & Extinction*, is about a moth which has survived by changing its colour from white to black to avoid predators:

> Industrial Revolution and Evolution taught
> the moth to black its wings and not get caught
> where all of Nature perished, or all but.
>
> when lichens lighten some old smoke-grimed trees
> and such as Yorkshire's millstacks now don't burn
> and fish nose waters stagnant centuries,
> can *Biston Carbonaria* relearn,
>
> if Man's awakened consciousness succeeds
> in turning all these tides of blackness back
> and diminishing the need for looking black,
>
> to flutter white again above new Leeds?[6]

Beneath the colloquial zest of the word-play and the informal rhyming the feeling is in many ways traditional: industrial Leeds has become another 'deserted village'.

One reason that, despite such decline, Harrison's Leeds is still a living place (as beauty spots like Rye are not) is that it reflects the changing nature of contemporary England, in particular its new aspect as a multi-racial society. His long poem *V* is an elegy not only for his parents but for their companionable, corner shop society. The wry pathos of its picture of the poet's father shopping is a cameo of an England whose old habits are dying away in a new world:

> And growing frailer, 'wobbly on his pins',
> the shops he felt familiar with withdrew
> which meant much longer tiring treks for tins
> that had a label on them that he knew...
>
> The supermarket made him feel embarrassed.
> Where people bought whole lambs for family freezers
> he bought baked beans from check-out girls too harassed
> to smile or swap a joke with sad old geezers.
>
> But when he bought his cigs he'd have a chat,
> his week's one conversation, truth to tell,
> but time also came and put a stop to that
> when old Wattsy got bought out by M. Patel.[7]

Harrison is a popular poet but not in the same sense the 'Liverpool poets' are popular. His verse is also highly literary, even here. Though the scene spells loss and dislocation the feeling still cements a connection between past and present Englands. Beeston Cemetery in Leeds sometimes reminds us of the more picturesque churchyard where Gray wrote his 'Elegy':

> Though I've a train to catch my step is slow.
> I walk on the grass and graves with wary tread
> over these subsidences, these shifts below
> the life of Leeds supported by the dead. (*V*)

The footballing term 'supported' reverts to an older meaning. Even the graffiti on the graves become symbols of time's passing.

Harrison seems a more 'contemporary' poet than Hill but his work is closer to *Mercian Hymns* than it looks at first. Both poets share a strong interest in other literatures and both like to work through literary and historical allusions. They also take their present as a cue for probing the past. (Neither Hughes nor Larkin have been so committed to studying how that past has shaped the present.) Both invite nostalgia without succumbing to it. Looking back is part of their present, not an escape from it. To cut oneself off from nostalgia might be to cut oneself off from history. Feelings that now look sentimental (and Harrison welcomes sentiment) may in time seem redemptive. They may help us to face up to the facts of where we live. Meanwhile, Hill and Harrison both remind us how hard it has become to keep faith with our history without breaking faith with our present. This is what saves them from thinking of England as a museum to house itself, as Larkin did in 'Going, Going'. Larkin's pessimism is an inverted reassurance, a way of letting us off the hook by capitulating. 'Englishness' must be something to explore, almost 'another country', not the epitome of a finished state.

This book is meant to be a flame-thrower, not a compendium or a literary history. It will have achieved its object if what it says about the writers it discusses sparks off thoughts about the writers it appears to ignore. I believe that similar conclusions about the pressure of the past, our proneness to nostalgia, the difficulty we have in imagining how a future can grow out of the memory-soaked present, might have been reached by considering different writers. This does not mean that I think of all recent English writers as being in the same boat. There are, for instance, distinctly different sorts of writer in the period; some could be seen as 'natives' (the Georgians, Newbolt, Thomas, Amis) and others as 'cosmopolitans' (Roger Fry, Eliot, Adrian Stokes come to mind). Not all English writers have been Little Englanders and it has even been possible to be both a 'native' and a 'cosmopolitan' at one and the same time, as Herbert Read was. In the 1930s, Henry Moore was able to celebrate the 'Englishness' of English stone *and* respond creatively to the stimulus of Picasso and the Surrealists. Much remains to be explored. In a longer book there would have been time to diagnose more precisely both the kind of patriotism which most writers defined themselves against and the kind of patriotism they actually felt. The influence of Europe, particularly at the time of Eliot and Pound, might also have figured more prominently. I hope that this book will at least have showed why such studies are necessary. But, within these limits, and faced with the variety – even the fragmentation – of our writing, I believe that the diagnosis of our nostalgia provides a basis to start from.

Some recent work on 'Englishness', such as Colls's and Dodd's useful collection of essays, gives the impression that it is something we now have sewn up, something to look back on and estimate. Yet 'Englishness' is only an interesting subject if we still feel sufficiently close to it to have trouble in pinning it down. If we know what we mean by it before we begin to write there is no point in writing about it. Flaubert liked to remark that 'L'ineptie consiste à vouloir conclure', an aphorism particularly true of discussions of nations and nationalities. If this book shows anything it is that 'England' is too large and too various to be a fixed concept. It has changed so fast in our time that it is hard to be sure, at any given moment, *which* England is in question, its present or its past. There may still be an England in which the English can meet but the only route to it is through our personal and eccentric starting points of class, religion, and region, precisely those things that divide us from a more general sense of our 'Englishness'. Moreover, criticism has to leave something to the imagination, as poetry does, not to try to dot the 'i's and cross the 't's for itself. This book has, in any case, left enough gaps in the story it has to tell to spare its readers any further conclusion.

NOTES

(Place of publication is London unless otherwise stated)

1 Hugh Kenner, *A Sinking Island: The Modern English Writers* (Barrie and Jenkins, 1988), p. 245.
2 *Ibid.*, p. 263.
3 *Coasting* (Pan Books, 1987), p. 210.
4 *Ibid.*, p. 268.
5 *Ibid.*, p. 276.
6 *Selected Poems* (Penguin, Harmondsworth, 1984), p. 177.
7 *V* (Bloodaxe Books, Newcastle, 1985), no page numbers.

Index